1970

This book may be kept

THE AMERICAN MAGAZINE:

A Compact History

Other Books by John Tebbel

An American Dynasty

The American Indian Wars (with Keith Jennison)

Battle for North America (editor)

The Compact History of the American Newspaper

The Compact History of the Indian Wars

Epicure's Companion (with Anne Seranne)

From Rags to Riches

George Horace Lorimer and the Saturday Evening Post

George Washington's America

The Inheritors

Life and Good Times of William Randolph Hearst

Makers of Modern Journalism

The Marshall Fields

Open Letter to Newspaper Readers

Red Runs the River: The Rebellion of Chief Pontiac

THE
AMERICAN
MAGAZINE:

A Compact History

John Tebbel

HAWTHORN BOOKS, INC.   PUBLISHERS
NEW YORK

for Elaine

Preface

TO COMPRESS THE HISTORY OF AMERICAN MAGAZINES into so short a space, and still make it a volume one hopes will be useful, requires a number of compromises. Foremost of these is the necessity to omit any more than a mention of some magazines that perhaps deserve lengthier treatment, and to leave out others entirely. Consequently, no one should suppose that a "compact history" can replace or in any way supersede the lengthy, scholarly studies already available or the work of those researchers who have made studies in depth of individual magazines or periods.

What I am offering here is a narrative history that necessarily depends in large part on the scholarship of others, but does what the others were of course not intending to do, that is, to tell the story of the magazine business in America from 1749 to the present, within the scope of a single volume, in terms the general reader, and especially the preprofessional reader, will find helpful to his study and understanding.

While I have used many volumes in preparing the first two-thirds of the book, I have relied chiefly, as everyone must do who writes magazine history, on Frank Luther Mott's four-volume *A History of American Magazines*. The sheer magnificence of this Pulitzer Prize-winning work has often been noted, but as one who has been through its pages for perhaps the third time, I cannot resist expressing again my profound admiration for the late Dr. Mott's work. One can only stand in awe at the magnitude and quality of his research, and marvel at the skillful way he made these dead bones live again, often with wit

v

and charm. If he had left nothing else behind him, this history would have made him preeminent among the historians of journalism.

In the latter part of the book, I have relied on the other major figure among historians of the magazine, Dr. Theodore Peterson, of the University of Illinois, whose *Magazines in the Twentieth Century* (revised edition, 1968) is unexcelled in its field, nor is it likely to be. Peterson begins where Mott stops (a fifth Mott volume dealing fragmentarily with the twentieth-century scene was recently published posthumously), and brings the story up to date with the same high standard of research and felicity of style.

However, in these later chapters, I have also been able to draw on my own magazine experience as writer and editor, and on a long acquaintance with a good many figures in the magazine business, an experience derived from nearly a quarter century of firsthand work with and observation of the magazine business in New York City. For material in the last two chapters, I have drawn on several articles written for the Communications Section of the *Saturday Review,* to whom I am grateful for the opportunity during the last five years to broaden my knowledge of the magazine scene, along with other areas of communication. The chapter on Curtis, Bok, and Lorimer is a fresh view of material first used in my 1948 biography, *George Horace Lorimer and the* Saturday Evening Post.

Since this is not meant to be a scholarly book, I have dispensed with the usual bibliography and source notes, but I have appended a short list of recommended reading that I hope will be helpful to the students who may use this book.

I should like to express my gratitude to the Magazine Publishers Association for their many courtesies in providing me with up-to-date material, to the library staff of the R. R. Bowker Co. for the use of their materials, and to my daughter Elaine for her swift and efficient typing job on the manuscript, done under pressure from her father, who is more accustomed to deadlines.

JOHN TEBBEL

New York City
July, 1969

Contents

PART FOUR: MAGAZINES OF THE TWENTIETH CENTURY (1905–   )

PART ONE

HOW MAGAZINES BEGAN

(1741–1825)

one

The First Magazines

WRITING TO THE REDOUBTABLE Philadelphia publisher Mathew Carey, in 1788, George Washington remarked that he hoped magazines would be successful in America because, "I consider such easy vehicles of knowledge more happily calculated than any other, to preserve the liberty, stimulate the industry and meliorate the morals of an enlightened and free people."

Washington had reason to wish magazines well. Attacked by newspapers from the time he was a young colonel of Virginia militia, assailed by both the Tory and the patriot press through the Revolution, slandered outrageously by the Jeffersonian papers during his presidency, Washington was in a sour state of mind about the press when he wrote to Carey. After his second term, he left the Capital in such a rage at the newspapers that he canceled all his subscriptions for a time. There were understandable reasons, then, for his support of magazines, but he expressed what a good many other men in public life were saying in the postrevolutionary years when he noted the potentials of the "easy vehicles of knowledge."

Magazines were incomparably better purveyors of knowledge and entertainment than the newspapers of Washington's time. Because the magazines were so imitative of English periodicals, and lacking in sophistication and originality, it is easy to underestimate these eighteenth-century publications, but they were an important element in advancing the state of culture in America.

Magazines had been the last of the print media to appear in this country. The first periodical, in 1741, arrived a century after the first book, *The Bay Psalm Book*, emerged from the press at Cambridge in 1640, and fifty-one years after Benjamin Harris's initial, and abortive, attempt to publish a newspaper, *Publick Occurrences Both Foreign and Domestick*, in Boston in 1690.

There were excellent reasons for the long wait. The other media had risen out of necessity, but there was no immediate need for magazine reading, which was essentially a leisure-time occupation of the upper classes. Books had come first because there was a need for printed laws and proclamations, and for volumes that would advance both the religious and the political interests of the colonies' founders. Newspapers rose as soon as towns became too large for information to be conveyed by word of mouth. Magazines had to wait until the literary and practical arts in America had developed enough to create an audience sufficiently large to justify publication.

Even so, the magazines of the eighteenth century were heavily dependent on their British counterparts; the scissors and pastepot were indispensable tools of the first editors. These editors, nevertheless, were determined to put America's best foot forward as often as they could, and they sincerely meant to serve the interests of cultivated men everywhere in the colonies by providing as broad a spectrum of subjects as they could. Many regarded their publications as an extension of books, and considered it suitable for subscribers to bind the issues and add them to private libraries.

In founding magazines, the prospective publishers appealed for support to the educated and cultured men of the colonies, who were a relatively small group numerically but of an unusually high order of intellect. Out of the ranks of these potential readers—ministers, lawyers, historians, educators, and doctors, for the most part—came the publishers and editors as well. They were men of the caliber of Benjamin Franklin, Andrew Bradford, Isaiah Thomas, Thomas Paine, Noah Webster, and Mathew Carey. These men, through their own writings and what they selected from the work of others, were to influence literature and thought in eighteenth-century America.

Their readers were inconsiderable in number; subscribers never exceeded 1,600 for any one magazine, and the average was closer to 500. It was 1780, or later, before the total number of magazines printed at any one time exceeded 2,500. Consequently, the considerable work for printers involved in magazine publishing was not highly profitable. The printers at the time worked mainly on newspapers and to a lesser extent on almanacs, job printing, and a slowly growing number of books.

The mechanical limitations were, of course, severe. For a long time, paper and ink had to be imported, and the handpresses, relatively unchanged since the fifteenth century, were painfully slow to operate, printing one page at a time, after which the type had to be redistributed and a new page set. It was an expensive business, too; and with so few subscribers and so little advertising, magazines made a negligible economic dent in the publishing industry.

It was no wonder that most of the first magazines were short-lived. The greater number disappeared after a year or less; only two lived as long as eight years in the period before 1800. All the more credit should be given to those printers, writers, and editors who persisted in the face of so much discouragement and so little reward. They were driven partly by national pride, partly by the intellectual's urge to preserve and advance culture, and occasionally no doubt by the demands of their own egos.

Certainly there was enough to write about in these early years. Before the close of the eighteenth century in America, three wars had been fought: King George's, the French and Indian, and the Revolution itself. These events raised large economic and political questions, like taxation, the power of the state, Indian treaties, money, and the growth of industry and commerce. The magazines dealt with all these and similar questions, interpreting contemporary history for their readers. This kind of interpretation became especially important in the years after the Revolution when, for a time, the uncertain new republic seemed in doubt about itself, economically and politically. The conflict of interests was intense, and the magazines faithfully recorded it, to the great benefit of future historians.

The historians have found an equally valuable record provided by the magazines in social history. Education, for example, was argued about widely in the periodicals, and the great debate over slavery began in their pages. Prohibition was discussed 150 years before the

Volstead Act was passed. Crime and punishment were analyzed and discussed endlessly. Philosophical inquiries into the nature of the new government, and the character of government itself, were common topics. Differences were splitting apart the dominance of the old, established religions. The magazines spoke of these, and about medicine, natural phenomena, and other aspects of materialism.

As for literature, the magazines languished somewhat. They were still in the cultural embrace of England, and there Addison and Steele, chief purveyors of the essay, which was the dominant literary form, were so preeminent that everything else was imitative. In lesser hands, these imitative essays turned out badly more often than not. Nevertheless, the form was eagerly embraced and exploited in magazines by such American intellectuals as John Jay, Alexander Hamilton, Thomas Paine, and John Dickinson, among others. Franklin was the master, but writers like Philip Freneau, Timothy Dwight, and Noah Webster were giving a new polish to the literary essay in America, even though most Americans writing in that form consciously or unconsciously imitated the celebrated French and English authors of the day. It would have been difficult, indeed, to avoid being influenced by contemporaries like Voltaire, Rousseau, Bacon, Locke, Hume, Swift, Chesterfield, Goldsmith, Johnson, and men of like intellect and talent.

With such masters as models, it was not surprising that American magazine writers were hesitant about producing literary criticism, even of the small but growing output of native work. Noah Webster was the first editor, in 1787, to venture anything substantial in that direction, but there were other writers who felt themselves competent at least to discuss the classics, or to talk about rhetoric and etymology. Not much was said about fiction, because that art form was still embedded substantially in the essay. Magazines did, however, print excerpts from plays, and one reproduced a complete drama. Stories, when they were used, were ruled by "sentiment and sensibility," the watchwords of the day. As the magazine historian, Lyon N. Richardson, puts it, the themes were "the preservation of female chastity in a world of rakes, the tendency of wealth to breed avarice and arrogance, and the sad, ineffectual reactions of over-sensitized souls. . . ." Most fiction and poetry was reprinted from British periodicals, and even when native work appeared, it was usually indistinguishable from the British.

The magazines offered their readers more than words. There were "embellishments," as the editors called them when they advertised their wares to subscribers—meaning copperplate engravings for the most part, although woodcuts were frequent, too. There were music plates, cartoons, pictures of noted public figures, homes of celebrities, depictions of ceremonies, displays of America's scenic wonders, illustrations of scientific discoveries and invention, and scenes from whatever fiction the magazine might carry. Paul Revere was one of the first of a long series of engravers who gave their talents to magazine work, among other and perhaps more profitable outlets.

In establishing the first magazine in America, Benjamin Franklin and the Philadelphia printer Andrew Bradford ran what was nearly a tie. Probably Franklin, the universal genius, was first to conceive of such a project, in 1740, but it was a year later, in 1741, before he was able to issue his periodical, *The General Magazine, and Historical Chronicle, for All the British Plantations in America.* Meanwhile, three days before Franklin's magazine appeared, Bradford had issued *The American Magazine, or a Monthly View of the Political State of the British Colonies.* Franklin and Bradford had been rivals in the publication of newspapers, rivals for the postmastership of Philadelphia (Bradford had been fired and Franklin appointed to that position), and contestants in virtually every other field of publication. Franklin, a man of genius, naturally held a substantial edge in the rivalry.

Looking over the potential circulation for a magazine in 1740, Franklin was encouraged to start one when he observed that there were more than 13,000 people living in Philadelphia alone, and more than 100,000 in Pennsylvania. Life in the colonies was turbulent, but Franklin reasoned that this could only increase the public interest in what he proposed to print.

Since his own interests were so varied, Franklin entrusted the editorship to someone else. Unwisely, he chose John Webbe, who had been writing for Franklin's *Pennsylvania Gazette,* but had once been Bradford's lawyer. Webbe promptly took the plans for the magazine entrusted to him and showed them to Bradford, who hired him at a higher salary for the same job on his own publication. The quarrel that this maneuver generated was carried on by means of acid charges and retorts in the two publishers' newspapers, and elsewhere. In the end, Franklin won; Webbe, as editor, was nowhere near the stature of his rival. Bradford's *The American Magazine* lasted for just three issues, although it produced a truly surprising amount of original material.

Franklin's *The General Magazine,* in fact, was closer to English models, but its scope was far larger and it enjoyed the inestimable advantage of its publisher's own writing and editing. It carried the usual essays as principal stock-in-trade, along with poetry, letters, articles about current events, and extracts from American books and pamphlets. Consequently it was a much better reflection than Bradford's magazine of what was being produced in American literary life, not only in the Middle Colonies but in New England and the South as well.

The General Magazine ran for six issues, a total of 426 pages, of which a little less than 10 percent was original material. Its difficulty was that it had little to offer beyond what the weekly newspapers were already carrying. It was not a profitable venture, and Franklin was not one to carry a dead weight for no good reason. Apparently he must have had little regard for the magazine himself, because he did not even mention it in his *Autobiography*.

Franklin and Bradford did, however, give Philadelphia the honor of being the birthplace of magazines. Yet Boston was the cultural hub of the colonies (if not of the universe, as many inhabitants believed) and it was only a short time before three new magazines appeared in that city, which then had a population of 18,000 and was at the peak of its first period of growth. More than a thousand vessels sailed in and out of its port every year.

The comparative success of the first magazines in Boston, however, were not so much the result of its cultural eminence as it was the still close relationship of the city (and the colony) to England. Bostonians felt themselves bound to the mother country by strong traditional and cultural ties, and they welcomed *The American Magazine and Historical Chronicle; for All the British Plantations*, which was a kind of *Reader's Digest* of several British magazines, with articles from the leading English periodicals abridged to provide a cross section of what was being talked about in London and Edinburgh.

The American Magazine first appeared in March 1743, and lasted for three years. Earlier in March, two other publications emerged, with the intent to rival it. The first of these, the *Boston Weekly Magazine*, lasted only three issues. But the second, *The Christian History*, was more solidly based; it rode the crest of the "Great Awakening," the revivalist movement sweeping New England and battering at the doors of the conservative, established church. Several earnest and eloquent ministers served *The Christian History*. Their determination and abilities enabled it to survive for two years. But in the end the conservatives won; and the revival, if not the spirit behind it, died down, and the magazine—if indeed, it could be called one in the ordinary sense—expired with it. Nevertheless, it was a landmark: the first religious magazine in the colonies.

After these Boston experiments, the focus of magazine publishing shifted to New York City, where the medium had not flourished at all before. Nor did it flourish now, in any real sense, since the only worthwhile magazine published in the entire decade between 1747 and 1757 was a four-page weekly, *The Instructor*, appearing in 1755. Three years earlier, however, another four-page weekly, *The Independent Reflector*, was introduced, and this folio, although it lasted only about a year and was otherwise undistinguished, did bring essay writing in American periodicals to a new peak. Its successors, *The Occasional Reverberator* (1753) and *John Englishman* (1755), carried on the tradition.

New York was already a growing, busy city, foreshadowing what was to come, but magazines had been slow to develop there because more than half of its population was Dutch, with no interest in the English literary tradition, and many of the remainder were blacks who could not read. Around the community itself, nestling at the end of Manhattan Island, stretched the manors of the Dutch patroons. Many of them were highly cultured men, but with no particular interest in English or American magazines.

Another hindrance was the close rein on New York held by the Crown, which discouraged frank expression of opinion, literary or otherwise. This explained the relatively short life of *The Independent Reflector*. It was not meant to be a radical journal, but its publisher, a young man named James Parker, who had learned the printing trade under the elder William Bradford, found that what he advocated was more and more an attack on the Episcopal Church's exertion of its power to establish King's College (later Columbia University). Hugh Gaine, the fiery newspaper publisher, was on the opposite side, and so the controversy drew public attention.

The Independent Reflector was outstanding during its brief life because of the brilliant work of its editor, William Livingston, descendant of a distinguished New York family, Yale graduate, member of the bar, a writer of both prose and poetry. His essays were exemplary —clear, direct, and fair.

But once more the magazine scene was shifting. New and outstanding editors were coming on the scene as the medium began slowly coming into its own. The focal point was again Philadelphia, and the magazine begun there in 1757 was nominally the product of William Bradford, the publisher (he was the nephew of Andrew, the first magazine publisher in America), but in reality it was edited by William Smith, provost of the College and Academy of Philadelphia, later the University of Pennsylvania. This Scotsman, a doctor of divinity, was so outspoken in attacking the peace program of the Quakers in Pennsylvania and in supporting new military action against France that he found himself twice in prison after the magazine was founded.

His publication, *The American Magazine, or Monthly Chronicle for the British Colonies,* was no mere propaganda organ, however. Many of its contributors came from the universities, and they were not confined to the middle colonies; several were Southerners. Their varied contributions made the magazine the most original and vital of all the literary magazines published before the Revolution. The work of the best American poets, men like Francis Hopkinson, appeared in its pages. For no published reason (perhaps because Smith went on a trip to England) *The American Magazine* discontinued publication after its first year.

It remained for that all-around publishing genius Isaiah Thomas to produce the first magazine of distinction in America, which he began in January 1774, on the eve of the Revolution. Thomas was already operating his *Massachusetts Spy*, probably the best newspaper in the colonies, and certainly the one most effective in its support of the patriot cause. The magazine Thomas produced, *The Royal American*, had as subtitle *Universal Repositor of Instruction and Amusement*. It was the first periodical to appear in the colonies for more than a year, the first of a general type in four years. Forty pages and well printed, as befitted a craftsman like Thomas, who was a master printer, it carried on the *Spy*'s patriot propaganda, but also printed a wide selection of essays and other pieces, along with the usual piratings from English magazines.

Thomas did not remain *The Royal American*'s editor for long. Occupied with the events growing out of the closing of Boston's port by the British, he relinquished the editorial direction of his project to an elderly friend, Joseph Greenleaf, who made it less militant. Greenleaf appealed to the "sons of Harvard" to contribute articles about improvements in "mechanical arts, husbandry, in natural and experimental philosophy, and the mathematics"—all of which, he hoped, would make the world "better as well as wiser." One of his major accomplishments was to print the first really important engravings, a series of twenty-two executed mainly by Paul Revere, who was paid about three pounds for each one. *The Royal American* was also first in carrying the words and music of a song, and the first to print the kind of confessional, sentimental love stories so dear to the readers of English magazines.

On the night before the Battle of Lexington, Thomas ferried his press and types across the harbor from Charlestown, loaded them in a wagon, and drove them to safety in Worcester, which thereafter became his publishing headquarters. *The Royal American*, however, ended with Lexington; Thomas did not renew it in Worcester.

Four months before that initial skirmish of the Revolution, another magazine, *The Pennsylvania Magazine; or American Monthly Mu-*

seum, was launched in Philadelphia. Its famous editor, Tom Paine, made it noteworthy. Robert Aitken, its publisher, was a printer and bookseller with, as Paine remarked in a letter to Ben Franklin, "little or no turn that way himself" in the direction of periodical editing. But he was astute enough to hire Paine as editor, at a salary of fifty pounds a year.

Paine contributed his own pungent, vigorous prose to the magazine, although Aitken sometimes had to coax it from him with liberal applications of brandy; Isaiah Thomas tells us that after the third glass, Paine wrote "with great rapidity, intelligence and decision: and his ideas appeared to flow faster than he could commit them to paper." Under the signature A.B., Paine wrote everything from poetry to Addisonian essays and descriptions of inventions, so that his role became more than that of a contributing editor. Although he undoubtedly wrote much of the revolutionary material in the magazine, Paine (and Aitken) did not permit *The Pennsylvania Magazine* to be simply a propaganda organ. It contained a wide variety of other pieces, and enough original material to make it outstanding among magazines of the century.

There were few others among the early magazines that were of much interest to other than later scholarly historians. Mathew Carey, with four partners, began the *Columbian* in Philadelphia in 1786. While he was active for only about three months, the *Columbian* in its three and a half years of existence became the best looking of the eighteenth-century American periodicals (one of the partners, John Trenchard, was an excellent engraver), and it was beginning to do what magazines would soon do superlatively—reflect the national life. The *Columbian* performed this function especially well in its re-creation of the Revolution in narrative and documents. It was equally preeminent in its coverage of its own times.

Mathew Carey, only four months after he helped launch the *Columbian,* began another magazine on his own, the *American Museum;* and the two periodicals, which curiously enough came to an end at the same time in 1792, shared the distinction of being the nation's first successful magazines. At the end of the first year, the *American Museum*'s subscription list of about 1,250 included such distinguished names as George Washington, John Dickinson, Timothy Dwight, John Randolph, Hopkinson, and Bishop William White, among others. Washington, in a letter of commendation, declared that the magazine had been conducted "with taste, attention, and propriety."

Frequently in trouble financially, since its noted subscribers were not always prompt in their subscription payments, the *American Museum* did a valuable service in reprinting revolutionary pamphlets, like Paine's *Common Sense*, and in printing new work by Franklin, Hopkinson, and Benjamin Rush. It touched on antislavery from time to time, discussed education, and, like so many of the early magazines, devoted considerable space to advising women about their role in society. It was Federalist in its politics, but not fervently so. As time went on, the magazine became more original and more literary. Certainly, with the *Columbian*, it was among the best of eighteenth-century American magazines.

While these periodicals were flourishing in Philadelphia, New York was making its first attempt at a monthly magazine. It was the product of another fertile and various mind, that of Noah Webster, who was then only twenty-nine and already the author of a spelling book destined to instruct millions of Americans, a prime mover in the beginning struggle for copyright laws, and a thoughtful writer on constitutional matters. Turning in a fresh direction, his *American Magazine* appeared in December 1787, a large duodecimo of seventy-two pages, costing its subscribers $2.50 a year (magazines were increasing in size and cost). It lasted twelve issues. Besides the customary reprints from English publications, it had the benefit of Webster's talented pen, from which flowed Federalist articles about the nature of government, and about education, another of the editor's primary interests. Webster was against using the Bible in the schools, and against the traditional classical education. Webster liked girls, as his diary shows, and there is a great deal about them in his magazine. In short, his periodical showed great promise, but his active mind was already leading him elsewhere, toward the founding of a newspaper, and he simply lost interest in his project.

Soon after Webster turned to other things, Isaiah Thomas made a third attempt at magazine publishing, this time in the *Massachusetts*

Magazine. This was not only the second longest-lived in the century (the *New York Magazine* lasted a month longer) but ranked with the best, although Thomas never made money from it—unusual for a man who was the first publisher to die rich. The *Massachusetts Magazine* was not a literary giant, but its remarkable variety gave it a vitality unusual in eighteenth-century periodicals. In its pages the American short story began to develop, and a full-length play was reproduced. It was full, too, of foreign and domestic news, proceedings of the Massachusetts legislature and of Congress, and other news of the most varied kind, as though it were more newspaper than magazine.

By the end of the century, as the life of the new republic gained momentum, magazines were still struggling. Many were dull, few lasted beyond a few months, and they were still heavily imitative of English models. But more and more they were reflecting social and political life, and they were influential well beyond their meager circulation figures, which themselves had increased 100 percent per capita on the average since 1741. Magazines were still not universally read, but those that now appeared were well thumbed and read by many people other than their subscribers.

The magazine business was fairly well launched, and on its way.

two

Magazines of the New Nation

AMONG THE WORST OF THE DIFFICULTIES eighteenth-century magazines had to face was the high cost of distribution. Not only was the mail service erratic, often over roads that were no more than rough wagon trails, but postmasters and the government itself gave magazines no consideration whatever. One of Andrew Bradford's complaints about his rival Benjamin Franklin was that, as postmaster of Philadelphia, Franklin had sent out his own magazine without paying the nearly prohibitive postal rates demanded of others.

In the Postal Act of 1794, the government grudgingly recognized the new medium, stating that magazines "may be transported in the mails when the mode of conveyance and the size of the mails will permit of it.'" In other words, magazines were transported or not at the whim of individual postmasters, few of whom had any particular regard for the medium.

When the mailmen deigned to carry them, periodicals were expensive to deliver. It cost eight cents per copy for a sixty-four-page octavo magazine to be carried more than a hundred miles. After that, the rates fell slightly: six cents for fifty to one hundred miles, four cents for less than fifty miles. That meant the cost of distributing this typical magazine would be anywhere from forty-eight to ninety-six cents, depending on the distance. The subscriber paid this cost.

Nor did the rates decline as roads became better, postal routes were extended, and transportation in general improved. In fact, when the aftermath of the War of 1812 precipitated a general rise in rates of all kinds, postage went up 50 percent for every category.

Nevertheless, magazines increased in number, although until 1875 at a painfully slow rate. There were a dozen magazines at the turn of the century, where there had been only five in 1794. By 1810 there were forty, and the figure had climbed to nearly a hundred by 1825. In the first quarter of the new century, somewhere between five hundred and six hundred periodicals were published in the United States.

Easily the most important magazine after 1794 and before 1825 was Joseph Dennie's *Port Folio*. Dennie was the first magazine editor in the modern style, a man of charm and wit who had begun his career as a writer for and editor of the *Farmer's Museum*, a newspaper in Walpole, New Hampshire. A Harvard graduate, Dennie had been a lawyer but then found himself drawn irresistibly to literature. He was a rather short, slender man who loved to dress elegantly and whose beautifully written essays were signed "Lay Preacher."

Dennie's work habits as editor of the *Farmer's Museum* were described with admiration by the paper's printer's devil, Joseph T. Buckingham, later to become a noted editor himself:

"Dennie wrote with great rapidity," Buckingham reported in his *Specimens of Newspaper Literature*, "and generally postponed his task until he was called upon for *copy*. It was frequently necessary to go to his office, and it was not uncommon to find him in bed at a late hour in the morning. His *copy* was often given out in small portions, a paragraph or two at a time; sometimes it was written in the printing-office, while the compositor was waiting to put it in type. One of the best of his lay sermons was written at the village tavern, directly opposite to the office, in a chamber where he and his friends were amusing themselves with cards. It was delivered to me by piecemeal, at four or five different times. If he happened to be engaged in a game when I applied for copy, he would ask some one to *play his hand for him while he could give the devil his due*. When I called for the closing paragraph of the sermon, he said, 'Call again in five minutes.' 'No,' said Taylor, 'I'll write the improvement for you.' He accordingly wrote the concluding paragraph, and Dennie never saw it till it was put in print."

The "Taylor" in whom Dennie put so much trust was his friend, Royall Tyler, also a former lawyer, who wrote the first comedy, *The*

Contrast, to be performed on the American stage. Tyler was only one of Dennie's literary friends, who formed a circle around him in which each shone in the other's reflection.

Dennie might have stayed happily in Walpole, playing cards and drinking with his friends, writing his "Lay Sermons" for the *Farmer's Museum*, but in 1799 he was made private secretary to Secretary of State Timothy Pickering and at the same time was offered a job on the Federalist newspaper *Gazette of the United States*, which Hamilton had founded in Philadelphia. Even with these tasks, Dennie had more than enough energy and inclination remaining to carry on his "Lay Sermons" in a new form. The vehicle was to be a magazine, the *Port Folio*, and it began its long career on January 3, 1801, destined to run until December 1827. It sold at an initial price of five dollars a year. With the founding of the magazine, Dennie also assumed a new pseudonym: Oliver Oldschool, Esq.

Besides Dennie's own polished writing, the *Port Folio* benefited from a most distinguished list of contributors, although names were not signed to the articles. The first number carried a continuing "Journal of a Tour Through Silesia," by John Quincy Adams, and some unpublished letters written to the novelist Tobias Smollett by Boswell, Samuel Richardson, Hume, and others. No wonder that within four months the paper was selling two thousand copies a month. For eight years it remained a monthly and attained the literary heights of its career; after that it became a monthly and diminished in importance and interest.

Politically, of course, the paper was Federalist in the violent style of the day, heaping invective and ridicule upon Jefferson, Jefferson's friends and all his works. As far as Dennie was concerned, "democracy" was a failure in America and the election of Jefferson a ruinous seal of doom on the new nation. These sentiments, expressed in his usual forceful way in a series of articles in 1803, resulted in his indictment by a grand jury on a charge of seditious libel. After numerous postponements of the trial, he was ultimately acquitted in 1805 and immediately went back to baiting the Democrats. After 1809, however, the *Port Folio* became nonpartisan, and soon dropped politics entirely.

The heart of the magazine was Dennie's "Lay Preacher" essays, seventy-seven of which appeared in its pages between 1801 and 1808. Their topics covered the range of Dennie's numerous interests—literature, politics, morals, manners—and they were all graceful, witty, informed, and perennially entertaining. As for the work of the other contributors, essays predominated, but there were also humor, travel, biography, comments on American speech, and satire. The tone was English and vaguely antiAmerican; Dennie was a great admirer of the British.

As the most successful literary periodical up to that time, the *Port Folio* was no more financially profitable than its predecessors. Dennie himself died on January 7, 1812, and the magazine passed into other hands. It never again commanded the impressive list of contributors Dennie was able to summon from the ranks of his friends—writers like Charles Brockden Brown, Tyler, John Quincy Adams, Gouverneur Morris, and others of like talents.

One of Dennie's group, Charles Brockden Brown, was responsible for the second most important contribution to magazine history in these early years of the century. He began a series of periodicals in April 1799 with the *Monthly Magazine and American Review*, published in New York, which was succeeded in 1801 by the *American Review and Literary Journal*, in turn followed by the *Literary Magazine and American Register,* published in Brown's native Philadelphia. Then, in 1807, Brown began a semiannual called *The American Register or General Repository of History, Politics and Science,* which he edited until he died.

Brown, who was a singularly talented man, is sometimes called America's "first novelist," although that is a matter of dispute and of definition. *Wieland,* his first novel, was published before he became an editor. He had also been a magazine writer in Philadelphia. But he was eager to found an American literary magazine, an ambition that was to end in frustration and his death. His first effort, the *Monthly Magazine,* was chiefly distinguished for Brown's own contributions, and lasted little better than a year and a half. The quarterly *American Review,* which followed it, beginning in January 1801, lasted only until the final quarter of the following year. Its purpose, unlike its predecessor, appeared to be more to instruct than entertain, and the instruction in literature, arts, and science seemed to readers, and no doubt to Brown himself, less than fascinating.

The project was abandoned, but not the publisher's ambitions. A year later, in October 1803, he tried again with the *Literary Magazine and American Register*, a semiannual, this time with better luck. The magazine survived until 1807, in spite of such a severe dearth of contributors at the beginning that for the June 1804 issue Brown, with a single exception, had to write everything. He continued to write for his new venture—his novel, *Carwin the Biloquist*, ran as a serial through the first three volumes—but other contributors did appear, and about half the later contents was original, including some exceptional pieces like "A Rural Walk," a poem by the ornithologist Alexander Wilson.

Eventually, however, the *Literary Magazine* went the way of its predecessors. It became more informational and less entertaining. The sucessor Brown devised, *The American Register*, was encyclopedic in tone, a semiannual of about five hundred pages, and almost purely informational, hardly more than an almanac in most respects. Disappointment in his work and in his private life as well, combined with the drudgery of what amounted to hackwork in getting out *The American Register*, hurried Brown to an early death.

But other editors were rising out of the intellectual stirrings of the new nation. Joseph T. Buckingham, who had observed Dennie so admiringly from his lowly status on the *Farmer's Museum*, was now an editor in his own right in Boston. *Polyanthos,* his magazine, begun in 1805, was not an important publication, but it sparkled with the prose of its publisher and of his chief contributor, Royall Tyler. Men of intellect were constantly being attracted to editorial chairs, although often they did not stay long. Washington Irving, for example, served briefly as the guiding hand of *The Analectic Magazine,* begun in 1813.

While the monthly general magazines were the most important aspects of the burgeoning magazine scene, the weeklies were the most prolific. These sprang up in every part of America; there was scarcely a community of any consequence that could not boast its own weekly, even though it might linger for only a short time. These weeklies were cheap quartos, and made no pretense at enlightenment; they were meant to entertain. If they could find no original entertainment, they felt free to borrow from other publications at will.

As they proliferated, the weeklies, by the law of averages, produced a few grains of wheat along with the chaff. One of these grains was the *Saturday Evening Post,* a descendant of Franklin's *Pennsylvania Gazette,* although that paper had been gone half a dozen years before the *Post* appeared. The *Post* began its long, spectacular career on August 4, 1821, the enterprise of a twenty-four-year-old printer, Charles Alexander, and another printer, Samuel Coate Atkinson. The partners took over the printing plant where Franklin's *Gazette* had once functioned, a two-story brick structure behind 53 Market Street, Philadelphia, and from their attic editorial department (the rest of the building was occupied by a pressroom and two composing rooms) they began to turn out a four-page small-folio, without pictures and only five columns to the page. Most of the *Post*'s contents in its first five years was clipped and pasted from other publications by its editor, Thomas Cottrell Clark, who also did a few pieces of his own.

This was the modest beginning of what would become one of the giants of magazine journalism. It passed through a variety of ownerships and tribulations before Cyrus H. K. Curtis rescued it from imminent extinction near the close of the century and turned it over to George Horace Lorimer, who made it for years the most successful magazine in America.

Another important weekly was the *New-York Mirror,* founded in 1823 by two poets, George Pope Morris and Samuel Woodworth. Both were young men; Morris just twenty-two. Before it ended its career, about 1857, after various changes in ownership and title, the *Mirror* had not only conveyed a relatively truthful reflection of New York society but had also laid the foundations for the comfortable literary tradition that permeated what came to be known as the Knickerbocker period in New York life, before the Civil War.

Of the other weeklies, the only one of major consequence was the *Minerva, or Literary, Entertaining and Scientific Journal,* a lively miscellany of fiction, criticism, poetry, book reviews, and drama criticism, edited by George Houston and James G. Brooks. It, too, had other titles and other editors, but it remained one of the brightest and best of the literary weeklies.

Imitation of English models and of each other was still a prevailing mode in magazine publishing. The quarterlies were inclined to fashion themselves after the prototypes in London and Edinburgh. As in the United Kingdom, they attracted a coterie group of intellectuals as editors and contributors, many of them from universities like Harvard, such as Jared Sparks and Edward Everett. Those publications content to exist entirely and frankly on the work of others—the eclectics— drew on British periodicals for the most part.

As magazines developed, they continued to diversify and reflect the multiplying interests of the new nation. Religion was especially well represented in an era full of splintering and controversy, in which every new faith sought to have its own voice. Those who were spreading the word inland found printed publications an ideal messenger because they could be kept and read by any number of people. The secular magazines could hardly ignore the religious arguments that occupied the minds of so many people, and the fervor of evangelism often seeped into their pages as the revivals swept westward.

By 1824 there were at least twenty-one monthly religious magazines, and a good many newspapers published by different denominations. Their number grew rapidly in the next decade. As they grew, so did the other specialized magazines, reaching out now to new audiences—farmers, teachers, lawyers, doctors, musicians and theatrical people, college students, scientists, mechanics, and historians. Increasingly popular with everyone were the comic magazines, stemming from the comic almanacs and jest books turned out by the book publishers.

The vast audience of women was beginning to be tapped, but these early attempts were tentative and subject to early collapse. Women's magazines were soon to be a major factor in the business, but their time was not yet. Meanwhile, women were argued about pro and con in the pages of other periodicals. Frank Luther Mott, in his *A His-*

tory of American Magazines, quotes from the *Monthly Anthology* of January 1804, on the subject of the influence of French fashions, which the magazine viewed with alarm.

"We have imported the worst of French corruptions, the want of female delicacy," the *Anthology* grumbled. "The fair and innocent have borrowed the lewd arts of seduction. . . . What must we say of some, whom we daily observe, whose dress is studiously designed to display the female form? Why do they solicit our gaze? I will not charge them with the design of kindling a lawless flame. They will shudder at the suggestion. But I warn them. . . ."

Women found a friend, however, in Charles Brockden Brown, who, anticipating the feminists of a later day, defended their rights as human beings. Even Brown, however, was inclined to take a highly romantic view of women, in the manner of the day. A writer (probably not Brown) in his *Literary Magazine* declaimed: "All the virtues that are founded in the sensibility of the heart are theirs. Pity, the attribute of angels, and friendship, the balm of life, delight to dwell in the female breast. What a forlorn, what a savage creature would man be without the meliorating offices of the gentle sex!"

When Brown himself was doing the writing, his feminist sympathies were undisguised. In a dialogue on "The Rights of Women" in the *Weekly Magazine,* Brown asks a lady, "Pray, Madam, are you a federalist?" She replies:

"While I am conscious of being an intelligent moral being; while I see myself denied, in so many cases, the exercise of my own discretion, incapable of separate property; subject in all periods of my life to the will of another, on whose bounty I am made to depend for food and shelter; when I see myself, in my relation to society, regarded merely as a beast, as an insect, passed over, in the distribution of public duties, as absolutely nothing . . . it is impossible I should assent to their opinion, so long as I am conscious of moving and willing. . . . No, I am no federalist."

Some magazines seriously debated the subject of physical education for women. The *American Journal of Education,* for instance, deplored gymnastics as "unfeminine" but granted that riding and walking were not harmful, although it appeared to consider the best exercise for women spinning and household chores.

Periodicals for children were also emerging, and they were generally as humorless as the books provided for them, devoted mostly to teaching religion and morality. The stilted, heavy-handed style in which most of these magazines were written must have been truly discouraging to any child looking for innocent amusement. A literature for children was developing in America, but slowly. There was no lack, however, of magazines concerned with how to educate them. The chief argument was over the standard classical education, as opposed to the new studies in science and mathematics that, some complained, were crowding Greek and Latin out of the curriculum. On this subject, Brown was again the most controversial of editors. He had a low opinion of colleges. An article, probably from his pen, deplored the "mania" for establishing colleges. "Three fourths of the colleges in the United States," he declared, "have professors wretchedly unqualified for their station. . . . I have known young gentlemen going home with A.B. affixed to their names without being able to construe the diploma which certified their standing." On this subject, Brown was not on sound footing.

Such were the magazines in the early years of the nineteenth century, breaking new ground, making exploratory starts in directions that would soon be exploited to the limit. Unaware of it, magazines in 1825 were standing at the brink of a Golden Age.

three

Editors and Editing

"WE WISH TO IMPRESS UPON EVERY MIND, a true value of the dignity of our national character. This dignity is promoted and upheld by nothing more than learning." So spoke the editor of a magazine called *Portico* in the summer of 1816, and his was the voice of the new nation, trying in its literature as well as its politics to present itself as a state worthy of taking its place in the older, established community of the Western world.

America got little encouragement from abroad. In the eyes of Europeans, and particularly of Englishmen, the United States was essentially uncivilized and absurdly pretentious about its infant culture. There were self-doubts at home, too, as recent scholarship has pointed out. By the time the first quarter of the nineteenth century ended, there were prophets of doom among the intellectual elite, whose oratory and writings began to reflect a nostalgia for the past, along with doubts about the future of such concepts as "freedom" and "democracy" in a rapidly expanding society that was already beginning to lose its peaceful Jeffersonian agricultural character. Many of these doubts were strikingly similar to those of today, and they shared the same root cause: Man's adjustment to a new technological society.

Some of this discontent filtered into the magazines, but primarily the editors were interested in doing what they could to develop a national literature. Since there was not always enough material at hand to make that possible, however, they, too, clung to the past by continuing to imitate the British periodical press. Nevertheless, the tone of many magazines was doggedly patriotic and defensive against at-

tacks made on American culture. There were frequent oratorical flights like that by Robert Walsh, a founder of the *American Review*, who wrote: "The unshackled genius of the new world is now exerting itself with gigantic vigour, aided by the treasures of nature, to strengthen its powers, increase its commerce, its resources, and its wealth. No other quarter of the globe, much less a single nation, will eventually be able to dispute the empire of the seas with the new world. . . . The eyes of the world are upon us."

It was the age of great orators—Clay, Calhoun, John Randolph, among others—and the oratorical style flourished in the magazines. While oratory in prose was acceptable if done well, it was less than inspiring in poetry, particularly if the poetry was long-winded and declamatory, as it often proved to be. "One of the surest methods" to elevate standards, asserted the *Literary Gazette*, of Philadelphia, was to "make our poetry national and peculiar, to hang its flowers around our history, to interweave it with our local attachments, to dye it deeply in the grain of our prejudices and passions."

Not all editors held this point of view. Some were highly critical of American literature, and not only were unwilling to abandon the literary mainstream of Great Britain and the Continent but actively opposed such schemes as Noah Webster's to establish an "American language." (Amusingly, even editors like Walsh, announcing the exertion of the New World's "unshackled genius," still employed English spelling in noting the nation's "gigantic vigour.")

Most of the editors, however, were peculiarly sensitive to criticism of America, American writing, and of American magazines in particular, when it came from traveling critics—the first wave of those visiting English lecturers and observers who came, saw, and returned to deride the promised land. William Tudor, in the *North American Review*, soon to be the nation's leading intellectual periodical, spoke for most when in 1816 he declared angrily that "the travellers who described us have with very few exceptions been so ignorant or so profligate, that we almost despair of an able and unprejudiced account of the United States from a European." There were even those who thought the foreign critics were part of a paid conspiracy to ruin the United States industrially and economically.

Some of the guns fired in the war of words between English and American writers can still be heard today. On both sides of the Atlantic, the *Edinburgh Review*'s lofty and disdainful question "Who reads an American book?" strikes sparks even now. Americans are often infuriated to find, more than a century and a half later, that few English bookstores stock American books, that these books are regularly clubbed to death in the British quality newspapers and periodicals, and that American magazines are widely regarded as essentially vulgar, although some of those most derided are widely read in their international editions.

In the verbal war of the early nineteenth century, there was no cousinly love lost on either side. The British *Quarterly Review*'s observation that "Americans are inherently inferior" intellectually to Europeans was answered by the American *Atlantic Magazine*'s advice to treat such "rhapsodies" about the "barbarism of the United States" with "laughter at their blunders, if made ingenuously and with commiseration, if they proceed from malice." Joseph Dennie's *Port Folio* was far less charitable. It called the English travelers "those unblushing miscreants—those slanderers by profession . . . whose very names are offensive to the ear of virtue. . . ." Dennie himself was dead when these words were published in 1815; alive, he had taken a far more indulgent view.

In spite of some strong French sympathies in America, there was little more forbearance on the part of the editors toward France and its literary spokesmen. American editors often warned about French novels and French "atheism," and spoke of French "literary decay." Nevertheless, some magazines continued to review French literature and to reprint both poetry and prose from France.

Toward the Germans, however, there was much more cordiality. Edward Everett, editor of the *North American Review,* for example, was one of those American intellectuals who had traveled in Germany and could read German literature in the original. He was among those who helped make the work of such writers as Goethe and Schiller known to America.

The editors of early-nineteenth-century magazines had more serious practical problems than defending the nation against foreign critics.

They were confronted with the basic difficulty of finding able contributors. Sometimes these were so scarce that the editor, if he was capable of it, had to write a good part of the magazine himself. Otherwise, he had to resort to clipping and pasting.

The reason for the difficulty was that there existed no writing class as such, no group of professional writers who made their living by the pen. That was not so much because of a lack of talent as it was the nature of the magazine business itself. It was still less a business than a leisure occupation for gentlemen, and the bulk of the readers were still an educated elite. Consequently, the editorial affairs of a magazine were conducted in a haphazard way. Submitted articles were read and responded to when the editor got around to it; it might be a long time before the hopeful author knew whether he had been accepted or not. Payments were small—nonexistent until 1819—and, even worse, were not made until the piece was in print, which sometimes might be a year or more after it was accepted. Moreover, writing, like acting, was not considered quite a respectable occupation. A gentleman might write for amusement and distraction, as Charles Brockden Brown put it, but to write for money would be vulgar. As for poets, the editors of the *Monthly Anthology* complained, they were "either uneducated females, or men, who write rather from motives of vanity than the impulse of genius."

Usually an editor had to depend on his friends for much of the contributed material, and these friends were often members of a literary club that more or less supported the magazine they favored. The talent of the membership suffered the usual variation in quality, and the average was not high in this nonprofessional period. Style tended to be heavy, wordy, and too often plain dull. On the other hand, if the editors tried to lighten up the contents they were likely to be accused by some readers of frivolity.

Since writing for publication was considered not quite respectable, articles were mostly unsigned or pseudonyms were used, in the old manner. Thus, again, there was little incentive to write, even as an outlet for ego. Worse, the editors considered it their obligation to exert absolute control over what they printed to the extent of making any changes in the contributions they might think necessary, without consulting the author. Announcing his new *Christian's Magazine,* the editor, John M. Mason, declared: "As the object of this magazine cannot be attained without the editor's control over its materials, he will feel himself not only at liberty, but under obligation, to make such alterations in the pieces which may be offered for insertion, as he shall judge expedient."

Editors, as well as contributors, shared the financial poverty of magazines. The first magazine to pay for submitted pieces, the *Christian Spectator,* proposed a fee of a dollar a page when it appeared in 1819, and others followed. But not all contributors would accept. Those who still considered writing a gentleman's amusement would not take money even when the editors tried to bless the payment by calling it an honorarium. The dollar-a-page rate was, for a time, the standard payment when it was accepted.

As for the editors, they were often not paid at all—they were expected to do the work in their spare time or as relaxation from the task of guarding a private fortune, or if they *were* paid, it would be a salary in proportion to whatever success the magazine might have. Sometimes magazines were published by firms engaged in other occupations, and the editors took on their chores as part of whatever regular job they were paid for. The few professional editors were paid salaries so small that they could be, and were, called honorariums. Consequently editing was a part-time occupation for most editors. Clergymen or seminary professors edited the religious periodicals, and professors from colleges like Yale, Harvard, and Princeton served as editors of many of the intellectual periodicals.

A few editors managed to extract a fairly respectable amount for their work. Joseph Dennie, for instance, was paid £110 a year for editing the *Farmer's Museum* in 1796 (reduced to $400 two years later), and perhaps as much as $2,500 for his work with the *Port Folio* after he had to give it up as his own property in 1808. More typical was the salary of $1,000 annually paid to the poet William Cullen Bryant for editing the *New-York Review* in 1825.

Even if customs had been different, however, neither editors nor contributors could have hoped for much from the financially struggling periodicals of the early century. Their life expectation was short, in most cases, and their circulations small and fluctuating. The situation was well described by a friend of the *Atlantic Magazine*'s editor, who wrote: "There is too great a flock of magazines, foreign and domestic, of all sizes and materials and colors, flying about, like the ecclesiastics in limbo—red, blue and green, 'with all their trumpery.' The number of past abortions, and rickety, short-lived productions, has put the 'pensive' subscribing public on its guard, and the fondness for newspapers is too great and too general."

The result usually was circulations numbering in the hundreds; the *Port Folio*'s 2,000 and the *New York Missionary Magazine*'s 2,434 (achieved through the efforts of clergymen in getting club subscriptions) were exceptional. Often the failure of subscribers to pay up was enough to ruin a magazine before it could win its audience. Successful collection was beyond the resources of most publishers. Since there was so little advertising, these entrepreneurs had nowhere else to turn for cash.

In spite of every difficulty, circulatory and editorial, magazines continued to exist, and even to grow in number, largely by virtue of support from local groups of intellectuals or other people with common interests, grouped within relatively small areas. The idea of a national magazine was yet no more than an idea, although by 1825, periodicals like the *North American* were reaching out to broader horizons, and consequently enriching their circulation lists.

Magazine publishing was concentrated in the East, primarily in Boston, New York, and Philadelphia. The last for a time was the political capital of the new nation, and it later considered itself to have taken over from Boston as the cultural center—"the Athens of America," as the British writer John Neal called it in 1824. There was some basis for this claim: its citizens included scientists like Alexander Wilson and Benjamin Rush, universal geniuses like Franklin, artists like Benjamin West, writers like Brown, Dennie, Philip Freneau, and Washington Irving, although the last two could be claimed only for brief periods.

Boston and New York looked askance at Philadelphia's pretensions. Boston, with more than a little reason, looked upon itself as the intellectual capital of the New World. But expanding, bustling New York was beginning to surpass the other cities in growth, especially as a business center; and as the *business* of publishing developed, whether in books, magazines, or newspapers, it came to be increasingly centered there as time went on. By 1825, New York was already the center of book publishing, and had drawn even with Philadelphia in the number of magazines published. One Charleston, South Carolina, publisher moved his magazine to New York in 1806 because, as he said, he wanted to "stand at the confluence of the greatest number of the streams of knowledge." A New York literary group that was then beginning to develop and that would soon be perhaps the most important in the country lent weight to his words.

Yet Boston, though suffering from a decline in both trade and population, was far from relinquishing its literary eminence. Not only was it the home (there and in its environs) of some of the best minds in the nation, and the best writers as well; it was also the seat of several of the most important magazines, like the *North American Review* and the *Atlantic Magazine*. These periodicals were constantly fed and refreshed by contributors and graduates from the Boston area's great natural resource, Harvard College.

Boston looked upon the rest of intellectual America much the way the British looked upon their upstart former colony, and if there was one thing that Philadelphia and New York editors had in common, it was resistance to Boston's often proclaimed superiority. They made common cause against their New England neighbor. Of the failure of a Boston magazine in 1800, one Philadelphia editor remarked: "Many attempts have been made to establish periodical works in that small town; but miscellaneous readers ask in vain for a magazine, a review, or a literary journal in the capital of New England. The poverty of the inhabitants is the probably cause of the deficiency."

In the South, Baltimore was probably chief among the cities aspiring to be the literary capital of that region. Its literary weeklies were lively but inclined to be short-lived. However, it could boast two magazines that would survive and be famous: *Niles' Weekly Register* and the *American Farmer*. Nor were its resident writers inconsiderable:

Edward C. Pinkney, Francis Scott Key, Rufus Dawes, and T. S. Arthur, among others. Jared Sparks, too, was a preacher and editor there for a time.

Richmond and Charleston were other centers of southern culture and of magazine publishing, although Richmond was still a small town (less than 15,000 population in 1825), and hardly able to support adequate circulations; its newspapers carried most of the literary burden. Even smaller than Baltimore, Charleston nevertheless had the first magazine south of that city. It could not yet produce anything but tentative efforts toward periodical publishing, however. As one historian has noted: "Before 1825 the physical and economic conditions of the southern states were such as to render the production of a southern literature a practical impossibility."

In the West, physical and economic conditions were even more primitive, yet there were the beginnings of culture and of magazine production. Lexington, Kentucky, became the first center for periodicals, probably because Transylvania University attracted so many able men to its faculty. The Lexington *Medley, or Monthly Miscellany,* published during 1803, was the first general magazine west of Pittsburgh. Later, the *Western Review and Miscellaneous Magazine* became Lexington's most notable product, well above the level of what might have been expected of a frontier publication.

Cincinnati, another of the numerous American cities to regard itself as a latter-day Athens, still had little to justify its self-imposed title of "Athens of the West" except for a medical journal and a literary weekly. Like other western cities, Cincinnati and Lexington shared the difficulties of circulation in a largely undeveloped region. Mail delivery was extremely slow, and the roads were often impassable. But the magazines tried their best to promote culture in the region, and eastern magazines informed their readers of the lands opening up beyond the mountains.

As the magazine business approached its Golden Age in 1825, there were other signs of vitality besides expansion beyond the eastern centers and the forum it created for intellectuals. Mechanically, magazines were becoming more attractive to their growing public, as an influx of English engravers began to make noticeable improvements in engraving on copper, and as the technology of pressmaking began to improve. Engravings were much more frequent in magazines, and of considerably better quality when they did appear. The *Port Folio* was especially outstanding in its advancement of this art, which it began in 1809 and continued for nearly two decades. Wood engraving was also beginning to appear in American magazines by 1825.

Magazines were slowly establishing themselves as something more than transient imitations of English models, or even thinly disguised patriotic broadsides. There were more of them; they were becoming rapidly diversified; and perhaps most important, they were beginning to reflect national life in a substantial way.

four

Reflecting the Nation's Life

AS THEY BECAME MORE DIVERSIFIED, magazines were especially useful as interpreters of the American scene. The specialized magazine,
directed toward a particular profession or occupation, mirrored the
state of whatever field it served, besides offering a valuable record of
its progress. What appeared in the general magazines was less authentic and often less interesting, notwithstanding that many made an
effort to cover major aspects of the life around them.

In science, the medical journal dominated. The *Medical Repository,*
a quarterly in New York edited by Professor Samuel Latham Mitchill,
of the Columbia chemistry faculty, became the nation's first scientific
journal in 1797. Its co-editor was Dr. Edward Miller, one of the first
senators from the state. The *Medical Repository* and other medical
journals were much preoccupied with epidemics, as well they might
be, considering the number and virulence of outbreaks that swept the
United States. The yellow-fever epidemics in New York and Philadelphia were historic events in themselves, and so were given considerable attention in general periodicals as well. Some of the best
descriptions of the horrors of these plagues appeared in the magazines.
Philadelphia was the home of a good many medical journals, and
would be the center of medical book publishing for a long time to
come.

The leading general science periodical, however, did not begin in
any of the recognized magazine centers. The *American Journal of Science* was a product of New Haven, and of a great editor, Professor
Benjamin Silliman, who, together with his son, and James Dana,

edited it from the time it began in 1818 until 1864. It had excellent illustrations, printed articles by the best American scientists, and in general did much to further the development of American scientific thought.

Scientific periodicals also covered what was occurring in agriculture; but in a country still predominantly agricultural, in spite of the threatening advance of technology, it was only natural that magazines directed exclusively to farmers would arise. The first of these, the *Agricultural Museum,* was issued on July 4, 1810, in Georgetown, D.C. Its busy editor was the Reverend David Wiley, who was also secretary of the Columbian Agricultural Society, postmaster, superintendent of the turnpike, a merchant, a miller, and mayor of Georgetown. His modest publication depended on the members of the society for its life, and they apparently could not or would not support it beyond one year and eleven months, in spite of the fact that Joel Barlow was among the contributors.

A more successful attempt was the *American Farmer,* begun in 1817 by John S. Skinner, the Baltimore postmaster, who announced it would deal with "rural economy, internal improvements, news, prices current." It had the influential moral backing of such successful farmers as Jefferson, Madison, and Thomas Pickering. Soundly edited, influential from the first, it had a long life and did not cease publishing until 1897.

Among the professions, lawyers were foremost in establishing magazines, if not in point of time at least in vigor and persistence. One of Dennie's contributors, John E. Hall, was probably the first to publish a lawyers' magazine, the *American Law Journal,* of Philadelphia. For a while Hall was editor both of the *Journal* and the *Port Folio.*

The law journals were rich in contributors, editors and patrons, and the profession contributed liberally also to the list of editors of general magazines and reviews. Some turned from the law to magazine editing—Dennie, Brown, Bryant, and Skinner, among those editors already mentioned. Lawyers were chief among the *Port Folio's* contributors, and the prestigious *North American Review* numbered many of them among its best writers. Its editor, Edward Everett, and his brother Alexander H., also an editor, were both lawyers. Benjamin Latrobe, in 1811, remarked that lawyers were the best patrons of the arts in America, and "among the most distinguished members of the Academy of Fine Arts are those men who are most eminent at the bar."

Lawyers and other professionals were prominent among those who first began to use the magazines as a forum for the discussion of slavery, and for the introduction of other, less momentous, reform movements. Before the grand climax in 1861, the periodicals would carry the chief burden of the pro- and anti-slavery arguments—a national sounding board for the great debate.

The first of the notable antislavery magazines was *The Genius of Universal Emancipation,* the creation of a remarkable man named Benjamin Lundy, who established it in 1821, in Mount Pleasant, Ohio, with no money and a subscription list numbering six. Lundy was the epitome of self-reliance. His paper was printed in Steubenville, twenty miles away, and he walked there to get the printed product, bearing it home again on his back. For a time he moved his little sixteen-page monthly to Greenville, in northeastern Tennessee, having walked halfway there from Mount Pleasant, but in 1824 he put his knapsack on his back and walked again—this time to Baltimore, where he re-established his magazine. There it did so well that he made it a weekly in 1826.

Lundy was hardly a radical by today's standards. *The Genius* called for only gradual abolition, and advocated eventual colonization elsewhere of black people, but it infuriated the Baltimore slaveholders and dealers, one of whom nearly succeeded in killing Lundy. He was not dismayed. On foot, he traveled through the states preaching his abolitionist doctrine, as well as continuing to publish *The Genius.*

One of the people Lundy met on his travels was young William Lloyd Garrison, soon to be one of the nation's leading abolitionists. Garrison began publishing an antislavery newspaper in 1828, in Bennington, Vermont. In this *Journal of the Times,* as Garrison called his brief effort (it lasted a little less than two years), he wrote of Lundy: "Within a few months he has travelled about twenty-four hundred miles, of which upwards of sixteen hundred were performed *on foot!*

—during which time he has held nearly fifty public meetings. Rivers and mountains vanish in his path; midnight finds him wending his solitary way over an unfrequented road; the sun is anticipated in its rising. Never was moral sublimity of character better illustrated." Garrison, in 1829, became assistant editor of *The Genius,* after Lundy had walked up to Bennington to persuade him.

The impetus behind the antislavery magazines was largely religious, just as the discussions of it in the general periodicals were far more sentimental than political. Religion, too, was implicit in the attack on drinking, which began in 1826 with what was probably the first temperance magazine, the *National Philanthropist,* although the subject had been debated earlier in the general magazines. Similarly, smoking was under assault in many periodicals, but this "reform" had no magazine of its own. The magazines also sought to condemn dueling, which persisted through the 1820s and beyond.

An entirely new class of magazines that rose before 1825 was the theatrical review. Although not the first, certainly the most remarkable in this category was the *Thespian Mirror,* of New York, which appeared in December 1805 and continued until the following March. Its thirteen-year-old editor was John Howard Payne, who became a noted actor and is remembered, not for his career on the stage, but for a single song, "Home! Sweet Home!" of which he thought little. As an editor, Payne made an immediate impression. The *Port Folio's* New York correspondent reported that "the little editor of the *Thespian Mirror* is almost the only topic of fashionable table-talk."

Most of the theatrical journals barely survived a theatrical season. The only one to do so was a monthly titled *Mirror of Taste and Dramatic Censor,* published in Philadelphia during 1810 and 1811 by Stephen Cullen Carpenter, an Irish journalist. Otherwise, drama criticism was confined to the general magazines and newspapers. But the theater, like magazine writing, was not in good repute generally, and the *Portico* summed up the opinion of most of its contemporaries in 1807 when it described the stage as "Nought but ignorance and vulgarity clamorously enjoying the lowest obscenity and farce."

Another new classification to appear in the early years of the century was the comic periodical. They were quite as transitory and ill-regarded as the theater magazines, but pioneered what would become one of the mass audience's chief pleasures.

The best of them, one that became famous in its own right, and served as a model for those to come after, was the *Salmagundi,* subtitled, *or, the Whim-Whams and Opinions of Launcelot Langstaff, Esq.* The reason for its eminence, of course, was its editors and writers, who included Washington Irving, his brother, William, and his brother-in-law, James Kirk Paulding. *Salmagundi* lasted only a year, between 1807 and 1808, and it did not appear regularly. The first of its kind in American literature, it was full of rather gentle satire, fun-poking comments about the theater and other institutions, a little verse, and some unflattering portraits of contemporary personalities. It was so successful, no doubt, because its young entrepreneurs did not take it or themselves seriously. As Paulding wrote to Irving, "I know you consider old Sal as a sort of saucy, flippant trollope, belonging to nobody, and not worth fathering." Paulding thought better of old Sal, however, and published her himself in Philadelphia between 1819 and 1820. It was not the same without Irving's master touch.

Quite naturally, as centers of intellectual activity, the colleges produced their own magazines. Probably the first of these was Yale's *Literary Cabinet,* its first issue dated November 15, 1806. Harvard followed in 1810 with the *Harvard Lyceum.* But it was to be a time before the college magazine would come into its own, and these early efforts were brief: Yale lasted not quite a year, Harvard even less, in spite of the fact that Edward Everett was one of the editors of the *Lyceum,* and its chief contributor.

The arts were not much better served. Music had no magazine of its own until later, in spite of a national interest in music that resulted, among other events, in a performance of *The Barber of Seville* in New York as early as 1826. Some general magazines published music criticism, and a few even made it a department. Art was neglected except for an occasional article or a piece of criticism. For a while the *Port Folio* had a fine-arts department, and there were art notes in the *North American,* but in general the arts would have to wait until a later day for the magazines to catch up.

Still another kind of publication on the rise in the early years of the century was the business periodical. They were slow to come before 1825; it would take the sudden burst of technology preceding the Civil War to bring them fully into being, but they were on the way. Their forerunner had been the publications known as "price-currents," appearing first in seventeenth-century Holland and England. The earliest of these had been distributed in Amsterdam in 1609, but England boasted the first to be published privately and sold for profit. Translated to the American colonies, they appeared first in Charleston, South Carolina, in 1774, and were virtually the only kind of business publishing until the War of 1812, although *The Useful Cabinet* had appeared in Boston in 1808, and the *American Mineralogical Journal* in New York two years later.

Philadelphia, if not the Athens of America, was at least its financial center in these early years, and business publications naturally centered there. The "price-currents" did not last much longer than other magazines; merchants, it appeared, would rather get this information from newspapers and the newsrooms of mercantile establishments. But the need for them grew as the century advanced, and it is worth noting that there was enough demand for business information in 1815 to warrant the establishment of the first daily business paper, *Daily Items for Merchants,* which began in 1815 in New York. "Price-currents" went on for some time, however, expanding from simply reporting commodity prices to coverage of all commerce for which figures could be obtained.

Real specialization was not far away. The year 1825 seemed to mark a real break in business publishing, as it did in other types of periodicals. In that year the founding of the *American Mechanics Magazine* in New York, and the *Journal of the Philadelphia College of Pharmacy* (later the *American Journal of Pharmacy*), which still exists, indicated the direction of a new era.

There were other stirrings in the magazines as the era of nationalism ended. Fiction was getting more attention in periodicals, although it would be some time before it dominated so many magazines. In the women's magazines and the weekly miscellanies, the short story was already a staple. Fiction's progress was impeded, however, by the same public intolerance that relegated acting and magazine writing to a place just above the gutter. All three were in the same class, as far as the new bourgeoisie was concerned, with dancing, gambling, cock-fighting and horse racing. Magazines themselves reprinted with approval a London periodical's article of 1797 titled "Novel Reading a Cause of Female Depravity." A good many sober, serious people believed in this kind of nonsense—just as many today believe there is a connection between reading matter and sexual behavior.

In the light of these depressing beginnings of literary intolerance, it is refreshing to find a writer in the *Western Review,* of March 1821, referring in his breezy outlands way to the "bigots" who called the novel "the primer of Beelzebub." The same magazine, a few years later, termed the outcry against novels "mere wretched cant, utterly unworthy of the least pretension to mental enlargement, and fit only for men, who could have presided over a judicature for the trial of witches, or an ecclesiastical legislature to enact 'blue laws.' "

The meat-and-potatoes of many magazines was biography, as it has been in one form or another ever since. Mostly the periodicals printed the lives of heroes, military and political, and borrowed heavily from English magazines for similar portraits of those abroad. In carrying biographical material, obviously, the magazines were also purveying history to their readers, who increasingly turned to them as the past receded and the national self-doubts of the period before the Civil War developed. They found there information and reassurance that the American past had, indeed, been glorious. No American magazine of the time would have dared to tell them anything different.

Besides essays and biography, magazine readers were particularly fond of travel stories. The *Port Folio,* as noted earlier, had carried John Quincy Adams's account of his journey through Silesia, and the other magazines were soon publishing letters from Americans traveling in Europe. Much of the travel writing, however, consisted of excerpts from books, of which there were nearly as many as there were travelers.

Books of American poetry were much less frequent—so rare as to be an event—and so the magazines became the chief outlet for poems. They were a bad lot, on the whole, but not entirely without merit. As noted, Alexander Wilson's *The Foresters* was published in the *Port Folio*; it had to be done serially because it was two thousand lines long. Some of the short-lived literary weeklies and monthlies printed Longfellow, Halleck, and Bryant, among others, while the first American appearance of "Thanatopsis" was in the *North American Review* for September 1817. Lydia Huntley, a minor but much read poet, began the magazine phase of her literary career in the *North American* in 1816, about a year after the publication of her first book.

There were, unfortunately, also a quantity of poetical hacks like William Biglow, who, according to the editor of the *New-England Galaxy,* would "turn out any quantity of rhymes, *to order,* on any subject, and in the shortest possible time." Some magazines printed large quantities of such junk.

In any case, American poets were not much admired compared with the devotion given to English poets, who were published here both in book and magazine form. Darwin and Burns were popular in the United States before they were at home. Milton, Shakespeare, Pope, and Cowper were read in America by those who lived in huts and farmhouses, as well as by those who inhabited the fine Georgian mansions in the cities and the eastern countryside.

As soon as Scott arrived on the scene, however, he eclipsed all the others. The *American Review* observed in 1811 that no poet's works had been "more widely circulated or read with more avidity in this country than those of Walter Scott, who is now as a poet, on the highest pinnacle of fame and popularity." He soon attained the same fame as a novelist. Only Byron rivaled Scott as a popular poet in America. The *Portico* declared that "the popular voice" had hailed Byron as "the first poet of the age." For those who could not stomach Byron's personality or personal life, Thomas Moore became a substitute favorite. Moore contributed to the *Port Folio,* and even wrote a few stanzas about its editors, who were among his firmest American admirers.

Coleridge and Wordsworth were other poets widely read in American magazines, and widely criticized, too, a fate that did not escape any of the others, even Scott. But, then, literary criticism in America was pretentious, shallow, and often self-serving. There were not yet any major critics in the nation.

This was the state of American magazines on the brink of their Golden Age, a development that occurred in the quarter century between 1825 and 1850, and was one of the most remarkable in the history of communications.

PART TWO

THE GOLDEN AGE

(1825–1850)

five

How the General Magazines Began

THE YEAR 1825 WAS A TURNING POINT in both Europe and America. Abroad there was a rising wave of revolutionary movement in many countries, and a strong tide of reform was running. Change was the order of the day. It was also the primary fact of life in America as well, where the House of Representatives' denial of the Presidency to Andrew Jackson after he had won both the popular vote and the electoral vote, although by insufficient margins, paved the way for the coalition of South and West that sent him triumphantly to the White House four years later.

Jackson's accession was more than a Populist triumph, a grass-roots revolt that momentarily broke the hold of Easterners on national political life. It was the beginning of a new era in American politics, with large and far-reaching consequences that were not immediately foreseen. The nation had asserted itself as a nation for the first time. There was a suddenly awakened public consciousness of the continent—"the land was ours before we were the land's," as Robert Frost put it so many years later at another inauguration. The Erie Canal was a symbol of the change. It was finished in 1825, as hardworking immigrant laborers began to lay the rails westward for the Baltimore and Ohio Railroad.

Out of this ferment—and particularly the rapid spread of education, the reduction of illiteracy, the improvements in printing machinery, and the rise of the cities—came the nearly incredible expansion of the magazine business from its modest beginnings to mass market size. America itself was expanding in every direction, but no aspect of it was growing faster than magazines.

"These United States are fertile in most things, but in periodicals they are extremely luxuriant," said the *New-York Mirror* in November 1828. "They spring up as fast as mushrooms, in every corner, and like all rapid vegetation, bear the seeds of early decay within them. . . . They put forth their young green leaves in the shape of promises and prospectuses—blossom through a few numbers—and then comes a 'frost, a killing frost,' in the form of bills due and debts unpaid. This is the fate of hundreds, but hundreds more are found to supply their place, to tread in their steps, and share their destiny. The average age of periodicals in this country is found to be six months."

While the *New-York Mirror* may have underrated the general durability of the new magazines, it did not exaggerate the state of their proliferation. Figures for the period are as incomplete as they are unreliable, but there were about six hundred periodicals existing in 1850 where less than a hundred had been published in 1825, and in that quarter century it seems probable that somewhere between four and five thousand were published. Nothing like this gigantic wave of publication has ever been seen since.

In a time of highly significant changes and innovations in the business, perhaps the most important was the dramatic rise of the general monthly magazines. They had existed before, of course, but now they would climb to a preeminence of which their earlier entrepreneurs had not dared to dream.

One of the first ventures in this field proved to be also one of the most important. It began with the founding in 1826 of *The Casket: Flowers of Literature, Wit and Sentiment* by Samuel C. Atkinson and Charles Alexander, publishers of the *Saturday Evening Post.* ("Casket," it may be added, was a favorite name for magazines; the word was used in the sense of being a repository, with no somber connotations of funerals unless one considered that "literature, wit and sentiment," or whatever else editors had to offer, was "laid out" in these repositories.) As a sister publication of the *Post,* the *Casket* continued for a dozen years, with frequent interchanges of material between the two publications, until 1839, when Atkinson, who had remained as publisher after Alexander left the partnership, decided to sell it to a hustling young man named George R. Graham.

Graham altered the *Casket*'s character by changing it from a rather cheap-looking miscellany to a well-printed, entertaining magazine. Then, in another year, he bought the *Gentleman's Magazine,* which had been edited as an offstage amusement by the noted actor William E. Burton, who now needed the money for his real career. Combining the two, Graham in 1840 began issuing his new periodical, which he forthrightly if immodestly called *Graham's Magazine.* As Dr. Mott says of it in his *History,* it "not only became one of the three or four most important magazines in the United States but, in the five years 1841–45, displayed a brilliance which has seldom been matched in American magazine history." (More will be said of it in Chapter 9.)

In Boston a new magazine emerged, the *New-England Magazine,* edited by Joseph Dennie's youthful admirer, Joseph T. Buckingham, and his son Edwin. This venture became notable if for no other reason than its publication of fifteen pieces by Nathaniel Hawthorne.

A more enduring periodical, which became successful and famous after a rocky start in 1833, was the *Knickerbocker Magazine,* edited after 1834 by Lewis Gaylord Clark, who became known to generations of New Yorkers as "Old Knick." Drawing on the rich pool of literary talent then in the city—writers like Irving, James Fenimore Cooper, Bryant, Halleck, Paulding, and Nathaniel P. Willis—Clark added such notable New England names as Longfellow, Hawthorne, Whittier, and Holmes until he was producing a magazine difficult to surpass.

Clark introduced something new in magazine format—a section titled "Editor's Table," in which he talked in a light fashion about topics of the day, and especially happenings in New York City, for whose citizens the magazine was intended. This department was the ancestor of the present-day *New Yorker* magazine's opening "Notes and Comment" section, and, in a more general way, of the "Editor's Easy Chair" department in *Harper's* magazine and similar sections in many other magazines. It gave the magazine a more personal voice, besides providing the editor with a platform for his views and observations about contemporary life.

Of equivalent importance in the development of periodicals during this exuberant Golden Age was the rapid rise of magazines for women. Earlier attempts to reach this audience were dwarfed by the giants that now arose, challenging the general magazines and arousing not only their competitive antagonism but also the ire of those who thought it preposterous to serve women with magazines at all. Charles A. Dana, soon to be one of the most famous of newspaper publishers, deplored in the *Harbinger* for August 8, 1846, the assumption these magazines "constantly put forth of being designed for *ladies,* and of representing in some way the women of the country. . . . Heaven protect us from such literature!"

The women for whom the magazines were intended disagreed. Though some of the material in the new periodicals might be appallingly bad, there was plenty of good reading, too, and women were delighted with the idea of large, well-printed magazines directed especially to them.

After a few tentative starts in that direction, the first really successful women's magazine was produced in Boston, in 1828, by Sarah Josepha Hale, a formidable woman who left an imprint in more ways than one on national life. Mrs. Hale looked like everybody's mother— an ample, full-bosomed, pleasant lady who yet had a no-nonsense air of efficiency about her. She called her new publication the *Ladies' Magazine.* It was meant not only to entertain but to promote Mrs. Hale's deeper interests, which lay in the direction of "female education." Perhaps that was why her publishing efforts sometimes met with such savage attacks. In an era when men did not regard women as having any legitimate interest in life other than keeping house and raising children, Mrs. Hale wanted them to be trained as teachers, and to educate them in "female seminaries." Other magazines for women had been sickly and sentimental and domestic. The *Ladies' Magazine* boldly campaigned for women's rights.

After nine annual volumes but only an indifferent financial success,

Mrs. Hale merged her magazine with its chief rival, *Godey's Lady's Book,* going along with it as an editor. In its issue for March 1837, the *American Annals of Education* noted the deal with disapproval: "*The Ladies' Magazine,* which has been for nine years devoted, in part, to female education, has recently lost its identity, and, like many a 'better half,' assumed the name of a worse one. It is united with the *Lady's Book,* a periodical of much interest; but far less important, in its tendencies on sound literature, morals, and education."

In its feminist zeal, the *American Annals* sadly underrated Louis Godey's excellent magazine, which was certainly the best of the women's magazines before the Civil War. Its contributors numbered the finest writers in the country, and it did what other magazines had not done, except for *Graham's,* by paying them liberally. By 1850 it was selling 40,000 a month—the highest any magazine had yet achieved.

The influence of *Godey's Lady's Book* on other magazines was substantial. Publishers and editors were made to realize that the female market was more important than they had realized and that reaching this market would substantially increase the circulation of any magazine, particularly the general monthlies. Consequently the astute George Graham, for one, changed the content of his magazine until half of it, or more, was intended for women. Others did likewise, and went even further by copying *Godey's* directly, to the annoyance of its proprietor. It was even imitated as far away as London.

Of these many imitations, the most successful was *Peterson's Ladies' National Magazine,* founded in Philadelphia in 1842 by a *Saturday Evening Post* editor, Charles J. Peterson. The editor of *Peterson's* was Mrs. Ann S. Stephens, one of those tireless ladies who wrote endless fiction serials for the magazines and who now turned a good part of her efforts toward her own periodical. Both *Peterson's* and *Godey's* continued until 1898, when they died simultaneously; by that time *Peterson's* had passed its rival in circulation, if not in prestige.

There were other imitators of a minor kind. The most successful were those monthlies intended to be bound at the end of the year as gift-book annuals, usually under such titles as *Ladies' Wreath* or

Lady's Wreath or *Ladies' Garland,* and selling for a dollar. A few weeklies for women were also published, but they were of little consequence.

In sheer numbers, the literary weeklies outnumbered the women's magazines and the general monthlies. They were cheap, and most of them soon died. One of the best, and therefore able to survive for a time, was the *New-York Mirror,* begun in 1823. Before it died in 1846, it presented to its readers a fascinating running commentary on the morals and manners of the times, done with wit, grace, and style.

Another weekly, which forecast a style of the future, was *Paul Pry,* edited in Washington, D.C., by an eccentric, witty woman, Mrs. Anne Royall, who wrote down her observations of Washington life in a way that has survived to our own time in the gossip columns and society columns of newspapers, and in magazines like *Confidential* and *Whisper.* Mrs. Royall may not have been as sensational as these later successors, but in the context of the times she was fully as outspoken about politics and society in Washington, about which she had few illusions. *Paul Pry* began in 1831. Five years later, when the energetic editor was seventy-one, she dropped her successful magazine for no special reason and began a new one, *The Huntress,* which continued to shoot its barbed shafts until 1854.

As many stories, most of them apocryphal, were told about Mrs. Royall as appeared in her magazines. A favorite, repeated for years, was her alleged pursuit of the elusive President Madison for an interview. She was said to have happened upon him while he was swimming alone on a hot day in a secluded part of the Potomac, and sat on his clothes while he stood up to his neck in water and submitted to the interview.

If true, this maneuver at least demonstrated original enterprise at a time when the lack of international copyright made literary piracy highly profitable. It was practiced by magazine and book publishers alike, by most quite openly. The talented Nathaniel Parker Willis, with his friend Dr. T. O. Porter, launched in 1839 a magazine boldly called the *Corsair;* Willis had wanted to call it *The Pirate.* In his prospectus Willis declared frankly that he meant "to take advantage, in short, of the privilege assured to us by our piratical law of copyright; and, in the name of American authors (for our own benefit) 'convey' to our columns, for the amusement of our readers, the cream and spirit of everything that ventures to light in England, France and Germany." In spite of Willis's own brilliant efforts, and a trip to Europe to comb piratical possibilities there (he obtained some travel letters of Thackeray, but had to pay for them), the magazine ended a year after it started.

Piracy was made to pay, however, in a historic series of episodes beginning in 1839, with consequences going far beyond the periodicals themselves. Two young men, Park Benjamin and Rufus W. Griswold, who had learned their trade as editors on Horace Greeley's *New-Yorker,* begun in 1834, started a cheap fiction weekly called *Brother Jonathan* in July 1839. It contained a little original material, but most of it was given over to serials pirated from the works of Dickens, Bulwer-Lytton, Captain Marryat, Paul de Kock, and others. Even the woodcut illustrations were stolen from other magazines.

Six months later, Griswold and Benjamin had to relinquish their venture to the printer-publishers Wilson and Company, but they immediately began another publication of the same stripe, which they called *New World.* It was first issued on June 6, 1840. The format was unusual: pages four feet long and eleven columns wide on occasion, although in six months or so the magazine began to appear in a quarto edition as well.

The struggle between these two competing pirates was an epic one. They quickly swallowed up available English fiction, and soon were competing fiercely to beat each other on the street with novels fresh off the boat from England. Book-publishing houses and some of the other periodicals were playing the same game, but *Brother Jonathan* and *New World* beat them by publishing complete novels in a single issue. They were called "extras." Taken off the boat in their original hard-cover form or in sheets, they were rushed into print by day-and-night shifts in sweating composing rooms, then hawked in the streets like newspapers at ten cents a copy. They were difficult to read in closely set type on quarto pages, but readers seemed not to mind when they could get for ten cents what would cost them a dollar from the book publishers.

The method soon spread to Boston and Philadelphia, but the two
New York papers were more energetic than any rival. To those who
protested the morality of the piracies, *New World* replied piously that
its "ample pages are unsoiled by profane or improper jests, vulgar
allusions, or irreligious sentiments."

Benjamin and Griswold had discovered a way to make a great deal
of money, until the Federal government noticed that both magazines
had been going through the mails at newspaper rates. In April 1843,
the post office ordered much higher pamphlet rates applied to the publications, and two months later they lost their Canadian distribution
when British copyright laws were invoked against them. Within a year,
both had expired, although *Brother Jonathan* resumed later as a
twenty-five-cent monthly.

It had been an amazing episode. Assessing it with some indignation,
E. A. Duyckinck, writing in the *American Whig Review* for February
1845, observed: "Native authors were neglected, despised, insulted;
foreign authors were mutilated, pillaged, and insulted besides. . . . The
good writers were not only taken possession of, their works altered
and thrown upon the public without their just honor and responsibility, but they were made the cover for the worst licentiousness. . . .
The cupidity of the publishers over-stocked the market, and the traffic
fell. . . . Doubtless a taste for reading was diffused. . . ."

Not only was the taste diffused, but the "extras" showed book publishers the way to new publics and larger profits. In competing with
the magazines, they began to issue series of paperbound books of their
own, sometimes complete, sometimes long novels in parts at prices
ranging generally from twenty-five cents to fifty cents. Thus was the
paperback book born, and this first "revolution" flourished before the
Civil War, and has recurred in tremendous surges four times since.
Today paperbound volumes are an industry, and the racks upon racks
of these books we see owe their origins to *Brother Jonathan* and the
New World.

There were other cheap magazines, however, with a different purpose. These were the so-called "knowledge magazines," offering all
kinds of factual information. The first was the *Magazine of Useful
and Entertaining Knowledge,* a monthly published during 1830–1831

by N. Sargent and Abraham Halsey, members of the New York Lyceum of Natural History. Imitators followed, until there was a profusion of "family" and "penny" periodicals with titles often containing the phrase "Cabinets of Instruction."

How well they instructed was doubted by their contemporaries. Summarizing them in 1835, the *Family Magazine* deplored these "cheap publications," and continued: ". . . In the zeal of competition . . . many stale and useless works were imprudently admitted into some of the publications, and the smallness of the type and bad quality of the paper rendered many of them unsatisfactory and almost worthless. Many of the cheap magazines, also, became satisfied with making up their pages with fragments of ephemeral news, rather than with substantial Knowledge, alleviating their dullness by introducing here and there a worthless tale, and only taking care to impose the trash upon the world with the catch-penny glare of engravings."

Among the quarterlies before 1850, the *North American Review* continued upon its majestic way, although it suffered from the editorship of men who, though brilliant in other ways, were not good editors. Its principal rival was the *New York Review,* edited successively by its 1837 founder, the Reverend Francis L. Hawks; Caleb S. Henry, professor of philosophy at New York University; and the Astor librarian J. G. Cogswell. It nearly matched the *North American Review* in scholarship, and stood well ahead of its other competitors.

No doubt the most famous of the quarterlies, although it made no particular attempt to compete with its contemporaries, was *The Dial,* Margaret Fuller's journal of transcendental opinion and writing which she began to publish in July 1840. Ralph Waldo Emerson edited it during the second part of its four-year existence. It was not a magazine for the general public. As Dr. Mott puts it, it was "a mystification to the uninitiated, caviare to the general, and a butt of ridicule for the irreverent." Nonetheless, it contained work by some of the best minds in New England, much of which later emerged in book form.

Church periodicals before 1850 were inclined to be quarterlies, and while they naturally devoted much of their space to theological argument, since it was a time of the most intense religious controversy, some at least devoted their columns to secular interests, and a few could hardly be distinguished from the magazines published by and for the laity.

More and more, as churches discovered what an ideal platform magazines could be for dissemination of the faith, they turned to this medium as a primary outlet, while also starting their own book-publishing houses. Thus the religious press became one of the most rapidly growing and active in the entire publishing business. The Congregationalists alone had at least twenty-five periodicals, and the Catholics as many as forty or fifty. The *Biblical Repository* asserted in January 1840 that "of all the reading of the people three-fourths is purely religious . . . of all the issues of the press three-fourths are theological, ethical and devotional." Eight years later, New York City alone could boast fifty-two religious magazines. According to the census of 1850, there were 191 religious publications in the United States, about half of them newspapers.

The use of magazines as a platform for theological argument led to their use as platforms for secular interests. It was in magazines that the great issues of the day were debated before the Civil War engulfed the nation.

six

Periodicals as a Political Platform

IN THE TURBULENCE OF THE JACKSON ERA, with the menacing cloud of the slavery debate moving ever closer, Americans were preoccupied with politics. As Timothy Flint observed in the *Western Monthly Review* for May 1830, "In travelling through our land, little interest or excitement is seen in any thing, but electioneering and politics.... The columns of our newspapers are occupied with little else...."

The columns of the magazines, however, were not so single-minded, primarily because those intended for women and children were not at all politically oriented, and the religious press was nonpartisan, at least for a time. But the political struggles of the period were so fundamental that they inevitably overflowed into the pages of the periodicals, existing side by side in uncomfortable juxtaposition with *belles-lettres*. There was little attempt to be neutral. The magazines were partisan, sometimes violently so.

Wherever one looked, there was controversy. There was the question of the National Bank, and economic issues raised by the Panic of 1837. The Mexican War was as bitterly opposed as it was supported. A nation pushing its boundaries outward was certain to run headlong into disputes, like the arguments over the annexation of Texas and the boundaries of Oregon. South Carolina raised the issue of nullification. And with swiftly increasing momentum, the debate over abolition began to overshadow everything else.

Both sides of political issues often found powerful supporters in the magazines. Advocates of a National Bank, fiercely opposed by the states'-rights believers, were grateful for the aid of so influential an organ as the *North American Review* and writers like George Bancroft to argue the case. When the Mexican War became a national issue, much of the opposition to it found its voice in the magazines, where a respected thinker like Ralph Waldo Emerson could say bluntly, as he did in the *Massachusetts Quarterly* in December 1847, "We have a bad war. . . ."

The argument over the war was strikingly like the national division over Vietnam in our own time. "It seems surprising all men cannot see that such a glory is only shame," Theodore Parker said in the same issue that carried Emerson's uncompromising statement. "Poor, unhappy Mexico!" an article began in the *Knickerbocker* of July 1847. The *Whig Review* declared that the war "might and should have been avoided," while the same magazine carried an article by Daniel D. Barnard, just retired from Congress, who asserted: "We have been plunged into this war by the blunders, or the crime, of those who administer the public affairs of our own country."

On the other hand, some of the influential magazines were purposefully silent on the issue, whether out of patriotism or in deference to the known sympathies of their audiences, it is difficult to say. Whatever reticence there may have been in some periodicals about the slavery question, however, disappeared in time under the heat of controversy. On the other hand William Lloyd Garrison's *The Liberator,* founded in 1831, was by far the most eloquent, and served as the voice of the New England Anti-Slavery Society, begun in 1832 and a year later changing its name to the American Anti-Slavery Society. Other abolitionist organizations had their magazines or newspapers, but none of the others, of course, had Garrison's fiery pen to command it. Few magazines had ever been so ardently loved or hated as *The Liberator*; today scholars regard it as a publication of both literary and historical importance.

In spite of those who despised it, *The Liberator* was safe enough in Boston at first. The abolitionist journals nearer the South, in the border states, were not so fortunate. The office of the *Cincinnati Philanthropist* was raided twice by an irate mob in 1837, and yet again four years later. Its editor, Dr. Gamaliel Bailey, started another abolition paper in Washington in 1847, the *National Era*, and this magazine soon gained a wide reputation for itself, first because of the literary work it carried by Nathaniel Hawthorne, including "The Great Stone Face," and then for its serialization of *Uncle Tom's Cabin* from June 5, 1851, to April 1, 1852. Harriet Beecher Stowe, for whom the writing of the book was a great emotional experience, found herself unable to stop, while her Boston publisher fretted at its growing length because he wanted to bring it out in a single volume, for reasons of economy. Mrs. Stowe at last wanted to end it with Tom's death, but when the question was put to the readers who were following the tale with utter absorption, they begged her to go on. Jewett finally had to publish the book in two volumes.

Some magazines, like Bailey's and Garrison's, were devoted to the slavery question. Others, both the general and the specialized, discussed it more and more, especially the religious reviews and weeklies. They were far from uniformly abolitionist, of course. The debate was dividing the churches, north and south, as it was the rest of the nation. The Presbyterian *Biblical Repository*, for example, quoted the Scriptures to attack the abolitionists and defend the institution of slavery, even after the war began. On the other hand, the *North American Review*, which ordinarily spoke in a calm and reasoned voice, printed in capitals the Jacksonian battle cry: THE FEDERAL UNION—IT MUST BE PRESERVED. That was as early as January 1833, during the early argument over South Carolina's nullification action.

But it was *The Liberator*'s strong voice that stirred passions more than any other magazine. "We hold slavery to be a blot upon our national escutcheon," it declared sternly, "a libel upon the Declaration of Independence, A SIN AGAINST GOD which exposes us to his tremendous judgments, and which ought to be immediately repented of and forsaken." Such talk began to stir up those who thought the abolitionists were going too far, and there were mass meetings in New York and Boston to protest what was regarded by many as an unwarranted revolutionary provocation. The result of the tumultuous meeting in Boston was mob violence against Garrison and the destruction of his press, while in Charleston another mob rifled the mailbags and burned the northern antislavery papers they found there.

At least some of the magazine press believed that the newspapers, reflecting the interests of the businessmen who were generally in favor of the *status quo*, were inciting the mobs. After the sacking of *The Liberator,* the great Methodist organ *Zion's Herald,* a newspaper itself, came flying to Garrison's defense with an outraged cry: "And this is the land of LIBERTY! Our soul is sick at such hypocrisy! . . . Who are the authors of this riot? The daily press of this city. . . ."

Oddly enough, there was less passion in the articles supporting slavery that appeared in such southern magazines as the *Southern Quarterly* and *Southern Literary Messenger,* which felt they could hardly avoid the question but did not often raise their voices when they were discussing it. Their reserve began to wear thinner, however, toward 1850, as the number of abolitionist journals continued to increase in the North, although most of the leading magazines there still opposed abolition, and prominent editors refused to believe that the question would not be resolved peacefully before long.

When they were not discussing slavery, the magazines found other political questions to occupy their pages. Tariffs were always good for columns of argument, and for many the Oregon question was of more moment than abolition. Some even favored fighting England for the territory, if it proved necessary, while others were inclined to share a Boston magazine's verdict, "The territory of Oregon is not worth much," separated as it was from the rest of the country by a "desert two thousand miles broad and a range of lofty and precipitous mountains." Many of the periodicals that held this view, however, changed their minds after gold was discovered in California in 1848. The West was seen to have some value after all. In fact, gold fever filled the pages of a good many magazines for a time.

The physical problem of getting westward stimulated articles by the hundreds, as the frenzy to extend the rail ribbons reached a peak in the 1840s, with nearly three thousand new miles of track being laid every year. This was a relatively nonpolitical subject that stirred everyone's imagination, and the editors took full advantage. "Even if the art of flying should be invented," exclaimed the *Illinois Monthly* in 1830, "who would endure the trouble of wearing a pair of wings and the labor of flapping them, when every gentleman may keep his own 'locomotive' and travel from the Mississippi to the Atlantic with no other expenditure than a teakettle of water and a basket of chips!" Some southern writers even saw in the linking of the Ohio River and the Atlantic by rail a force that would unite North and South "by the endearing bonds of mutual sympathies and common interests."

The railroads soon had their own periodical, the *American Rail-Road Journal*, published in New York as a weekly beginning in 1832, later a semimonthly and finally a monthly, existing today as *Railway Locomotives and Cars*. It was not the first in the field, however. A year earlier, in Rogersville, Tennessee, the *Rail-Road Advocate* had a brief life. Two other railroad magazines were founded before 1850, and half a dozen others had emerged by 1865.

Once slavery, politics, and transportation were disposed of, the magazines before 1850 gave rather short shrift to such other problems of the day as immigration, poverty, and labor conditions. A few writers were becoming concerned about the social problems of the new society being created, but there were few who shared the *Democratic Review's* alarm in 1849 over the fact that "fortunes of $1,000,000 are now not rare, and some reach $20,000,000, while thousands of starving beggars throng the streets and crowd the public charities." There were many more editors who preferred to cite the favorable situation of American labor as compared with the lot of workingmen in Europe. The French Socialists were quoted and written about, but infrequently read with any ardor. Nevertheless, there were some who could not look upon the thriving New England factories without fear of what they might be doing to the structure of society.

There was a good deal of trivia in the magazines, too—endless prose dealing with the fads and fancies of the day, as well as with the innumerable attempts at "reform." It sometimes appeared that the entire American society was split into groups intent on improving the morals and manners of every other group. Temperance at times excited as much passion as slavery; there were nearly a hundred temperance societies by 1828. Most editors, however, sympathized with the opinion of the *Knickerbocker* writer who confessed: "I for one have *drank moderately,* when it suited my feelings and caprice, for twenty years. I feel in no danger."

Smoking was also debated, pro and con, but it was easier to argue the merits of chewing, where feelings on both sides were stronger. Nevertheless, there was a continuing agitation against tobacco, strongly supported by some magazines, and in 1851 Boston, at least, made it an offense to smoke on the streets and specified a fine for violators. The mayor, however, a smoker himself, made an exception of Boston Common and provided a circle of seats there in a special corner where tobacco lovers could puff away in peace.

In rapidly growing New York, magazines like the *Mirror* and the *Knickerbocker* were complaining about obscene pictures, the rudeness of omnibus riders, wandering pigs in the streets, and traffic. Most of all —a familiar cry echoing down the centuries—they were perennially upset about the continuous destruction and rebuilding of the city, making it, as one complained, "a city of ruins"—as it remains today.

Another mild crusade carried on in the magazines was the effort to get Americans to take baths more often. "Of all the inhabitants of the globe," the *Mirror* complained, "we Americans are, as a people, the least addicted to bathing; and among all the Americans we of New York have the least claim to the character of a self-washing race. . . . Here the bath is merely a summer luxury for a vast majority of the citizens, enjoyed perhaps once a week during the hottest weather, and it may be some half dozen times during the rest of the year. How many houses are there in this city furnished with bathing rooms? . . ."

The ladies' magazines declined to join in this crusade. As the *Christian Parlor Book* warned, "It is quite certain that the practice, in extremely cold weather, of leaping from a warm bed and suddenly extracting all the caloric by cold water has been ruinous to multitudes of delicately organized ladies."

Still another issue discussed in the magazines has a familiar ring today. The subject was hair—beards, to be specific. Before the early 1840s they had been absent for a long time, almost a century, but suddenly they revived and became a fad. The Secretary of the Navy eventually had to take notice of it, and issued his celebrated "Whisker Order," defining the limits of hair on the face and thereby nearly precipitating a mutiny.

One of the specializations beginning to develop in the periodical press was the sports magazine. The *Turf Register* appeared in Baltimore in September 1829, reflecting an American interest in racing, a sport that dated from colonial times. Racing had been brought over from England, where it was as passionately followed in the seventeenth century as it is today.

A sporting paper of more dubious reputation, although it has survived into our own time, was the *National Police Gazette*, begun in 1845 in New York. Its specialty at the beginning was not sport but crime, promising "a most interesting record of horrid murders, outrageous robberies, bold forgeries, astounding burglaries, hideous rapes, vulgar seductions, and recent exploits of pickpockets and hotel thieves." Along with these juicy attractions, the *Gazette* also printed some sporting news, but its readers, which included criminals and those in the city government who protected them, were often outraged, and not infrequently wrecked its offices. Later the *Gazette* was bought by a former police chief, and as the decades went on it passed through various metamorphoses, although always retaining its special, fragrant blend of sex, scandal, and sports. A staple of barbershops at the turn of the century, it lost ground steadily as the present century advanced and introduced periodicals that made it look like a Sunday-school journal.

Of all the reformers, major and minor, who argued and fought in the magazines before the Civil War, probably those who were for or against women's rights were the most vociferous. Women were emerging from domestic slavery. They were in the thick of the abolitionist battle; they were writing for the magazines, and contributing many of the hugely popular novels of the day; and they were struggling openly, in and out of their magazines, for some kind of parity with men. The first Woman's Rights Convention took place in 1848, at Seneca Falls, New York.

Seven years before that event, when women abolitionists had been refused admittance to the World's Antislavery Convention in London, Sophia Ripley summarized the conflict in the *Dial*: "There have been no topics for the last two years more generally talked of than women, and 'the sphere of women.' In society, everywhere, we hear the same oft-repeated things said upon them by those who have little perception of the difficulties of the subject; and even the clergy have frequently flattered 'the feebler sex' by proclaiming to them from the pulpit what lovely beings they may become if they will only be good, quiet and gentle, and attend exclusively to their domestic duties, and the cultivation of religious feelings, which the other sex kindly relinquish to them as their inheritance. Such preaching is very popular."

It is difficult today for us to believe that the idea of women voting should ever have shocked Americans, especially the educated, cultivated men who edited the best magazines. Yet the *New-York Mirror* protested, "The eternal wrangling of discordant opinions about men and offices, and the petty details of elections and caucuses can have little charm for the refined taste or polished judgment, and lend no charm to the intercourse of the domestic circle. . . . No, there can be no excuse for a female deserting her allotted privacy and volunteering to encounter gladiators in the political arena." Even most of the women's magazines were opposed to suffrage for their sex.

Those women content to stay at home with their children found that the mania for starting magazines had extended to periodicals designed for the young, and while many of these journals were dreary moralizers, the new trend toward entertainment that had already begun in books was also evident in the periodicals. The indefatigable Nathaniel Willis began *The Youth's Companion* in Boston in 1827, and served as its editor for three decades while it established its just reputation as one of the best and most popular periodicals for young people of all time. It survived into the twentieth century and died in 1929, a victim of the Crash.

In 1833, that mountain of energy Samuel G. Goodrich, who was equally successful as publisher and writer, began his *Parley's Magazine* in New York. Goodrich had to sell it a year later because of ill health, but "Peter Parley," as he signed himself, continued to delight generations of children with the books he produced for them. In 1844

Parley's was merged with another magazine Goodrich had started in 1841, *Merry's Museum for Boys and Girls.* It was distinguished because it was edited by Louisa May Alcott, who also contributed to it.

Magazines, proliferating as they were, by 1850 had become a national platform for every kind of argument and reform movement. They were more affluent and varied than ever, and for the first time they offered a career to writers.

seven

The Coming of the Magazinist

MAGAZINE EDITORS TODAY DEPEND for what they print, beyond the output of their own staff writers and contributors, on the work of a hard core of free-lance writers, numbering from three to four hundred, who supply material for most of the general consumer magazines and many of the specialized periodicals as well. Only a negligible percentage of what the magazines print comes from unsolicited, over-the-transom contributions.

The creation of a body of professional magazine writers is largely the product of the twentieth century, but the roots of the profession are in the pre–Civil War magazines, in whose pages the work of writers, as a class, first began to appear. The growing number of specialized magazines were able to continue with the natural practice of drawing contributions from the ranks of their own audience—doctors, farmers, clergymen. But the general magazines were victims of the condition described in 1835 by Park Benjamin in the *New-England Magazine* when he wrote: "With the exception of those whom Fortune has placed beyond the necessity of exertion, there are no authors by profession. The efforts of American writers are, for the most part, made in hours of leisure, set aside from business." Or, as *Brother Jonathan* put it in 1842, "the man who depends upon literature for a living is little better than a fool."

Not long after these words were written, the policies of the new magazine proprietors began to change this condition. Publishers like Graham and Godey were astute enough to realize that by raising payments to contributors substantially they would be providing an incentive likely to produce a wider choice of work, and they were right.

Nathaniel Parker Willis has long been regarded as the first successful, professional free-lance writer—or "magazinist," as he was called in the nineteenth-century idiom. Willis wrote for both *Graham's* and *Godey's*, and for a good many other magazines as well. He had the essential characteristics of a good free-lance writer today: he was an excellent reporter, able to work in a variety of fields, and the possessor of a light, smooth, readable style that was a refreshing contrast to the pretentious prose of the day. He wrote both prose and poetry, fiction and nonfiction; it seemed there was nothing he could not make at least a creditable attempt to do.

Willis readily acknowledged that he was the leader in his field; modesty was no part of his nature. In dress and manner, he seemed a dandy, and he annoyed even his friends by his excellent opinion of himself. Nevertheless, he was not the highest paid magazine writer in the country without reason, and his exuberant personality overflowed into his lively prose style. Few writers of his day would have had the brash confidence to begin a story: "I have a passion for fat women. If there is anything I hate in life, it is what dainty people call a *spirituelle*. Motion—rapid motion—a smart, quick, squirrel-like step, a pert, voluble tone—in short, a lively girl—is my exquisite horror! I would as lief have a *diable petit* dancing his infernal hornpipe on my cerebellum as to be in the room with one. . . ." Willis then goes on to describe in detail the heroine of his story, a fat girl whose name is, appropriately, Albina McLush.

A magazinist of far greater ability and much less income was Edgar Allan Poe, who contributed to more than thirty magazines and served on the editorial staffs of five of them during his tortured lifetime. His magazine life was, unfortunately, as melancholy as his stories and poems. For the contributions he made, some of which were enduring portions of American literature, he got as little money as the pay scales of the time allowed. For his work as editor, he was among the lowest paid. True, he was much less editor than writer, but even so, his genius placed him far above the general run of men who sat in the editorial chairs.

Among the other early magazinists could be cited writers like Park Benjamin, who was always busy as writer, editor, or both, and the Philadelphian T. S. Arthur, better known to us today as the author of *Ten Nights in a Bar-Room,* his most successful book. Arthur left a hundred books behind him, many of them filled with his magazine pieces. William Gilmore Simms, whom we remember more now as a poet, was the leading magazinist in the South, but he was so prolific that his work appeared in many of the northern periodicals, too.

The most indefatigable of the magazinists, like Arthur, were inclined to be book writers, and there was now, indeed, a natural flow between the magazine and book business—magazine contributions became books, books were excerpted or printed whole in magazines, just as they are today. No one was more deeply involved in this traffic than Mrs. Lydia H. Sigourney, who wrote steadily for fifty years, a tidal output of prose and poetry appearing in more than three hundred magazines, and resulting in fifty-six books. By her own count, Mrs. Sigourney contributed a minimum of two thousand articles to the periodicals. There was, in fact, a whole "writing tribe" of women who wrote for the magazines, but none of them approached Mrs. Sigourney in productivity.

If she had any near rivals, it was those "sweet singers of the West," as Whittier called them, Alice and Phoebe Cary, who began writing in the 1840s with an almost frightening ease. Alice was wildly understating the case when she told her editor, "We write with great facility." The sisters often produced two or three poems a day—and they wrote every day.

The rise of the magazinist did not come without internal struggle, and there was born during this period the feeling of mutual dependence and mutual conflict that characterizes so many editor-writer relationships in our own time. Agents are often the buffer zone between the disputants today, but there remain numerous nose-to-nose confrontations about rewrites, alteration of ideas, rejection of articles in manuscript that have been previously accepted as ideas—and always, of course, money. These disputes are an everyday fact of life to free-lancers, although naturally they are not characteristic of the relationship as a whole.

In the early days of the magazinist, however, there were no prece-
dents, and editors were likely to be uninhibited critics of the writers,
feeling free to improve them, with or without their consent, in ways
that would be considered completely impermissible today. Often the
writers fought back, as one addressed the editor of the *New-England
Magazine*: "Your impertinence is equalled only by your ignorance;
your wit is as mean as your capacity is questionable; and the profun-
dity of your self-conceit is in ludicrous contrast with the shallowness
of your intellect."

In reality, however, authors had few rights that editors were bound
to respect. Magazines freely reprinted from each other, without further
payment to the writer, until *Graham's* and *Godey's* began to put some
curbs on the practice in 1845 by copyrighting the contents of their
magazines. American copyright had achieved considerable strength
by this time; it was the idea of international copyright which was still
little more than an argument. Nothing was done, however, to limit
what appeared to many authors as a more serious interference with
their work—the absolute control editors exerted over what was submitted to them. They did not hesitate to rewrite as they pleased, without consultation, and sometimes added material of their own if what
they had seemed incomplete or did not please them. Even the fact
that the editors were his close friends did not save Emerson from being
edited without his permission by the proprietors of *The Dial,* Margaret
Fuller and George Ripley.

While payment was improving rapidly, and could support a magazinist if he wrote enough, it was still far from sufficient to compensate
for editorial tyranny. Rates still depended on the size and financial
condition of the magazine, and these factors also usually determined
when the contributor might get his money. A dollar a page, the *North
American Review*'s rate, was still something of a standard, but others
sometimes paid more. The *Knickerbocker,* for example, paid five dollars a page "for such contributions as we consider best," but another
contributor in the same issue might get nothing.

Graham's Magazine was a forecast of things to come. George
Graham did not lay down a fixed rate for contributions, but he paid

anywhere from four to twelve dollars a page for prose, and ten to fifty dollars for a poem. Higher prices were quoted for famous names, just as they are today. This rate scale had an inflationary effect on all the magazines able to afford it, and the result was highly beneficial for writers, notwithstanding that if *Graham's* page size was used as a measurement, a writer had to produce a thousand words for every page he was paid for. Thus an author could expect to get from twenty to sixty dollars for a five-thousand-word article—excellent payment by the living standards of the day.

Some of *Graham's* contributors could make enough from this scale, and the substantial additions if they were famous, to live very well indeed. Longfellow got fifty dollars a poem. Cooper got eighteen hundred dollars for an inferior novel, *The Islets of the Gulf*, a book that made about 250 pages in the magazine, and he got a thousand dollars for a hundred pages of articles about naval commanders. On a writing income of only five hundred dollars a year, Willis was able to tour Europe, but he was soon earning fifteen hundred dollars from his work for four magazines, and at his peak he became the highest-paid writer in America, with an annual income of ten thousand dollars—not all of it from magazines, however.

Poor Poe, as usual, was the lowest man on the totem pole. The best he could get from *Graham's* was four or five dollars a page. His famous story "The Gold Bug," sometimes cited as the first detective story in America, was bought for fifty-two dollars, or four dollars a page, but Poe withdrew it before publication so he could enter it in a contest run by another magazine, where it won a hundred-dollar prize. "The Raven," perhaps his most quoted poem, was bought for a mere ten dollars by the *Whig Review*.

George Graham had a profound effect on the magazine business. He demonstrated that by spending money for good writing a magazine would get good contributors, and thereby increase its circulation. The success of his magazine was convincing proof that he was right, and Graham had no hesitation in advertising his success and the reasons for it. In 1853 he pointed out that the magazine had spent "as high as fifteen hundred dollars on a single number for authorship alone," and added that this figure was "more than twice the sum that has ever been paid by any other magazine in America; while for years our minimum rate of cost, in relationship to the item of authorship alone, was eight hundred dollars per number." Dr. Mott estimates that Graham's editorial expenditures were about seven or eight dollars a page.

Graham boasted in 1852 that during the previous decade he had paid more than $80,000 to American writers alone—an estimate he increased to $87,000 a few months later. Godey had asserted earlier that *he* had paid American writers and artists "not less than two hundred thousand dollars" since he had called them to his aid. Godey did not mention, however, that he refused to pay anything at all to unknown writers.

Some observers, usually British, were not taken in by the boasts of American publishers. An American magazinist, however, Charles Astor Bristed, reported in 1848 in the *Edinburgh Review,* "In examining the causes of the inferiority of American periodical literature the most readily assignable and generally applicable is that its contributors are mostly unpaid. . . ."

For that matter, editors were still not well rewarded. Taking Poe's $780 a year as editor of the *Southern Literary Messenger* (he was later offered $1,040, his highest salary) as probably the lowest salary, the scale ascended scarcely at all to the thousand dollars a year offered to Rufus Griswold in 1842 as editor of *Graham's.* In that same year, however, it must be remembered that Willis earned more than the governor of Connecticut and that a college professor's salary was only about $600. Neither editing nor writing, then, was a way to get rich, even comparatively so, except in a very few cases, but it was possible for the writers who were paid, and the editors of the better magazines, to make a decent living, in the context of the times.

Magazines could pay more, when they did, because their general lot was improving, in spite of considerable difficulties. *Godey's* 40,000 circulation, a record, was no general reflection of prosperity; but the fact that it was possible to achieve such a figure showed that a new day was beginning for magazines. Meanwhile, most of the monthlies struggled along on 7,000 or less, and some of the more specialized journals were fortunate to reach a thousand. Moreover, much time and energy had to be spent collecting the money from those who did agree to subscribe. People were wheedled and cajoled to pay by every device known to the publisher or editor, just as they are urged to renew today, when it is the rate of renewal that is so important in magazine circulation. Many times the entreaties, no matter how heartfelt, did no good, and hundreds, perhaps thousands, of magazines died simply because subscribers did not pay up.

Circulation devices that would later be commonplace had already been introduced—"clubbing," or group subscriptions, and the premium system, for example—but these were not yet much help, and magazines were further drained by the practice of exchanging copies of a magazine for "reading notices" in newspapers—in a sense free advertising, but far too expensive when a magazine like *Godey's* began to carry as many as 1,500 newspapers on its exchange list.

Advertising had made only a tentative appearance, chiefly on the covers of the most expensive magazines and in four- or eight-page inserts, sometimes on colored stock. Bunching the advertising in unwieldy lumps at the beginning or the end of a magazine, or both, as was the practice later, set a pattern not broken until the time when advertising became important enough and plentiful enough to warrant linking it with reading matter through an entire magazine.

Another problem for magazines was the cost of production. This was the era of engraving on copper and steel, and it was expensive; yet because of the competition, a general magazine, at least, did not dare do without it. The *New-York Mirror* asserted that its full-page plates cost a thousand dollars, and no doubt they did, but it was also possible to have them done for as little as three or four hundred dollars. Still, it sometimes cost a publisher more for the "embellishment" in his magazine than it did for the editorial content. The ladies' magazines had fashion plates, in color, and possibly two or three other plates besides; the general magazines could carry no less. Yet the logic was inexorable: the magazines with the highest circulations were usually the ones with the most embellishments. Only the *Knickerbocker* did well without pictures. Woodcuts were gaining in popularity, and were already supplementing the engravings in the big magazines, but their day had not yet come.

With delinquent subscribers, the cost of production, and rising rates to authors, it is obvious that the Golden Age of magazines was golden in earnings only for relatively few publishers and editors. But as Dr. Mott has pointed out, the "variety, exuberance and abundance" of magazines in this period justified the phrase.

eight

Magazines and the Arts

MOST OF THE MAGAZINES in the Golden Age sought to encourage the arts in one way or another, and as a matter of national pride, they were especially anxious to serve the cause of American artists. Their anxiety, however, led them into a trap of which they themselves were only too conscious. Poe, speaking for his fellow editors, wrote in the *Southern Literary Messenger*: "We get up a hue and cry about the necessity of encouraging native writers of merit—we blindly fancy we can accomplish this by indiscriminate puffing of good, bad and indifferent."

The faults of the critics were numerous, as pointed out by other critics in the medium both used, the magazine. The chief sin, it appeared, was indiscriminate praise: it was difficult for an American book to get a bad review in an American magazine, although the British press somewhat made up for this deficiency. Moreover, the reviews themselves were often badly written, superficial, given to generalities, lush language, and padded out with long extracts from the book under review. Then, too, critics were often given complimentary copies of a book (standard practice now, but new then), and this appeared to dull their critical faculties. Sometimes the critic had to review the work of a friend or of another writer for the same journal, and that also discouraged real criticism. Other critics, it appeared, were afraid of venturing unpopular opinions; and some were simply lazy. As for newspaper criticism, said the *New-York Mirror*, it was "worse than worthless," whether British or American. "Weak tea and bread and butter

—milk and water—we cannot think of anything stale, diluted, insipid enough for a comparison. . . ."

Much of what the critics said of the critics was true, and to their complaints could be added the self-evident—criticism was far too often the product of regional as well as individual prejudices. Political and religious feelings helped make much criticism more diatribe than analysis. Yet, notwithstanding, there were good critics in the magazines, and they wrote well. Poe's own brilliance offset much of the inferior criticism he so disdained. And there were other distinguished names among the critics: James Russell Lowell, William Hickling Prescott, William Gilmore Simms, Richard Henry Dana, Margaret Fuller, Emerson, Longfellow, and John Motley.

If criticism was a major subject of controversy in the magazines, poetry was only slightly less so. There were those who scorned it as trivial when it was not pretentious, while others thought what was being written in America exceeded the best of English poetry, with the exception of Byron's. Certainly the scorners were on solid ground when they talked about the sentimental claptrap that filled so much of the ladies' magazines and the smaller literary weeklies. Even though much of this luxuriant verse came from women poets, it was a lady editor who figuratively threw up her hands in alarm over it in the *Union Magazine,* declaring, "It is fearful to think of the deluge of indifferent poetry at present!" Much of the poetry, indifferent and otherwise, that appeared in the magazines later reappeared in books, and formed a not insignificant part of the rapidly increasing number of new American books.

Readers were not nearly as addicted to poetry, however, as they were to novels, and fiction was rising to new levels of mass popularity. The magazines took little notice of this development except to deplore it. They were highly critical of novels and novel reading, even though many of them nevertheless carried such works as serials. People were reading mostly British, French, and German novels, since the number of American works was still comparatively slight. But these few revealed, in the purple light of historical romance, much of the remembered glory of the American past, once so close and now receding into the distance. Cooper was chief in this genre, but there were others of inferior quality who were read almost as enthusiastically.

Magazines continued to deprecate novel reading, however—possibly because people who were reading them were not reading magazines. The *Knickerbocker* professed to believe that the wildly popular works of Sir Walter Scott, who had captured the American imagination, had provoked a very injurious influence on both morals and manners, creating "an admiration of outlaws and freebooters, a respect for the license of barbarous ages." There were not many, one suspects, who took such criticism of Sir Walter seriously.

Probably a good part of the critical attack on novels was directed at a kind of publishing deserving of it—the so-called "cheap literature," which was not only cheap in price but without any visible literary merit, appearing both in book form and in newspapers. Cheap fiction also appeared in magazines, but not nearly in the same quantity.

In the furor over novels, the growing development of the short story as an art form was largely overlooked, perhaps because critics hardly knew how to treat it or even what to call it. Timothy Flint, in his *Western Monthly Review,* saw short stories as pitiful outcasts from the literary community: "Infinite numbers of these forlorn orphans are cast out on the arid highways, or to float on the lone waters, without even an ark of bulrushes to keep the feeble wailers from perishing. More than half are the fruit of foreign illegitimacy, and by no means as well worth raising, as our own home-born and honest bantlings. We should think charity began at home. . . . We have seen, during the past year, numbers of stories and tales and witty matters going the rounds of the papers, that might claim the premium for the highest attainable degree of vapidity and silliness. Editors, who commit such naughty actions, should be fined for debauching and stupifying [*sic*] public taste."

The magazines were blind to the virtues of American writers under their noses—masters of the short story form like Poe, Hawthorne, and Irving. Of these, only Hawthorne was given much recognition for short-story writing. Irving, the leading popular writer for so long, was considered so on the basis of his longer work. Willis, certainly not in a class with any of these writers, was mentioned by at least one critic as one of the few writers in the form worth talking about.

Rivaling fiction and poetry for interest among magazine readers, as well as booklovers, was biography, and the magazines had much to draw upon in satisfying their audience. Many of the most noted writers turned their hands to the biographical form—Cooper's "Lives of the Naval Commanders," in *Graham's,* Irving's *Columbus,* Jared Spark's excursions into the lives of many eminent Americans, and a host of others. Virtually every magazine carried some biographical writing, and a few, like the *North American,* made it one of their hallmarks.

History was a natural companion to the interest in biography, and with the work of historians like John G. Palfrey, Prescott, Motley, and George Bancroft available to them, magazine editors could make some significant contributions to national culture in this field, and the best of them did so. Already, too, Americans were interested in their genealogies; the great game of ancestor hunting had begun, and new magazines like the *New England Historical and Genealogical Register,* begun in 1847, sprang up to serve them.

Another kind of writing began to attain a prominence in the Golden Age that it had never enjoyed before. Humor, always so much a part of American life, had been given little notice in the magazines, which, in earlier days, had seemed to think it beneath them. Lewis Gaylord Clark, who was editing the *Knickerbocker* with his twin brother, Willis Gaylord, in 1846 was convinced that "the present age is emphatically the Age of Fun. Everybody deals in jokes, and all wisdom is inculcated in a paraphrase of humor."

No doubt the Clarks would have called New York "Fun City" if they had thought of it, and no doubt they would have been as sharply criticized for it as Mayor John Lindsay was more than a century later. There was little enough in New York to laugh at for a large part of the population. The city was already plagued with the urban problems that were never to leave it. Yet then, as now, there was a kind of wry humor prevalent, and the *Knickerbocker* reflected it. Nor was it simply a local humor. The magazine printed the best fun of the times, from Clark's own "Editor's Table" down to the newest primitive humorist. It was full of excellent satire, including a page designed typographically to look like a rural newspaper, in which local reporting was held up to gentle ridicule.

A distinctive kind of American humor was emerging, based on the "tall tale" and the stereotype, both of which persisted well into this century. In a remarkably perceptive analysis of this development, the *Democratic Review* said: "The sources of American humor are various and novel, the scheming Yankee, the wild Kentuckian, the generous Virginian, the aristocratic Carolina Planters, the camp meeting, the negro music, the auctioneers and orators, the fashionable clergy, life on the Mississippi and the Lakes, the history of every man's life, his shifts and expedients, and change of pursuits, newspaper controversies, fashions in dress, militia trainings, public lectures, newspaper advertisements, placards, signs, names of children, man-worship, razor-strop men."

While the humor of stereotype is all but dead in this age of black comedy, television and the comic strips have preserved the idea in their delineation of bumbling husbands and all-powerful wives, of dumb blondes and sexy brunettes, of the New York cabdriver and the California suburban dweller—or the suburbanite anywhere, for that matter.

Some forecast of things to come could be seen in the weekly called *John-Donkey*, edited by George G. Foster and Thomas Dunn English. This periodical, best of the comic magazines, was ahead of its time in its irreverence and total disregard for the dignity of famous personages. *John-Donkey* attained its best effects by denying it was trying to be funny; its satire, sometimes labored, was done with a straight face, which made it all the more irritating to those it satirized. No one was safe from its often brutal pen, not even Poe, who hardly deserved it, or Horace Greeley, who sometimes did. *John-Donkey*'s circulation mounted quickly to 12,000, but the nation wasn't ready for such humor, any more than were the objects of it. A rain of libel suits made it impossible for the publishers, G. B. Zieber, of Philadelphia, and George Dexter, of New York, to keep the magazine alive for any more than the six months between January and July, 1848.

Where the performing arts were concerned, the magazines did not yet serve them well. New York, by this time the national theatrical center, had only a few magazines that were devoted to the drama, and other areas had even fewer. There was some drama criticism in the general periodicals, more in the newspapers. A writer in *Arcturus* noted the "remarkable neglect . . . on the part of our periodical writers, in the department of theatrical criticism. We have no dramatic critics worth the name. The newspaper notices of plays and actors . . . are so extravagant, both in censure and praise, as to amount to nothing at all."

Music did a little better, for as John Sullivan Dwight, the leading critic in that field, remarked in the *Harbinger* in 1845, "Our people are trying to become musical. There is a musical movement in this country." Americans were discovering they had a native music, and although even the northerners took a plantation owner's view of them, Negro songs were hailed as indigenous, and delighted everyone. There was little to bolster black self-pride in such songs as "Old Zip Coon" and "Jump Jim Crow" and "Dandy Jim"—the work songs, the blues, the prison songs were not likely to be white popular music—but there was some truth in the *Knickerbocker*'s characterization of them as an "American national opera."

Notwithstanding the national interest in music, the founding of orchestras like the Philharmonic Society in New York, and the visits of renowned European virtuosos like the violinist Ole Bull, there were not many music magazines published, and those that were had little to recommend them. The best music critics appeared in the general magazines.

There was even less art criticism and art magazines, notwithstanding the tradition of American art that had been established in the eighteenth century. There were only occasional articles about art, or criticism of it, in the magazines.

If the arts had not yet inspired many periodicals to support them, the sciences did better. There were a good many agricultural and medical journals surviving from the earlier periods, and now more specialized journals began to appear. Philadelphia was increasingly becoming the center for medical publishing, both book and magazine, although

New York and Boston were also well represented. Louisville was the medical publishing capital of the West, while in the South the *New Orleans Medical and Surgical Journal* began a lengthy career in 1844.

Popular health magazines had begun to appear, full of sententious advice, most of it wrong, although it can now be seen that there was merit in the *Journal of Health*'s stout opposition to tobacco. In the general magazines, and some educational journals, attention was paid to physical culture, and the same things were being said about it that are said today, as witness Horace Mann's *Common School Journal* and its declaration: "The present generation is suffering incalculably under an ignorance of physical education." The same charge was made generation after generation, while American children grew stronger and taller.

One of the popular idiosyncrasies of the times, a harmless irrationality, was an interest in water and its healing properties, perhaps a part of the European cultural heritage brought over by immigrants who knew the great European spas. Americans were interested not only in mineral springs but also in water almost for its own sake. The book-publishing house of Fowler and Wells, in New York, began to publish in 1845 a curious magazine called the *Water-Cure Journal and Herald of Reform,* which acquired a circulation of fifty thousand in little more than five years. Its range of interests was relatively broad: physiology, pathology, hydrotherapy, and physical, moral, and intellectual development. Curiously, all these large and lofty concepts seemed to come down to the use of water, for whatever purpose, but primarily as a healing agent for most of what ailed the human system. There were enough earnest followers of this doctrine to give the magazine a life of fifteen years under its initial title, but then, under other names, it went on for a half century longer, dispensing further information and misinformation about health and hygiene.

Fowler and Wells were also the leading distributors of literature about phrenology, a fad that surpassed the water cure in popularity. This pseudoscience originated in Germany, flourished in Edinburgh, and was finally established in America in 1838 by a young Philadelphia medical student, Nathan Allen, who used the proceeds from his *Phrenological Journal,* begun in 1838, to put himself through medical school. When he graduated in 1841, he sold it to the Fowler brothers, O. S. and L. N., of New York, who combined in 1852 with Dr. Samuel R. Wells, a vegetarian and hydrotherapist, to establish Fowler & Wells. All three men, and the Fowlers' sister, Charlotte, who married Wells, were phrenologists. They lectured and wrote on the subject, and even taught it in a Phrenological Institute.

Phrenology, as a fad, reached the peak of its popularity and subsided after the Civil War, but the *Journal* had an astonishingly long life, existing until 1911, although in its later years it devoted more pages to general articles on health than to phrenology. The "science" was finally relegated to sideshows in carnivals and circuses, where it survives today.

It must not be imagined, however, that phrenology was confined to the self-serving promotion of a single magazine. Serious, talented writers and editors believed in it, and many of the best magazines devoted space to it. A relatively sophisticated man like Park Benjamin, then editor of the *New-England Magazine,* could write soberly in 1835: "We are devout believers in its doctrines. We cannot discover in its principles any incompatability with religious belief." And Edgar Allan Poe, reviewing a book on the subject in the *Southern Literary Messenger* during the following year, declared: "Phrenology is no longer to be laughed at. It *is* no longer laughed at by men of common understanding. It has assumed the majesty of a science; and as a science ranks among the most important which can engage the attention of thinking human beings. . . ."

Some magazines and editors, it must be added, refused to take phrenology seriously. The *Mirror* satirized it unmercifully, and the *Knickerbocker* remained skeptical and amused, printing in July 1850 a gently probing couplet:

> "Thou hast a noble cranium; what remains
> To make thee a great genius? Only brains."

nine

Editors of the Golden Age

THE IMAGE OF THE MAGAZINE EDITOR was beginning to be more clearly defined in the Golden Age, just as the modern newspaper editor suddenly emerged in the person of James Gordon Bennett, Sr., with the establishment of his New York *Herald* in 1835. Similarly, the book publisher as an entrepreneur was also acquiring definition— no longer primarily a printer, and not always a bookseller, but a man engaged in the search for and purveying of literature of every kind.

As a working individual, the magazine editor was still inclined to vacillate between writing and editing, as we have seen, and the concept of his job as generating and carrying out ideas was not yet developed. Yet the basic job of planning the magazine and working with writers was established, as was the task of dealing with business problems.

Preeminent among the magazine editors, and a prototype for others to follow, was George R. Graham. Only twenty-six when he became a full-fledged magazine publisher, Graham had started out in life first as a cabinetmaker, then as a lawyer, but he never really worked at either occupation. He seemed destined to be an editor, and began to be one as soon as possible, in the manner described earlier.

As an editor, Graham was endlessly inventive and innovative. If he did not invent the idea, he successfully promoted the practice of listing all his famous contributors on the cover and title page of *Graham's Magazine*—a practice that became, years later, the primary merchandising tool of Hearst's *Cosmopolitan,* and still later common practice on many magazines. Graham was not content to make impressions

83

from steel and copper plates already used elsewhere, as was the custom on the other monthlies; he insisted on new plates, engraved particularly for *Graham's,* a move that astonished and impressed some of his contemporaries.

In shaping his magazine, Graham proved to be not so much a literary figure, advancing the arts, but the kind of publisher familiar to us today. He was aware of the value of big names, and knew he must pay to get them. His higher rates to authors was the act of a publisher buying talent, not an editor, rewarding merit. Yet as editor, a post in which he functioned tirelessly, he had the valuable attributes of the best—a genial personality which attracted and held people and allowed him to iron out personal differences. Writers were loyal to him. He shared his success with them, as well as enjoying it himself. He lived in a fine house on Philadelphia's Arch Street, driving his bays down the street in a splendid carriage, entertaining the leading literary figures nearly every day in his home.

To those who worked for him and with him, Graham remained a figure of civility and kindness. But in the end it was Graham's own generous nature that led to his troubles. With the leading magazine in the country and the largest circulation in the world, his property yielding him $50,000 a year, Graham made a common mistake and embarked on an unwarranted and unnecessary expansion. He made the error of buying two newspapers. Graham, of course, had no precedent to guide him, but it is historically true that newspaper publishers who buy magazines, and vice versa, are seldom successful, even though notable exceptions like Hearst come to mind. Millions of dollars have been lost in the unsuccessful attempt to be two kinds of publisher. In Graham's case, the two merged Philadelphia papers became the *North American,* and he compounded his folly by financing a third paper, the *Evening Bulletin.* These ventures were steady money losers, and Graham lost still more by investing in mining stocks.

Graham himself diagnosed his mistakes accurately: "Had I not in an evil hour forgotten my own true interests and devoted that capital and industry to another business which should have been confined to the magazine, I should today have been under no necessity," he wrote in October 1848, when he had to sell the controlling interest in his magazine to Samuel D. Patterson & Co. He was so enterprising and talented, however, that in two years he regained control of it, and as he said, "I can yet show the world that he who started life a poor boy with but eight dollars in his pocket and has run such a career as mine is hard to put down." Nevertheless, he was not able to boost his magazine to its former heights. It continued to decline, and a bad review by Graham of *Uncle Tom's Cabin* in 1853 did not help; indeed, Graham believed that it was this sour notice at a time when Mrs. Stowe reigned as a national heroine that was the final blow to his property. A short time after it was written, Graham had to sell his magazine. He worked on newspapers for a time, nearly lost his sight, and had to retire on a pension provided, ironically, by George W. Childs, the eminent Philadelphia publisher, a man who had once looked up from sweeping the street before his employer's shop to watch, with awe and admiration, as Graham swept down the avenue behind his trotters. Graham died in 1894; his magazine lost its identity in 1858 and became a short-lived ladies' monthly.

Timothy Flint was a different kind of man. His *Western Monthly Review* began in May 1827 as the *Western Magazine and Review*. Flint did not become a magazine editor until he was forty-seven. He had begun as pastor of a Congregational church in New England, then went west as a missionary. Meanwhile, he had written extensively for the magazines. As a Harvard man, he was well educated, and his literary work included at least half a dozen books, one of them a novel. He was a lively, witty writer of more than ordinary talent.

He put his whole family to work on the *Western Monthly Review*— son Hubbard was publisher, son Micah P. was a poetry contributor, daughter Emeline translated from French and Spanish. No one worked harder than Flint. At the start he wrote most of the magazine, and later on about three-quarters of it.

Flint was belligerent and outspoken—"the donkey of Cincinnati" one New York paper called him—but he was honest, a rare enough quality in any age, and his magazine was valuable both as a recorder and interpreter of western Americana. Like so many other periodicals, the *Western Monthly Review* was at last the victim of its nonpaying subscribers.

The publisher of the magazine that ranked in importance with *Graham's* was nothing like either Graham or Flint. Louis A. Godey in another era might have been called a "ladies' man," although not in the sense of a sexual adventurer, to be sure. Godey was the kind of man who would have been at home in any domestic gathering of the ladies of his time, talking to them in their own language. He was a simple, chubby, benign soul whose attitude toward women was in the best tradition of gallantry. His audience were "fair ladies" or "fair readers." He spoke to them as one good friend to another in the pages of his *Lady's Book:* "We have received a note from some fair Lady, we presume, requesting us to give another description of Love than that found in the February number. This shall be done, and another fair Lady has it now in charge." It was no accident that Godey capitalized "Lady" and "Love."

Beneath this amiable, courtly exterior, Godey was an excellent businessman, who ran up the circulation of his magazine to a record 150,000 before the outbreak of the Civil War, and left more than a million dollars behind him when he died. He knew exactly what his ladies wanted. When he wrote, "Nothing having the slightest appearance of indelicacy, shall ever be admitted to the Lady's Book," he was stoutly reaffirming the incredibly mawkish morality of an era in which the breast of a turkey could only be referred to as its bosom, and the legs of a grand piano at a concert had to be adorned with pants (or "inexpressibles," as they would have had to be called) lest the word "leg" be suggested to the minds of delicate females in the audience.

Godey acquired a decided asset in 1837 when he bought Mrs. Sara Josepha Hale's *Ladies' Magazine* in 1837 and succeeded in persuading Mrs. Hale herself to join his staff. What better assistant could he have than a woman of whom it was said: "Her whole life was a tribute to the respectabilities, decorums, and moralities of life."

What Mrs. Hale did for her great cause, "female education," which she began crusading for in her own magazine and carried on in *Godey's,* has been overshadowed by her reputation as the author of "Mary had a little lamb," and by her persuasion of President Lincoln to adopt her idea of declaring Thanksgiving a national holiday. But she did much more. Mrs. Hale was a pioneer and a prime force in getting women into the teaching and medical professions. As a writer, she produced a good and popular cookbook, among other volumes, and edited several anthologies and annuals while she was editing *Godey's* for its publisher. Her title was Literary Editor, but although she was second in authority to Godey himself, she ran the magazine.

Although the two assembled a distinguished list of contributors, *Godey's* was never a literary success. It was a sentimental success, and that was what its publisher intended. Godey died in 1878; in 1877 Mrs. Hale, at the age of eighty-nine, had reluctantly given up her editorial duties, and Godey's sons took charge. As is usually the case in such circumstances, the magazine declined and finally lost its identity in 1898 when Frank Munsey bought it.

Graham and Godey made such an impressive start toward establishing the pattern of modern magazine publishing that other efforts often seem less interesting, but there *were* entrepreneurs as notable in their own way. They were men, for example, like Joseph Buckingham, whose *New-England Magazine,* beginning in 1831 and running for a little less than five years, was the best literary periodical in that part of the country before *The Atlantic Monthly* began.

The idea of this magazine came from Buckingham's tubercular son, Edward, who must have been a most persuasive editor; he was able to lure writers like Longfellow, Holmes, Whittier, and Everett to write for him at a dollar a page. When Edward died, little more than a year after the magazine began, his father continued it for a time, although he had no taste for the job. Nonetheless, it continued to be, as the *New-York Mirror* put it, "a journal of which the country may be proud." One of its accomplishments was the publishing of Mathew Carey's autobiography. The magazine was sold in 1834. Park Benjamin edited it for a year, until it merged with the *American Monthly Magazine,* of New York, by the end of 1835.

In New York, the most prominent editor was unquestionably Lewis Gaylord Clark, the "Old Knick" of the *Knickerbocker Magazine.* Like the other successful editors of his time, Clark was a popular man with his contemporaries. He was a humorous, handsome, curly-haired, animated individual. As a friend wrote admiringly of him, "He was never else to the world but light-hearted, always kindly disposed, and ever discovering amusement not only in trifling but the most serious events of life." In addition, along with all good editors, Clark could recognize talent, and had a great capacity for attracting and holding writers as friends. The result was an admirable list of contributors, the lifeblood of magazines. Among the contributors was his twin brother, Willis Gaylord, who also served as associate editor. Clark retired as editor in 1861 and died in 1873; the magazine preceded him in 1865.

Among the lesser known editors—or perhaps just less remembered —of the Golden Age was John L. O'Sullivan, who with his partner and brother-in-law, S. D. Langtree, founded and edited the *Democratic Review*, which began in 1837 as the *United States Magazine and Democratic Review*. Both founders were, as O'Sullivan recalled later, "very young, very sanguine, and very democratic."

O'Sullivan himself was an appealing figure. Julian Hawthorne describes him as: ". . . A cosmopolitan of Irish parentage on his father's side, and one of the most charming companions in the world. He was always full of grand and world-embracing schemes, which seemed to him, and which he made appear to others, vastly practical and alluring, but which invariably miscarried by reason of some oversight which had escaped notice for the very reason that it was so fundamental a one. He lived in the constant anticipatory enjoyment of more millions than the Adelantado of the Seven Cities ever dreamed of; and yet he was not always able to make his income cover his very modest and economical expenditure. . . ."

But the fact that O'Sullivan and his partner were "very democratic" paid dividends almost immediately because no less a democrat than "Old General Jackson" took a great interest in the magazine and became its first subscriber, a well publicized act of tremendous promotional value. The *Democratic Review* remained faithful to Jackson, and to Martin Van Buren after him, even though O'Sullivan failed to get any of the government's official printing. That was one of the reasons the magazine suspended for six months in Washington, where it began, then resumed again in New York, where O'Sullivan was its sole editor for the next five years, and succeeded in attracting such contributors as Whittier, Longfellow, Lowell, Hawthorne, and Walt Whitman, who signed himself "Walter."

By 1846, however, O'Sullivan's great expectations of financial glory were still unrealized, and he had to sell his magazine. In other hands, and under other titles, it survived until 1859.

A man of quite different character, who left a much more permanent mark on the magazine business, was Eliakim Littell, a man who began making periodicals in 1818, when he was only twenty-one. After selling his interest in a clip-and-paste publication, the *Museum of Foreign Literature,* in 1844, Littell left Philadelphia and went to Boston, where he founded *Littell's Living Age,* a magazine destined to last well into the twentieth century. He had the help and support of some eminent men—Judge Joseph Story, Chancellor James Kent, the historian William H. Prescott, and John Quincy Adams, among others—and with their help he carried the art of clipping and pasting to its highest point.

The *Living Age*'s circulation never went much beyond 100,000 during its long life, but then it had little editorial overhead—Littell simply subscribed to the English periodicals, then clipped them with an editorial skill and discernment sadly lacking in the earlier days of magazines, when such operations were commonplace. In the usual sixty-four pages of the magazine appeared the best fiction, poetry, essays, and comments the discerning eye of the editor could find.

The best he could find was not always superior; the fiction, particularly, was inclined to be second- or third-rate from time to time, but the overall average of excellence was high in every department. The magazine became a kind of literary *Reader's Digest,* offering American readers a selection from such leading British periodicals as the *Edinburgh Review,* the *Quarterly Review, Westminster Review, Blackwood's Magazine,* and in time the *Cornhill Magazine.* Lighter material came from the less serious magazines, like *Household Words,* the periodical edited by Dickens; and Anthony Trollope's *St. Paul's.* Weeklies like the notable *Saturday Review* were also clipped. Littell was adept at finding material of interest to American readers, especially pieces about American life.

After the founder died in 1870, the editorial chore passed to his son Robert, who continued as his father had done until his own death in 1896. The magazine came into the hands of the Atlantic Monthly Company in 1919, and other able editors carried it on. The scope of *Living Age* had by that time broadened to include what was being published in the magazines of France, Germany, Italy, and Spain. Asian countries were added in time. Changed to a monthly in 1927, the magazine eventually came to a bizarre end after it was bought in 1938 by Joseph Hilton Smyth, who later proved to be an underground propaganda agent for the Japanese government. Smyth bought *Living Age* for a mere $15,000, supplied by his Japanese employers, and a few months later acquired what remained of the *North American Review*. As propaganda organs, the venerable publications were failures. The *Review* suspended in 1940, *Living Age* a year later.

These were some of the editors responsible for the Golden Age. From them emerges the broad outlines of the magazine editor as a type—an individual of strong personality and many talents, blessed with ideas, armed with determination, and much involved in the society he lived in. Like the men who were founding the great newspapers at the same time, they were powerful, sometimes eccentric people. The giants of the newspaper world may have been more powerful and more eccentric, but the magazine editors were also beginning to make a name for themselves as interpreters of the American scene.

PART THREE

RISE OF THE MAGAZINE BUSINESS

(1850–1905)

ten

Periodicals and the Civil War

A DARKNESS FELL ON THE LAND IN 1861. Four years later, when it lifted, the nation was not the same, nor would it ever be again. The Union was saved, the slaves were freed, but the United States had gone through an emotional experience so profound that the fabric of national life was altered in fundamental ways. The wounds that were opened have never been healed, the basic questions raised never really answered.

The floodtide of Civil War books in our time has documented this period as no other era in American history. Many of these books have relied on magazines as source material, because they were among the foremost recorders of the struggle. And this is one of the authentic miracles of publishing history, since magazines were hit far worse by the emergencies of the war than newspapers. Further, they had just come through the bad times of the Panic of 1857, which had ended the careers of prominent periodicals like *Graham's,* the *Democratic Review,* and the *New-York Mirror.* The others had no more than recovered when the war came, bringing with it soaring costs, manpower problems, and the severe disruption of distribution.

For northern magazines, the last difficulty was the worst. Overnight, or nearly so, they lost their southern subscribers, particularly disastrous to magazines like *Harper's* and *Godey's Lady's Book.* Only the popularity of some magazines in the Federal Army saved them from extinction. There was also a Civil War equivalent of World War II's *Yank Magazine.* It was called the *Soldier's Casket*—gruesome unless one recalled the old meaning of the word "casket" as it was used in magazines—begun in Philadelphia in 1865, not long before the war ended.

For magazines in the South, the war meant absolute disaster. Most of their supplies, like ink, paper, and machinery, came from the North, and although their circulations were much more local, they soon did not have the physical means to carry on business in many cases, nor did they have the manpower as the war dragged on. Others could not afford the ruinous postage rates imposed by the Confederate government. In spite of these enormous difficulties, both magazines and book publishing survived, and there were some periodicals that managed to get through the war, missing issues only rarely. Astonishingly, there were even a few new starts, although none survived long.

Newspapers prospered where magazines could not during the war, because the papers were selling a commodity, news, that was in great demand. Several of the magazines also offered news of the war, and people were eager to read their accounts of events and personalities, and to study eagerly the illustrative woodcuts they carried. But for immediate news they turned to the newspapers to learn the outcome of battles, to scan with anxious fear the daily casualty lists. Both media gained in circulation during the war, but newspapers did better.

(Some help, though still inconsiderable, came from increased advertising, to which more attention was being paid by those who created the ads. The prophecy of a day soon to come was embedded in the satiric words of *Vanity Fair* in 1860 when it said: "A model Advertisement-Writer in the *Herald* calls the sewing machine 'a swift-fingered sister of love and charity.' Let us hereafter speak of the Cooking-Range as the warm-hearted minister to appetite and contentment; of the Daguerreotype Apparatus as the bright-faced reflector of beauty and worth; and, among other ingenious contrivances, of the Model Advertisement-Writer as the soft-headed distributor of mellifluous soap." The first magazine devoted to the business of advertising had already been in existence nearly a decade when these words were written. It was *Pettingill's Reporter,* the house organ of the ad agency of that name.)

Naturally, during the war the tone of the magazines was quite different than it had been. Before the war the debate over slavery and states' rights rose to a furious tempo and made magazines more political than they had ever been. War itself could only intensify this situation. One result was an increase in both magazines and newspapers, as the disputants sought to find new voices for themselves. But before the war some magazines were convinced it was their duty to rule out political argument. Consequently, the great issues of the day do not appear in *Harper's, Graham's,* or many of the ladies' magazines, in the years before the conflict.

In the campaign of 1860, however, when national passions were coming to the boiling point, even the general magazines engaged in the battle swirling around Lincoln. James Russell Lowell, editor of a new magazine, *The Atlantic Monthly,* assessed the times correctly when he wrote that the election was "a turning point in our history." The eastern magazines were generally disappointed in Lincoln's nomination, and some of them ridiculed him unmercifully. He was, said *Vanity Fair,* "a longitudinal person with a shambling gait . . . slab-sided . . . He has a thin, almost nasal voice, and his grammar is not so far above suspicion as Caesar's wife is reported to have been."

The debate over slavery itself was virulent and exhausting. Among those exhausted was Charles Francis Adams, who wrote in *The Atlantic Monthly:* "What is coarsely but expressively described in the political slang of this country as '*The Everlasting Nigger-Question*' might perhaps be considered as exhausted as a topic of discussion if ever a topic was." That was written in April, 1861, and the "Question" had barely been raised.

There were ponderous debates on the descent of man, and where the Negro came in. The Bible was invoked or rejected, depending on the magazine, to justify slavery or to condemn it, and the southern periodicals talked of how much worse it was to enslave labor by means of money than by the beneficent system of the South. Slavery was even defended by some journals in the Far West. There was a veritable rash of antislavery sentiment in many of the North's church periodicals, led by *The Liberator* and the *National Era.* Two Negro magazines joined the attack: *Frederick Douglass' Paper,* and the *Anglo-African Magazine.*

When war finally came, magazines plunged into the conflict with the remainder of the press. Every issue of the general magazines had material of some kind about the war. Some became violently partisan; the *Knickerbocker,* for example, changed from a gently satiric review of New York life to a rabid Copperhead journal. Even periodicals devoted mostly to literature, like the *Southern Literary Messenger,* followed the progress of the war closely.

Probably because they were more in competition with the newspapers, the weeklies made an effort to cover the war in depth. Outstanding was *Harper's Weekly,* which had its correspondents and artists on the battlefields, writing and sketching; their reports ranked with the best war reporting done by anyone. *Frank Leslie's Illustrated Newspaper* was not far behind in picture-text coverage, but *Harper's* still stands today as prime source material for eyewitness accounts of the fighting.

The more virulent of the magazines on both sides hesitated at nothing to keep hatred of the enemy alive during the war. Capitalizing on a widely believed myth that southern ladies used the bones of dead Yankees to decorate their homes, a poet in the *Continental* magazine wrote:

> "Silent the lady sat alone:
> In her ears were rings of dead men's bone;
> The brooch on her breast shone white and fine,
> 'Twas the polished joint of a Yankee's spine;
> The well-carved handle of her fan
> Was the finger-bone of a Lincoln man.
> She turned aside, a flower to cull
> From a vase which was made of a human skull;
> For to make her forget the loss of her slaves
> Her lovers had rifled dead men's graves.
> Do you think I'm describing a witch or a ghoul?
> There are no such things—and I'm not a fool,
> Nor did she reside in Ashantee—
> No, the lady fair was an F.F.V."

"F.F.V." means the lady belonged to one of the First Families of Virginia, a social level located at a truly dizzy altitude.

The more violent of the magazines kept steady pressure on the President to emancipate the slaves. *The Liberator* quoted an ecclesiastical exhortation in Roxbury, Massachusetts, which advanced the idea that "God has become an abolitionist!" Unfortunately, said the orator, "Mr. Lincoln does not yet even see that God is an abolitionist."

Those who opposed the conflict not only were able to maintain their own press, both newspaper and periodical, but this Copperhead press, as it was called, existed in the heart of the Union. The *Day Book,* both a daily and a weekly, had begun as early as 1849 in New York. Its editor, N. R. Stimson, said he meant to make his weekly magazine "saucy, racy, and spicy," but it failed to convey enough of these promising ingredients, and failed in 1863. The other major Copperhead journal was the *Old Guard,* a monthly that choked to death on its own passion.

In the South, the magazines were inclined to take a grand, dramatic, even romantic view of the war. In one of them appeared these almost incredible words in January 1861: "With all its attendant evils—with all its tragic horrors—with all its mighty retinue of sorrows, sufferings, and disasters—war—civil war—war of kindred races—is not the greatest calamity that can befall a people. . . . There is in war a sublime and awful beauty—a fearful and terrible loveliness. . . ."

This tribute appeared in the pages of *De Bow's Review,* one of the South's leading periodicals, which had a relatively long and respectable career running from January 1846 to June 1880. Its founder was James D. B. De Bow, educated at Charleston College, who began his career as a lawyer.

De Bow was an enlightened southern leader who saw that the best hope for the South lay, not in political action, but in developing her industrial resources. If southerners worked together toward that end, he and others believed, the region would one day rival the North, and the obvious deep economic inequity between them would no longer exist. De Bow concluded that the best way he could promote the idea was to found a new magazine, and he did so with the *Commercial Review of the South and West,* as it was called originally when it first appeared in New Orleans, where De Bow thought it would have a better chance than in his native Charleston, where so many periodicals had died.

The new magazine was devoted chiefly to trade, commerce, agriculture, manufacturing, and internal improvements, but its publisher did not wholly neglect literature. For a while the venture struggled, and once had to be rescued from extinction by a friend's generosity. After various vicissitudes, it was truly launched in 1853 as *De Bow's Review*.

For all his vision of a new South, De Bow was no renegade to the Lost Cause. In fact, in an 1857 speech, he came out strongly for reopening the African slave trade, and two years later he was elected president of the African Labor Supply Association. As the war approached, *De Bow's* abandoned its earlier distaste for political action and seemed to be almost looking forward eagerly to the conflict, drifting with the secessionist tide.

During the war, De Bow was made the Confederacy's cotton-buying agent, and moved his magazine to Richmond, where he was now employed. There he endured all the difficulties of trying to maintain operations in wartime, with the enemy steadily closing in on the capital, until he finally had to suspend the magazine in August 1862, noting wryly that as "more than half of our subscribers are in Texas, Louisiana, Arkansas, and in parts of the other states held by the enemy, and to them, for some time to come, it may be our fate to be voiceless."

Voiceless De Bow was until after the war ended, except for a single number published in July 1864. The magazine was revived again in January, 1866, this time in Nashville, where De Bow had gone to live as president of a proposed new railroad that would go to the West Coast. He had a Presidential pardon in his pocket for his role in the Rebellion, and he now was solidly for Reconstruction, with a good many kind words to say for President Johnson.

But the difficulties of trying to revive the magazine and keep it going in postwar chaos was too much for De Bow. In March 1867 he wrote: "The expenses of the *Review* are three times what they were in former days! Even the most trifling sums are gratefully received.

We know, and make all allowances for, the necessities of the country; but there are numbers who, by a very small effort, or sacrifice, might aid us in this contingency."

It was too late for De Bow. Hurrying to the bedside of his dying brother in New Jersey in February 1867, he became ill himself and died within a week, a month before his brother. His wife continued the magazine for a time, but she soon sold it, and the rest of *De Bow's* story is a familiar one of declining fortunes and eventual demise.

De Bow's was one of the best of the southern journals. Highly partisan it might be, but it would never have printed a diatribe like the *Southern Monthly*'s shriek against the Yankees: "They are a race too loathsome, too hateful, for us ever, under any circumstances, to be identified with them as one people."

The war came to an end, and in the shock of Lincoln's assassination the chorus of hate died down and virtually disappeared from print, whatever may have gone on blazing beneath the surface. Lincoln had taken the worst abuse from the newspapers and magazines since George Washington, but now even those magazines that had attacked him most brutally, paid him tribute, whether anyone believed them or not.

Sharp differences between northern and southern magazines began to diminish, too, not only politically but in other respects—magazines were about to be far more national in nature; regionalism was dying. With the rise of the great national periodicals, some of which were rooted before the war, the modern era in magazine publishing was beginning.

eleven

Some Great Names, and How They Were Established

THE UPSURGE OF MAGAZINES after the Civil War (leading to a second "Golden Age") had much more of an air of permanence than ever before. The best of the new magazines, it appeared, had come to stay. There were a great many short careers, as there have always been, as periodicals flared across the literary sky like falling stars, but great names were being established. Some were already in business before the war, and were only now coming into full bloom; others were new ideas.

One of the old magazines to reach its full flowering was the *North American Review*. It was the oldest magazine of continuous publication in the country, having begun its long life in 1815, and in the first sixty years of its existence it had scarcely changed. The *Review* was widely respected, solid—and dull. From its native New England it drew the best of the academic writers and the finest literary names. These natural resources were not only its treasure but also its handicap, since they gave the magazine a provincial tone in spite of its extraordinarily high quality. Splendid as the contributions from Harvard College and the Boston intellectuals might be, they often gave off the dull glow of the scholar's lamp, and were more coldly informative than entertaining. As time went on, these characteristics had an effect on circulation, never large in any case, so that by 1876 the *Review* was still brilliant intermittently but had declined to the point of expiration.

Then came a radical change that transformed the magazine. As always, it was a change that could only be accomplished by the arrival of a great editor. He was Allen Thorndike Rice, who bought the magazine at a point in its career when its fortunes had declined so far that it had nothing much to sell except its distinguished name.

Rice was twenty-three, a native Bostonian who had been educated at Oxford and who therefore had the proper intellectual qualifications to head the *Review*. His other attributes were plenty of money and energy, and a keen mind. He paid $3,000 for his new property, for which he got a faithful subscription list of 1,200 people and an inherited annual deficit of alarming proportions.

As a first step, Rice made the magazine a bimonthly. Next, he moved it to New York, changing publishers from the book-publishing house of James R. Osgood & Co. to D. Appleton & Co., by that time one of the leading New York publishers. In this new climate, and with some new editors, the *Review* flourished, and by 1879 it was a monthly again, entering on a new era.

Rice did much more than change geography and publishers. He opened up the pages of his new magazine, so that it was no longer a regional intellectual publication but a forum for ideas, of which the United States had a plentiful supply at the moment. His magazine, said Rice, was to be "an arena wherein any man having something valuable to say could be heard." He believed, correctly, that new writing on topics of wide public interest was the formula necessary to restore the *Review*'s eminence.

For the next decade, during the eighties, the magazine rose to its grandest heights and best circulation figures as Rice filled its pages with the names of the world's great and with a swirling clash of opinion about the problems of the new industrial society rising in America. Henry George and David Dudley Field argued the theory of the single tax. Parkman attacked woman suffrage, and Lucy Stone, Julia Ward Howe, and Wendell Phillips, among others, defended it. J. A. Froude and Cardinal Manning debated the role of the Catholic Church, while Robert G. Ingersoll aroused a public outcry with his atheistic attack against religion in general. Walt Whitman contributed some essays. Richard Wagner talked about his life and career, and William Gladstone contributed more than a dozen articles about politics. General Pierre G. T. Beauregard reminisced about his Civil War experiences, and General Grant talked about the Nicaragua canal.

With this kind of liveliness, provoking discussion and quotation, the circulation had climbed to 17,000 when Rice died suddenly in 1889. It was then making an annual profit of $50,000.

Under a new editor, Lloyd Bryce, who had been Rice's friend at Oxford, the *Review* continued its climb. Bryce continued his predecessor's policies, and by 1891 the *Review* reached its all-time circulation peak—76,000, with subscribers paying five dollars a year. A rival magazine, the *Review of Reviews,* said of it: "It is unquestionably true that the *North American* is regarded by more people, in all parts of the country, as at once the highest and most impartial platform upon which current public issues can be discussed, than is any other magazine or review."

From this high point, the *North American Review* began a slow descent that stretched over decades, although it remained distinguished under the long editorship of Colonel George Harvey, who bought a controlling interest in it in 1899. As former managing editor of Joseph Pulitzer's New York *World,* and a businessman who had made a fortune in electric railways, Harvey did not seem at first glance like the literary man his new property required. But he proved himself a magazine editor of real ability, operating not only the *Review* but editing *Harper's Weekly* simultaneously from 1901 to 1913. He was also president of Harper & Brothers after its reorganization in 1900.

Harvey's first issue began with a long poem by Swinburne, a promising start, and he welcomed other poets such as Henley, Yeats, and many others. And the great names continued to appear in the table of contents: H. G. Wells, William Dean Howells, Henry James, Mark Twain. So it continued through the First World War, but it suffered a new decline as the 1920s began. By 1924 it was down to 13,000, and two years later it was sold to a lawyer, William Butler Mahony. It was sold again in 1935, became a quarterly, and not long after died, as mentioned previously, after being bought by an agent of the Japanese government.

As Dr. Mott says, its files are "unmatched by that of any other magazine of American thought through nearly a century and a quarter of our national life."

Nearly as old as the *North American Review,* but a magazine of an entirely different kind, was *The Youth's Companion,* founded in 1827 and published until 1929. Like the *Review,* it made no great splash in its earlier years, but after the Civil War it became one of the most popular magazines, and thoroughly entertained generations of American youth.

Like so many other magazines intended for the young in that earlier day, the *Companion* was founded with the intent to "warn against the ways of transgression, error and ruin, and allure to those of virtue and piety." It was an outgrowth of a Boston Congregational paper, the *Recorder,* one of the earliest religious weeklies, which had begun with the help of Nathaniel Willis. Willis and his partner, Asa Rand, originated the *Companion* after a children's department in the *Recorder* had proved the need for a new magazine for young people.

From the first issue, which contained, tucked away in a department called "Variety," a "little Hymn" beginning "Now I lay me down to sleep," the *Companion* was a success, although it was almost entirely a clip-and-paste job by Willis. Rand withdrew after three years. In common with other magazines (and books) for children, there was much material about dead and dying children, their essential goodness, and their repentance for sins.

Willis sold the magazine in 1857 to John W. Olmstead and Daniel Sharp Ford, who were publishers of a prominent Baptist paper called the *Watchman and Reflector.* The partners dissolved their relationship ten years later, and Ford became principal owner and editor until he died in 1899. Thousands of his readers knew him as "Perry Mason" because he called his organization "Perry Mason & Co.," rather than use his own name.

Ford set the pattern for the *Companion*'s rise to eminence. He bought more fresh, new work and got out of the clipping jungle as fast as possible. He bought much fiction, and although the emphasis still remained on morality, Ford's magazine moved away from being a Sunday-school paper. In ten years the circulation jumped from 4,800 to nearly 50,000. Famous names began to appear—Harriet Beecher Stowe, and others whose work for children was known and loved. Young readers themselves were invited to become contributors to a "Children's Corner."

In time the work in the *Companion* was of such high quality that parents as well as their children were reading it. To find articles by Gladstone, Lord Bryce, Thomas Hardy, Rudyard Kipling, famous presidents of universities and noted professors was unusual, to say the least, and Ford may have sometimes overestimated his audience. Sex, crime, or anything considered immoral were rigidly excluded. The emphasis was on action, adventure, humor, and what young people themselves were doing. New writers were welcomed, and it was this hospitality that first brought Jack London to public notice in 1899. The basic formula of the magazine was a mix of a serial with short stories, articles by the famous, science, anecdotes, and puzzles.

Magazine history was affected less, however, by the *Companion*'s content than by its circulation methods. It was the first magazine to use effectively the device of giving premiums for annual subscriptions, a practice it began in the late sixties. For more than a half century afterward, it issued every year in late October a "Premium List Number" containing pictures and descriptions of the treasures that might be had for obtaining two or three or whatever number of subscriptions. The list, which covered thirty-six pages of the *Companion* by the 1880s, included everything from magic lanterns to printing presses, from dolls to Elsie books.

There was no doubt about how well this method worked. Readers waited for the annual issue as eagerly as they awaited Santa Claus, and circulation gained until the *Companion* led all other magazines for a time, with a figure of 400,000 in 1887 and passing half a million in 1898. The subscription rate was not high; it remained at $1.75 from 1870 until nearly fifty years later. But the success of the premium method at the *Companion* spread through the magazine business until it raged like a fever, reaching the point of absurdity in many cases and even causing the premature death of some magazines. At its peak, the method would enable a super salesman to furnish a small store.

Most of those who used it had sense enough to give up the idea when its usefulness was exhausted. Only the *Companion* continued it successfully, until late in its career.

In the end, the *Companion,* like so many other old magazines surviving from the past century, was a victim of the changing times of the twenties. It could not change, and change was the order of the day. As a writer in the Boston *Transcript* remarked when the *Companion* died: "Ford's strictness was never entirely escaped. The modern *Youth's Companion,* whether or not the staff was aware of it, had inhibitions which held it back, quite imperceptibly perhaps." Nevertheless, when it died in 1929, merging with the *American Boy,* its circulation below 300,000, there were nostalgic tears shed by more than one adult who had stopped reading it years ago. It was the young who no longer needed it; they had gone on to other things.

Another early magazine that flourished into this century and is not yet dead is the *American Railroad Journal,* begun in 1832 and continuing under a variety of names up to its present title, *Railway Mechanical Engineer.* It was the first American railway periodical, and, at the time it began, was considered something of a joke. "You might as well have an *Aqueduct Chronicle,* or a *Turnpike Commentator!*" the *Journal* quoted its own critics. But its founder, D. Kimball Minor, a newspaper journalist, had faith in the railroads, and intended to use his magazine to encourage their growth. In time, the magazine went on to stimulate interest in the whole national public transportation system, then to reflect the changing interests of its own industry.

Still another long-lived magazine outside the general field was the *Scientific American,* begun in 1845 and alive and in better health today than ever before. Its founder, appropriately, was one of those inventive Yankees with great ingenuity, who became a stereotype. But Rufus Porter was no stereotyped individual. Apprenticed at fifteen to a shoemaker, he ran away, became apprentice to a cobbler for a time, painted gunboats, and blew the fife for the Portland Light Infantry in the War of 1812, later painted sleighs, played and taught the drums and even wrote a book on the subject, taught school, became an inventor, peddled a revolving almanac, went into portrait and landscape painting, returned to inventing, and in between bouts of invention began his journalistic career in 1840 by founding a new magazine, *The American Mechanic.* This led to the launching of his weekly, the *Scientific American.*

Porter could not stick to any pursuit for long. He sold his magazine in 1846 for a few hundred dollars to Orson Munn and Alfred Beach, the latter the son of Moses Y. Beach, publisher of the New York *Sun.* From then on, it began to record the scientific progress of the nineteenth century, and to support it against the assault of quacks and nonprogressives alike. The sons of the two owners carried on their work into this century. It became a monthly in 1921. Today, under the direction of a dynamic publisher, Gerard Piel, the *Scientific American* is probably the most highly regarded magazine of its kind in the world.

Of all the magazines begun in the nineteenth century and surviving to the twentieth, certainly the most prestigious and generally noteworthy would have to be the two started by the Harper brothers, whose great book-publishing house, of which the magazines were offshoots, is known to us today as Harper & Row. The first of their periodicals, *Harper's Monthly,* begun in 1850 as *Harper's New Monthly Magazine,* is still with us. *Harper's Weekly,* started seven years later than the monthly, came to an end in 1916.

The monthly was started, quite frankly, as an aid to the book-publishing business of the Harper boys, who used several pages of the magazine to advertise forthcoming books. Otherwise, it was to be a survey of contemporary English literature, as varied as possible, and with many different departments. Its first number was impressive: 144 octavo pages, printed on good stock, the contents including two short stories by Charles Dickens and fifty-eight other varied literary morsels, much of it clipped from other magazines. The British novels whose piracy had been an important factor in the foundation of the Harper business were to appear in the magazine, along with similar piratical plunderings of the British periodical press. Dickens and others were paid for their work in time, however, and Harper's published such noteworthy serials as *Bleak House, Little Dorrit,* Thackeray's *The Newcomes* and *The Virginians,* and George Eliot's *Romola.*

Harper's rivals cast it in the role of unpatriotic villain for its preoccupation with British authors—it was "a good foreign magazine," *Graham's* noted—but the Harper brothers saw no reason to forsake a good thing immediately. Slowly, however, the magazine began to change in the 1850s as American writers like Benson J. Lossing, Jacob Abbott, and Fitz-James O'Brien began to appear. In 1851 it began a department, soon to be famous, called "The Editor's Easy Chair," the first occupant of which was Donald G. Mitchell, whose amusing *Reveries of a Bachelor* became a best-selling book. He was succeeded in 1853 by George William Curtis, who for the next forty years made the "Easy Chair" the best department carried by any American magazine.

In the 1850s, *Harper's* was the most successful magazine in America with its combination of English serials, its wide variety of shorter work, and its many illustrations. Its first printing had been a modest 7,500; by the time the war began, it was 200,000, rich, and jealously abused by its enemies, the unfortunate competitors. *Putnam's* conceded resignedly, "Probably no magazine in the world was ever so popular or so profitable."

Since the monthly *Harper's* did not devote itself to the war, as the weekly did, its circulation declined rather sharply for a time, but as soon as the conflict ended, its lists were renewed, and for the same reason they had swelled before: serials like Wilkie Collins's *Armadale,* Dickens's *Our Mutual Friend,* and further serials by Anthony Trollope, R. D. Blackmore, Thomas Hardy, and others. Americans were not serialized in *Harper's* until the 1880s. They appeared often in the short stories, however, and came to dominate that form in the magazine.

As the magazine expanded in the later years of the century, it began to print advertising other than its own, beginning in the eighties, and soon was carrying as much as forty pages a month. By the nineties, *Harper's* had reached its peak as a general illustrated literary magazine, and as Dr. Mott remarks, it had probably "attained the very zenith of success among the world's periodicals of that class. . . ." It was achieving enormous popular successes with such serials as Du Maurier's *Trilby,* which set off a national craze, and Mark Twain's *Personal Recollections of Joan of Arc,* published anonymously. But

Henry Mills Alden, the editor, did not hesitate to edit out of Hardy's *Jude the Obscure* (published under the title *Hearts Insurgent*) bits and pieces he felt could not be "read aloud in the family circle." He had even dropped a whole chapter out of Henry James's translation of Alphonse Daudet's *Tartarin de Tarascon*.

Entering this century, *Harper's* continued on its distinguished way, printing the best of English and American authors. In 1919 Henry Alden retired after fifty years as editor, during which time, according to Poultney Bigelow, "the greatest editor of his age educated the English-speaking world from an editorial sanctum so small that he could reach everything therein without moving from his chair. His table was not visible because of the papers upon it." After 1925 the magazine became primarily a journal of opinion, its pages filled with the work of historians and philosophers like Charles A. Beard, James Truslow Adams, Bertrand Russell, Harold J. Laski, all these balanced and relieved by the short stories of Aldous Huxley, Wilbur Daniel Steele, and others. Its contemporary years will be recounted in a later chapter.

Although not as long-lived, *Harper's Weekly* was as distinguished in its own way. It provided a vivid picture-text history of American life from 1857 to 1916, the course of its lifetime. Pictorially and textually, it was nearly always interesting and often brilliant. The magazine was Fletcher Harper's "pet enterprise," and he managed it until he retired in 1875.

In format, the *Weekly* was somewhere between a magazine and a newspaper, and in fact called itself a "family newspaper." Its emphasis was on the news. The physical shape was a small folio of sixteen pages at the beginning. Unlike the monthly, it plunged into political discussion wholeheartedly before the Civil War and during it. Its pictorial coverage of the war was superb, particularly the work of the young artist Thomas Nast, which was neither downright realistic illustration nor the satirical cartoon he became famous for later, but rather the kind of mood drawing Bill Mauldin did so successfully during World War II. Lincoln could say of him truthfully: "Thomas Nast has been our best recruiting sergeant."

The *Weekly*'s circulation was a healthy 100,000 through the war.

It climbed after the war, and reached 160,000 by 1872. The editorials of George William Curtis, combined with Nast's pictures, were a powerful drawing card still. Like its monthly brother, the *Weekly* also printed English serial fiction, including Dickens, and articles by notable people. But as always, it was the pictures that held most fascination for the *Weekly* readers—illustrations and cartoons of contemporary life, and again especially Nast's political cartoons, which reached their climax in the seventies when he was a prime factor in the exposure of Tammany Hall's incredible iniquities.

After 1884 the *Weekly* began to decline, although it continued to improve in physical appearance and the display of its pictures, and it carried the work of many of the best English and American writers of the day. Nevertheless, it continued to slide a little every year toward eventual oblivion. When the Harpers sold it to S. S. McClure's organization in 1913, Colonel Harvey declared that it had been unprofitable for twenty years. Norman Hapgood, who had been spectacularly successful with *Collier's*, could not resuscitate the *Weekly*. As *Life Magazine* (the present *Life*'s humorous predecessor) said, "To the consternation of the *Weekly's* old friends, he took the first turn to the left, and drove the dear old paper down the hill. He also tipped her over and tipped out most of the old subscribers." In the end, the magazine was merged with the *Independent,* and lost its identity.

Another "great name" was *The Atlantic Monthly,* like the Harper publications the offshoot of a publishing house. For a century it has been bracketed in the public mind with *Harper's Monthly* as one of the two most distinguished literary periodicals in America. Both magazines have had their partisans who consider their favorite the better; sometimes the leadership has seemed to pass from one to the other, but over the lifetime of both magazines, most students of magazine history appear to agree that the standards of *The Atlantic* have been higher.

It was founded in 1857 by Moses Dresser Phillips, of the Boston publishing house Phillips, Sampson & Co. Lowell was its first editor, although he agreed to come only if Holmes became a contributor, which resulted in *The Atlantic*'s publication of *The Autocrat of the Breakfast Table.* Provincial at first, filled with good New England writing, it began to change when, in 1859, the magazine passed into the hands of another publisher, Ticknor & Fields, after Phillips's death. The price was a mere $10,000.

The Atlantic, in new hands, did not plunge into the war any more than did *Harper's Monthly.* It carried some reflective articles about the issues, however, including Emerson's "Emancipation Proclamation," and early began to devote considerable space to Reconstruction.

In 1869, while Fields was on a European trip, Mrs. Stowe submitted an article about Byron, intending, as one critic put it, "to arrest Byron's influence upon the young by overwhelming him with moral reprobation; instead of that, she has raised the interest in Byron to sevenfold intensity." By mercilessly exposing the poet's libido, Mrs. Stowe created the greatest magazine sensation since her own *Uncle Tom's Cabin* ran serially in the *National Era,* and in doing so she cost *The Atlantic* 15,000 shocked subscribers who refused to renew. The Panic of 1873 contributed further to the magazine's slipping circulation; it was down to 12,000 in 1881. By this time *The Atlantic* had a new publisher, H. O. Houghton, whose various publishing ventures had settled by 1880 into the prestigious Boston firm of Houghton, Mifflin & Co.

In the seventies, too, *The Atlantic* had a new and great editor, William Dean Howells, who broadened the horizons of the magazine. As he put it, "Without ceasing to be New England, without ceasing to be Bostonian, at heart, we had become southern, mid-western, and far-western in our sympathies. It seemed to me that the new good things were coming from those regions rather than from our own coasts and hills."

Howells himself contributed to the magazine, both fiction and criticism, which did much to increase its reputation. Among the other contributions, the most remarkable was Thomas Bailey Aldrich's *Marjorie Daw,* one of the most formidable popular successes of the day; nothing the magazine ever printed surpassed it in popularity. In 1881 Howells was succeeded as editor by Thomas Bailey Aldrich, who was more like Lowell in his tastes, and he in turn was succeeded by Horace E. Scudder, who, because of his intense interest in education, added more articles on social topics.

Until nearly the end of the century, however, *The Atlantic* had not yet attained its full powers. It did so, however, when Walter Hines Page became editor in 1896. Aggressive, young, a southerner, Page was foreign to everything *The Atlantic* had been, but he boosted its prestige and circulation by turning it to some mild muckraking and political controversy. Strange but distinguished names appeared in the magazine: Theodore Roosevelt, Woodrow Wilson, E. L. Godkin, William Allen White, Booker T. Washington, Jacob Riis. Page also secured a big best-selling novel as a serial, Mary Johnston's *To Have and to Hold,* which probably doubled *The Atlantic*'s circulation.

Page was succeeded by Bliss Perry. He in turn was followed by Ellery Sedgwick, who had helped to organize the Atlantic Monthly Co., which in 1909 was publishing the magazine. Sedgwick made it the lively, literary periodical, with a world view, that it remains today. Under his management, the circulation passed 100,000 in 1921. Recently, both *Harper's* and *The Atlantic,* in the new era of specialization, have entered upon new lives.

twelve

A New Breed of Editors

IN THE LONG DEVELOPMENT OF AMERICAN MAGAZINES from the end of the Civil War to 1905, a new breed of editors rose in the business. They deserve attention as a class, for they presage our own era.

They were, first of all, individualists. One thinks of the lonely figure of Edwin Lawrence Godkin, whose editorship of the tiny periodical *The Nation* was so powerful that although its circulation was never much more than 30,000, both he and the magazine were influential figures in America. Godkin was English-born, a cold, aloof man, with few friends, little known to his contemporaries. He was a paradox—a man who could not bear other people in his personal life, whose idea of hell was to mix with the lower classes. Yet his whole life was dedicated to trying to better the lot of these classes. He fought for the social reforms of his day with a razor-sharp style that made him the greatest editorial writer of his or any other time. As editor of *The Nation,* the weekend edition of the New York *Evening Post,* he created a crusading journal of ideas, many of them iconoclastic for the time. Godkin was more quoted, perhaps, than any other writer in America, certainly more than any other magazine or newspaper editor, during the last decades of the nineteenth century. Clergymen, educators, politicians drew on his editorials, and what he had to say filtered down from these opinion-makers, as they would be called today, and eventually were understood by the electorate, who translated much of what he advocated into political action.

At the opposite end of the scale was Dr. Josiah G. Holland, of *Scribner's Monthly.* Holland looked and talked like the popular magazine editor he was. His sympathies were not with the struggling masses, as were Godkin's, but with the upper middle class to which he himself belonged. A member of the class of original WASPs that now controlled the country, Holland was able to talk to a large audience in the pages of *Scribner's*, and he knew how to speak to them in their language. As a sentimental poet of note, he contributed to his own magazine, and into the remaining pages he instilled the moral, broad-gauged conservatism of his genial personality. That was exactly what his readers wanted to read. Though *Scribner's* was the great middle-class magazine of its day, its literary quality was high enough to rank it occasionally with *Harper's* and *The Atlantic,* particularly in its later days.

Godkin, Holland, and Howells were men of intellect, dealing with publications directed to an upper-level audience. The new mass market, however, created by the steady improvement in machine technology, particularly the rotary printing press, was the prime target for another kind of publication and another kind of editor, one who understood mass tastes. The first, and one of the best, of these mass editors was Frank Leslie.

Leslie's life could have been one of the semilurid tales his magazines carried. He was an adventurer, but one with a quick, lively mind and a driving ambition—and perhaps the first editor or publisher to understand the mass mind. He began working in his native England as a wood engraver, under his real name, Henry Carter. In 1848, at the age of twenty-seven, he emigrated to America with an idea germinating in the back of his mind. As a boy he had wanted to study art, but his father refused to help him in something so clearly useless, and the boy had to go it alone, drawing secretly in his room. He sent these drawings to his idol, the London *Illustrated News,* making sure to protect himself from his father's wrath if they were published by using a pseudonym, "Frank Leslie." They were, indeed, published, and Leslie was on his way. He moved to London from his home in Ipswich, telling his father he was going to be a clerk in a drygoods house. Instead, he went to work for the *News,* and soon was chief of its engraving room.

Leslie wanted to start such a magazine himself, but obviously he could not do it in London, without further alienating his family, and so concluded that he had no alternative but to go to New York. Once there, he had little difficulty finding work as an engraver, since they were much in demand. His best deal was with P. T. Barnum, who was about to manage Jenny Lind's tour of America. Leslie was given the job of preparing the illustrated programs for her concerts, and this pleasant task took him, following in her train, across the United States and as far as Havana. Then, after a brief interval in Boston with *Gleason's Pictorial,* he was back in New York again, scheming with Barnum to establish an American version of the *Illustrated News,* which unfortunately lasted only a few months.

By this time, however, Leslie was confident that he could operate such a magazine himself. He began with magazines for women, first *Frank Leslie's Ladies' Gazette of Fashion and Fancy Needlework,* which he began in 1854. It did so well that by the end of the year he was busy buying another magazine, a story paper called the *New York Journal of Romance,* which he reworked into his formula of pictures and text.

These ventures were not what Leslie had in mind. In December 1855 he made his real dream a reality. *Frank Leslie's Illustrated Newspaper,* in spite of its name, was actually a weekly magazine of a kind now plentiful all over the world, treating the news of the day with liberal pictures and some text. At the beginning it was only sixteen pages, priced at ten cents. Its pictures were something entirely new in magazine publishing—illustrations of an event no more than two weeks after it took place. Again like the news magazines and picture periodicals of our own day, it attempted to cover music, drama, fine arts, racing and other sports, and books, all in departments, and printed serial fiction besides.

Leslie had a large and well-organized art staff. At least five artists besides himself did the work, and he was able to produce big pictures in a surprisingly short time by dividing up the cuts into as many as thirty-two sections, giving a section to each man in his large crew of engravers. The accent was heavily on pictures. When the quota needed for news and fiction illustration was filled, pictures were run for their own sake. Some of them were so large, two by three feet, that they had to be folded into the magazine.

For Leslie, news meant sensation. He was not much interested in sober political events; with a true instinct for the mass market, he looked for the war in Nicaragua, the bloody conflict in Kansas, the sensational New York murder. It took nearly six months for this formula to penetrate the market, and during that time Leslie was nearly ready to give up, but then the tide began to change, and in its third year the *Newspaper* could claim 100,000 circulation. The delighted publisher immediately spawned a whole new series of magazines: *Frank Leslie's New Family Magazine,* 1857; *Frank Leslie's Budget of Fun,* a year later; *Frank Leslie's Ladies' Magazine,* in 1871.

The early years of the *Newspaper* showed what this kind of periodical could do to influence its audience—an audience able to absorb more from pictures than from words. With considerable courage, Leslie attacked one of the scandals of New York, the distribution of "swill milk." Cows in the dairies supplying the city with milk were fed with distillery refuse, which poisoned them and contaminated their milk, although they continued to produce until they died. Since the dairies and the distilleries were hand-in-glove with the Tammany political machine, and everybody was making money, all reform attempts had failed until Leslie's attack.

He had the weapon that worked. When his readers saw *in pictures* the incredible filth of the dairies, the grotesque, dying cows, and the milk being carted into New York in open barrels, there was a horrified outcry of public revulsion. The Board of Health tried to gloss over the scandal with a reassuring statement, but Leslie rejoined, "Every one of those cows has a vote!" and he sent off detectives in the wake of the milk wagons to record the places where milk was left, a list he published with an accompanying warning to the customers that they were poisoning their children. The politicians he attacked tried to have Leslie indicted for criminal libel, but a grand jury refused.

The end result was a complete victory for Leslie and his paper. The mayor was forced to permit a committee from the New York Academy of Medicine to make its own investigation, which completely confirmed everything *Leslie's* had reported. Two years later the state legislature passed a law ending the "swill milk" disgrace forever, and Leslie was presented with a gold watch and chain by a grateful public.

Leslie's was not always preoccupied with virtue, however. The publisher was not above capitalizing on sensational crime for the sake of circulation, and he gave space to prizefighting, a sport the paper occasionally deplored.

As the war approached, *Leslie's* caused a sensation with its drawings of the hanging of John Brown, and a week after the firing on Fort Sumter, it emerged with a four-page folding picture of the event. That was a forecast of its extraordinary role during the war years, when for week after week it produced a priceless history in pictures of the conflict. While its treatment did not have the literary luster of its rival, *Harper's Weekly,* *Leslie's* was more enterprising in its coverage of public affairs, and generally livelier. At the end of 1864, Leslie wrote: "We have had since the commencement of the present war, over eighty artists engaged in making sketches for our paper, and have published nearly three thousand pictures of battles, sieges, bombardments, and other scenes incidental to the war." The paper also had as many as a dozen correspondents in the field.

The cost of covering the war was great, and by 1865 the circulation of Leslie's was at a relatively low level of 50,000. It bounded up later to 70,000, then lost ground again to less than 40,000 during the depression of the seventies. This would have been large enough for the magazine to survive, and might even have rescued the weaker members of Leslie's magazine family if he himself had not lived so flamboyantly. But that was the manner of this good-looking, short but well-built man with the black beard. In the early seventies the man who had made so much money out of scandal in other people's lives found himself involved in one himself.

All had not been well at home with his wife of London days, Sarah Ann. They had separated at some time during the sixties, but were not yet divorced in 1867 when Leslie went on a junket to Paris as a United States Commissioner to the Paris Exposition, in the company of his managing editor, Ephraim G. Squier, and his wife, who was the editor of *Frank Leslie's Ladies' Magazine.* What happened between

Mrs. Squier and Leslie in Paris was told in titillating detail when Mrs. Squier divorced her husband in 1873, amid mutual accusations of adultery. Leslie, who had started and withdrawn two previous divorce actions, finally rid himself legally of Sarah Ann, and married his former traveling companion.

With this marriage, the editor began a new phase of his career. His new wife was redheaded, striking, as forceful and ebullient as he was, and together they made a handsome couple, whether they were in their grand Saratoga home, touring California in a private car with a retinue of writers and artists, or working together in New York. These extravagances, coupled with unfortunate excursions into Saratoga real estate, ended with his bankruptcy in 1877, although he was able to continue editing his properties, under an assignee, until he died in January 1880, at a time when his magazine had dropped to a melancholy 33,000 circulation, and half his other properties had been discontinued.

Mrs. Leslie succeeded her husband in the business, and proved herself at once to be as good an editor, or better, than her husband, paying off his debts and regaining control of the property. With a sure journalistic instinct, she stopped an edition already made up for the press, and remade the pages to cover the assassination of President Garfield, which earned the weekly a $50,000 profit. She improved the paper physically, too, with better stock and a more attractive cover, while she employed her formidable personality to attract new writers. Circulation began to rise again, and Mrs. Leslie became as much of a figure in New York as her late husband had been.

It turned out that she had been divorced one or more times before she had left Squier. It was said she had Creole blood, and she herself claimed to be of royal descent, with right to the title of "Duchesse of Bazus." A contemporary magazine described her at her desk "dressed in a French costume that is stayed and stiffened till it fits without a wrinkle or a crease. Her sleeves are poems, her back is a study, and her waist could be spanned by a necklace. She wears the tiniest of shoes, and carries a painted feather fan."

Mrs. Leslie sold her property in 1889; though it continued to be published, the heart had gone out it. It was more political and sober, less sensational, and as time went on, an unofficial organ of the Republican Party. However, under John A. Schleicher, who bought it in 1898, it combined politics, social comment, reviews, and art work so successfully that in the first years of World War I it reached a peak circulation of nearly 400,000. After the war, however, in the depression, it declined rapidly and died in June 1922, *Judge* getting what was left of its assets.

"Never shoot over the heads of the people," Frank Leslie's motto, was the key to the mass-market journalism being practiced on newspapers and magazines alike in the closing decades of the nineteenth century. Leslie's success was duplicated and excelled by other mass-market editors and publishers.

After the Civil War, with the population increase, the decline of illiteracy, the spread of education, and the modern printing machinery that made mass distribution possible, the magazine business grew rapidly. There were only about 700 periodicals in 1865, but by 1885 there were 3,300; in the two-decade period, some eight or nine thousand periodicals were published.

After 1885 the acceleration continued. A trade magazine, the *Journalist*, noted in 1889: "The rapidity with which magazines are started in this country is equalled only by the suddenness of their disappearance. Periodicals of all sorts and kinds and devoted to the interests of everything under the heavens . . . come and go. . . . By far the greater number either fail or ruin their proprietors." Six years later, *The Nation* reported the birth of magazines "in numbers to make Malthus stare and gasp," while in 1897, the *National Magazine* complained: "Magazines, magazines, magazines! The news-stands are already groaning under the heavy load, and there are still more coming."

There were, in fact, more than 4,400 magazines by 1890; five years later there were about 5,100, and five years after that, more than 5,500.

The Chicago *Graphic,* a journal of opinion, remarked in 1892: "The development of the magazine in the last quarter of a century in the United States has been marvelous, and is paralleled by no literary movement in any country or in any time. Every field of human thought has been entered and as the field has broadened new magazines have arisen to occupy the territory, and the magazine has become not only a school of literature but of science, art and politics as well."

It was this new "school of literature" that the new breed of editors had come to teach in, and as the century drew toward its close, they had done their job so well that *Literary Life* could say, "Our Magazines are outrivalled by none in respect to both text and illustration. ... We may boast of a weekly and monthly output that reaches the high-water mark of journalistic enterprise."

thirteen

The Second Golden Age

IN THE LATE, EXPANSIVE DECADES of the nineteenth century, when magazines were pouring out in a golden flood again as they had between 1825 and 1850, there was an increasing variety of periodicals, and in general a marked improvement on old formulas, along with some more or less new ideas.

A surprising number of the best magazines that were started survived well into the next century. Some did not, and perhaps the finest of these was *The Galaxy*, which began in 1866 as New York's answer to Boston's *Atlantic*. The rivalry continued until 1878.

There was reason to believe that New York could support a popular literary magazine, to rank with Boston's, and as soon as the idea was proposed, enthusiastic support came from critics and editors who thought *Harper's* was "sectional and dull" and *The Atlantic* "a New England coterie affair altogether." The prospective publishers were not altogether likely candidates for such a venture. They were brothers, William Conant and Francis Pharcellus Church, better known as "Colonel Church and his brother Frank," who had been publishers of *The Army and Navy Journal* during the war. Their postwar venture was an attempt to capitalize on the success of the *Journal,* and on the apparent demand for a New York literary magazine.

The Churches might have turned to literary men for help, and it was said that Edmund Clarence Stedman had been offered the job, but eventually they decided to edit the magazine themselves, surrounding themselves with a few able editors. The ablest by far was Mark Twain, who ran a department known as "Memoranda," for a few months between May 1870 and April 1871. Twain made a forth-right proposition to the editors: "If I can have entire ownership and disposal of what I write for the *Galaxy,* after it has appeared in the magazine, I will edit your humorous department for two thousand ($2,000) a year—and I give you my word that I can start out tomorrow or any day that I choose and make that money in two weeks, lecturing."

If the Churches gulped a little at the figure—at $17 a page, it was about twice their highest rate—they realized that Twain's name and work in the magazine would be worth it in circulation. In his first contribution, Twain announced with mock solemnity what he intended to do: ". . . In this department of mine the public may always rely upon finding exhaustive statistical tables concerning the finances of the country, the ratio of births and death, the percentage of increase of population, etc. etc.—in a word, everything in the realm of statistics that can make existence bright and beautiful.

"Also in my department may be found elaborate condensations of the Patent Office Reports. . . .

"And finally, I call attention with pride to the fact that in my department of the magazine the farmer will always find full market reports, and also complete instructions about farming, even from the grafting of the seed to the harrowing of the matured crop. I shall throw a pathos into the subject of Agriculture that will surprise and delight the world."

What emerged in Twain's department was a series of articles done in his best, savagely satiric manner, attacking some of the more irrational phenomena of the day: a clergyman's barring workingmen from his congregation because they smelled, the bad treatment of Chinese people in America, the minister who refused to bury an actor from his church. It was a task he enjoyed, but one he could soon see required more time than he had anticipated, and one he no doubt would have given up even if tragedy had not struck his family.

"I have now written for the *Galaxy* a year," Twain wrote in his valedictory. "For the last eight months, with hardly an interval, I have had for my fellows and comrades, night and day, doctors and watchers of the sick! During these eight months death has taken two members of my home circle and malignantly threatened two others. All this I have experienced, yet all the time been under contract to furnish 'humorous' matter once a month for this magazine. . . . I think that some of the 'humor' I have written during this period could have been injected into a funeral sermon without disturbing the solemnity of the occasion."

His presence in the magazine had meant much to *The Galaxy*; during that time it attained its highest circulation. Naturally, no one else could carry on his department successfully, and in time it was discontinued. Meanwhile, other contributors attracted attention, particularly Henry James, whose travel articles and literary criticism helped to increase his audience outside Boston. *The Galaxy* carried serial stories, although not of very high quality, except when Trollope appeared, or Rebecca Harding Davis, or translations from Turgeniev. In the poetry department, the magazine printed four by Walt Whitman (plus his essay on "Democracy"), and also work by Sidney Lanier, Bayard Taylor, Bret Harte, and Joaquin Miller. A section of William Cullen Bryant's translation of the *Iliad* appeared, too.

All told, *The Galaxy* merited more often than not the *New York Graphic*'s judgment that it was "more in accordance with the feelings of the reading public of America than any other magazine that is published." Nothing could have fascinated the public more, certainly, than such serials as General George Custer's *Life on the Plains,* which was still running when the events on the Little Bighorn cut it short.

In the end, however, *The Atlantic* won the contest between the two magazines, and in 1878 *The Galaxy*'s list of subscribers was quietly transferred to its rival, which graciously observed in welcoming them that "we shall aim to perpetuate the finest characteristics of a magazine which for eleven years has been a presence in our periodical literature so distinctly agreeable and useful that it could not wholly pass away without great public regret."

Of an entirely different pattern was *Harper's Bazar* (it did not take on its present spelling of "Bazaar" until 1929), still another product of the fertile Harper factory, and of Fletcher Harper's agile brain. Fletcher thought so much of his idea that he would have gone ahead alone if the others, reluctant at first, had not agreed.

Harper's Bazar appeared for the first time in November 1867, subtitled "A Repository of Fashion, Pleasure and Instruction," and very ably edited by New York City's historian Mary L. Booth. And Fletcher Harper was right—the magazine was successful, at least initially, rising to 80,000 in its first decade. What Miss Booth turned out, as Dr. Mott has observed, was "a ladies' *Harper's Weekly*." It contained English serials, plenty of double-page pictures, miscellaneous articles and stories, splendid art work, even Nast cartoons and other engravings from the *Weekly*'s artists.

Of primary interest, of course, were its fashion plates, which for years came directly from the magazine's great Berlin counterpart, *Der Bazar*, in the form of duplicate electrotypes. The German magazine also sent proofs of its text matter, describing the new styles abroad, and to this the New York staff added its descriptions of American designs. Women readers were also offered patterns, fancywork, and discussion of household problems, interior decoration, and garden planning.

Under various editors, *Harper's Bazar* went on erratically, surviving the Harper brothers' failure in 1899; but it had been a money loser for years, and a monthly since 1901, when it came to the attention of William Randolph Hearst in 1913. He bought it for his International Magazine Company, an empire he was then building, and his editors freshened it up considerably, making it much more sophisticated, and generally setting the tone it has now. As one of today's two leading high-fashion magazines, all that survives from the old days is a receptivity to good contemporary writing.

The kind of publishing represented by the Harper group of magazines was an antebellum development of real importance. This extension of book publishing allowed a flow of material between the two media that benefited the quality of both. Magazines started by the major publishing houses, moreover, were not likely to be so transitory, since they had the financial resources of a successful publisher behind them. Nearly all of them had long lives, and were of primary importance in carrying on the literary tradition of periodicals.

One of the best was *Lippincott's Magazine*, begun in 1868, a conservative periodical, and also one of the best printed and consistently of high quality in its contents. Its illustrations were not as numerous as some of the other magazines, but they were excellent.

Drawing on its own list of authors, as such magazines could do, as well as other writers, *Lippincott's* offered an impressive list, including Frank R. Stockton, Emma Lazarus, Brander Matthews, Henry James, Maurice Thompson, William Gilmore Simms, Sidney Lanier, and others. *Lippincott's* especially encouraged southern writers, and they were well represented, along with those who came from the magazine's native Philadelphia. Among the foreign contributions, "Ouida's" classic children's work (anguished over as much by adults), *A Dog of Flanders,* was an outstanding success.

Nevertheless, *Lippincott's* did not do well financially. Its advertisements were mostly for the publisher's books, and it would not disclose its circulation. Though changes were made in 1881 to make it a little lighter, it was still overshadowed by its mighty rivals, *Harper's* and the *Century Magazine.* It had a unique flavor, however, and *The Nation's* critic praised its "comparative freedom from staleness and routine." The publisher tried various devices to make it even fresher. Pictures were dropped in 1885, a single instead of a double-column layout was employed after 1886, and the following year it began to print a complete novel in each issue. One of them was Oscar Wilde's *The Picture of Dorian Gray,* and another, even more shocking to readers, was Amélie Rives's *The Quick or the Dead. Lippincott's* also introduced Sherlock Holmes to American audiences with *The Sign of the Four,* and climbed on the Kipling bandwagon with *The Light That Failed.* Paul Laurence Dunbar appeared among the poets, and there were high-quality short stories by Lafcadio Hearn, Anna Katharine Green, and Owen Wister. Still later, after the turn of the century, the magazine printed Mary Roberts Rinehart's first novel and Carolyn Wells's first detective fiction.

Lippincott's went quickly when it began to go. McBride, Nast and Company bought it in 1914, and it became *McBride's Magazine* later that year. But within eight months it, too, folded, and *Scribner's* became the ultimate beneficiary of *Lippincott's* list.

Another publishing-house venture with an even shorter life but a career distinguished in its own way was *Appleton's Journal,* which began publication in 1869 and soon established itself as a magazine of tremendous variety. At first, however, it reflected the chief interest of its editor, Edward L. Youmans, who was on the staff of D. Appleton & Co. and who wanted to popularize science. The public was apathetic about that; what it liked in the new periodical was the serialization of Victor Hugo's *The Man Who Laughs.* Youmans quit after a year and soon founded another Appleton magazine, the *Popular Science Monthly,* with which he was much more successful.

Other editors followed, but of particular note was Oliver Bell Bunce, a publisher and writer who turned out to be an excellent editor as well. Bunce originated in the pages of *Appleton's* the work that finally emerged in book form as *Picturesque America,* with Bryant's name as editor, although Bunce had done the work, because his distinguished name would help sell the book. The pictures and sketches that gave rise to the book began in the magazine. Other material appeared to be oriented to New York, except for the serials, which tended to be by British, French, and German novelists.

The magazine became a monthly in 1876, but in spite of its enticing variety, it never could seem to attain the distinction of its contemporaries, and after 1878 it was little more than a clip-and-paste review of English, French, and German magazines. Its loss in 1881 was not a serious blow to the magazine business.

Of far more enduring quality was the periodical brought out by the house of Scribner in November 1870. As noted earlier, Dr. Josiah Holland was its editor, but its founders also included Roswell Smith, the business manager, trained in publishing and the law; and Charles Scribner, head of the parent firm. The magazine operated under the roof of a company organized by these men, Scribner & Co. To give it a start, the subscription lists were taken over from another Scribner publication, *Hours at Home.* Then, a month after it began, *Scribner's Monthly* absorbed *Putnam's Monthly Magazine,* another publishing house rival; and the *Riverside Magazine for Young People,* a Boston publication intended for children.

Holland's strong personality, the personality of a great editor, along with the work of his associate, Richard Watson Gilder, and other first-rate editors like Richard Henry Stoddard, made *Scribner's* initially successful. Holland contributed poetry, and a good deal of serial fiction, along with his editing. He attracted to the *Scribner's* stable a long list of the best writers of the day, the star of whom in the early days was Helen Hunt Jackson, with Frank Stockton a close rival.

One of *Scribner's* most remarkable accomplishments was its long series "The Great South," by Edward King, with many illustrations by J. Wells Champney. It had been Roswell Smith's idea, and at its completion in 1874, Holland wrote: "It has been an enterprise involving an amount of labor and expense unprecedented in popular magazine literature. Neither pains nor money have been spared to make it all that we promised it should be. It has occupied, in all, about 450 pages of the magazine, and involved the production of more than 430 engravings. Mr. Edward King, who was written the papers, and Mr. Champney, the artist, who accompanied him and made the original sketches for the pictures, have traveled more than 25,000 miles in carriage, stagecoach, and saddle (in the latter, 1,000 miles), in personal survey of the immense tract of country presented, and our readers have the result of what has cost the magazine more than $30,000. ... The whole of the Southern papers will soon be republished in a beautiful volume."

On King's southern trip he discovered a young warehouse clerk in New Orleans who gave him some stories he had written about Creole life. He was George Washington Cable, the first of a parade of southern writers *Scribner's* welcomed to its pages—Joel Chandler Harris, Thomas Nelson Page, John Fox, Jr., among others.

Scribner's had another treasure in its art department, where the great printer Theodore Low De Vinne, was in charge of the magazine's printing from 1874 to 1914, and in that time made it the leading reproducer of wood engravings in the country, as well as distinguished it typographically. Later, on the *Century*, he made that magazine the best printed anywhere.

Except for *Harper's, Scribner's Monthly* enjoyed more success than any of the other publishing-house ventures. But in 1881 there was a falling out between the book publishers and the magazine publishers.

As a result, the magazine split off under Roswell Smith's direction and changed its name to the *Century Illustrated Monthly Magazine*. Holland died the same year, and Gilder succeeded him.

The *Century Magazine* got off to a spectacular start with a vast series of Civil War articles by the generals who had directed the battles and by such civilians as Mark Twain. Grant's pieces, four of them, for which the magazine paid him $1,000 each, later became the basis for his *Memoirs,* published by Twain. Converted into book form, the *Century* series became a famous set, *Battles and Leaders of the Civil War,* which the company published. It earned more than a million dollars, and the *Century* followed it with Nicolay and Hay's *Lincoln,* for which it paid $50,000.

Gilder remained editor of the *Century* for twenty-eight years, performing with increasing distinction as the magazine remained among the literary magazine leaders. With his death, as so often happens, the magazine declined under less capable hands, although it was still widely read and admired through the twenties, until it slipped quietly into quarterly publication in 1929 and died the following year, its circulation below 20,000. *The Forum* accepted it in a merger.

As for *Scribner's*, the publishing house had agreed not to start a new magazine in the same field for five years, as part of the dissolution agreement of 1881. It waited until January 1887, and then a new *Scribner's Magazine* emerged, with Edward L. Burlingame, a member of the publisher's staff, as editor. He had his work cut out for him, since he was in competition with *The Atlantic, Harper's* and the *Century,* all distinguished, all established. Burlingame had been given half a million dollars to make the magazine successful. He had a formula—dealing with popular topics in a literary way. Best of all, he used an economic bait—the new *Scribner's* would be twenty-five cents a copy, $3 a year; the other four were thirty-five cents, $4 a year.

It took nearly all the half million before Burlingame could make his formula work, but after that there was no further difficulty. Leading writers from both sides of the Atlantic appeared in its pages, rivaling the competitors, and in the first ten or fifteen years after the turn of the century the magazine hit a circulation peak of more than 200,000 between 1910 and 1911. It had already passed its rivals during the nineties. Moreover, its advertising, by this time a real factor in the life of magazines, was running more than a hundred pages a month, at $300 per page. In 1912, when *Scribner's* was twenty-five years old, *The Outlook* saluted its contemporary: "Ably edited, representing the best standards interpreted by the most original writers, thoroughly artistic in illustration, *Scribner's Magazine* must be counted not only among the publications which belong to periodical literature, but also as an important contribution to permanent literature."

Scribner's decline began after 1912, and circulation was down to 70,000 by 1924. Alfred Dashiell became editor in 1930, and the magazine had a brief reawakening, directed toward young intellectuals and oriented more to the Left. That, however, discouraged what remained of the old subscribers, and after a series of resuscitation efforts the magazine was suspended in May 1939. *Esquire* got its subscription list, and a magazine called *Commentator* obtained its name, publishing it as *Scribner's Commentator*. Under that title it fell into the hands of the Japanese propagandist Joseph Hilton Smyth, and reached the same disgraceful end as the *North American Review*.

These were some of the products of the second Golden Age. The magazine business now had quality as well as quantity.

fourteen

Rise of the Religious Press

RELIGIOUS MAGAZINES WERE A STAPLE of the periodical press from the beginning, but after the Civil War they proliferated even more, and came to constitute a large class in themselves. Their number doubled between 1865 and 1885, from 350 to more than 650. Circulation, however, was concentrated at least 50 percent in the Sunday-school papers, whose circulations sometimes passed the 50,000 mark. The reviews sold 10,000 when they did well, and the weeklies reached 100,000 only in a few cases.

Not many of these magazines were of high quality. The monthly and quarterly reviews were ponderous, dull, full of theological scholarship, while the weeklies were lively enough but so full of petty controversy they seemed provincial. Sometimes the weeklies went so far in their denunciations of each other, and of their common enemies, that the ruling bodies of the churches passed motions of censure against religious papers in general.

It is easy to see why they were provoked when one reads the tirade directed against the perfectly respectable New York *Evangelist* by Theodore Tilton, fire-eating editor of *The Independent*: "Take a man who can neither write nor preach nor keep his temper nor mind his own business; thrill his bosom day by day with twenty years of dyspepsia; flush his brain with the hallucination that his bookkeeping mind is competent to religious journalism; put a pen in his hand wherewith to write himself down a Pecksniff; set him like a dog in his kennel, to make a pastime of snapping at the respectable people of the neighborhood; and then, gentle reader, you have a specimen copy of the *Evangelist*."

The editors of nonreligious journals deplored this kind of journalism. They considered it unprofessional, and what might be expected from editors who were really clergymen and not journalists. Indeed, a writer in *The Galaxy* advanced the idea that journalism and religion were incompatible, and *The Atlantic*'s ordinarily austere editor, Lowell, termed the religious press "a true sour-cider press, with belly-ache privileges attached."

It was not, of course, as bad as all that. There was more than enough theological quarreling, but the tone was not generally in the style of Tilton's *Independent*—and *The Independent* itself was not always so raucous.

Perhaps the most consistently proliferating type of religious magazine was the Catholic one, representing a church whose growth itself was phenomenal. Catholics had some need of their own press, since there was a widespread Protestant fear of growing Catholic power. Anti-Catholic articles appeared even in the most respectable journals. Nurtured partly in self-defense, the Catholic press grew until by 1885 it surpassed by one the Methodists, who had led the field until that time. The score was Catholics, 74; Methodists, 73. Among the Catholic publications, *Catholic World,* founded in 1865, was the leader, followed by *Ave Maria,* which had its origins in Notre Dame University. Among the weeklies, the Boston *Pilot* and the New York *Tablet* led the field.

A great editor, Daniel D. Whedon, made the *Methodist Review* an outstanding monthly church publication after the war. The weekly leader was *The Christian Advocate,* in New York. The large number of Christian Negroes led also to the establishment by them of several journals, notably the African Methodist Church's quarterly, the *A.M.E. Church Review,* and the *Star of Zion,* the North Carolina organ of Zion Methodists.

The Baptists were more prolific than the Methodists, but because their publications were inclined to die sooner they were always behind the Catholics and the Methodists in total number. Among the Presbyterians, the press represented largely the divisions between conservatives and liberals, and between North and South. This kind of splitting up, particularly between liberal and conservative wings, was also a chief characteristic in the press of the other denominations, particularly among the Unitarians.

Aside from the established denominations, there was a wave of publishing among the Spiritualists, in whom there was renewed public interest, as there is during and after every war. Some of their magazines were edited by mediums, others by those who called themselves philosophers, especially the Swedenborgians, who were not, of course, Spiritualists but gave inspiration to that movement. There were also a good many undenominational journals, preaching church unity. Of these the best was probably *The Christian Herald,* a New York offshoot of a London journal. This general religious magazine has survived to our time. Other magazines were devoted entirely to sermons, and some to biblical scholarship or to missionary activity. Some were the organs of special interests like the Young Men's Christian Association and the Salvation Army, whose *War Cry* began life in New York in 1882 and continues today. Publications of tract societies and religious propagandists were numerous but unimportant except for the American Tract Society's *Illustrated Christian Weekly,* which ran from 1871 to 1892, edited for a time by Lyman Abbott, and proving to be nearly as good as some of the general magazines.

The religious press—and the general magazines, on occasion—debated such fundamental issues as evolution and the afterlife, especially the possibilities or the existence of hell. They had reason to be concerned, too, with the condition of organized religion itself, which was losing a great deal of its fundamentalist grip on the population. More and more people inside and outside religious faiths were demanding that the churches worry less about which people were going to get into heaven and more about the role churches should be playing in society. These feelings erupted, in both the secular and religious press, in popular novels like Mrs. Humphrey Ward's *Robert Elsmere,* and later in the fiction of the Reverend Harold Bell Wright. Writing for the *North American Review,* Oliver Wendell Holmes declared in

1881: "Creeds imperatively demand revision, and the pews which call for it must be listened to, or the preacher will by and by find himself speaking to a congregation of bodiless echoes."

It was now even possible for the agnostics and the atheists and the freethinkers of various stripes to be heard. "Bob" Ingersoll was attacked violently in many quarters, but his pleas for atheism were printed in the best magazines, and made him famous. There were at least half a dozen avowedly atheistic or agnostic magazines blooming in the latter part of the century, where there had been none before.

As the century drew toward its conclusion, all these trends were accelerated until it was clear that a great theological change was occurring in American life, brought on by unprecedented criticism of the Bible on historical and literary grounds, the inroads made by scientific thought on lay thinking, the growth of the idea of evolution, and a vast reevaluation of man's moral nature.

One offshoot of the new climate of opinion was the rise of the ethical culture movement, beginning with the founding of the Society for Ethical Culture in New York in 1876. This movement had its own periodical press, and with the beginning of the *International Journal of Ethics* in Philadelphia in 1890, it took on an international character.

Another result of the turmoil in the churches was a turning toward social problems, which many thought should be the chief concern of religion rather than saving souls for the hereafter. In time this movement had its own magazine, *Dawn,* founded in 1889 by the new Society of Christian Socialists. The publication's two subtitles breathed the reform spirit: "A Magazine of Christian Socialism and Social Progress," and "A Journal of Revolution Toward Practical Christianity." Similar publications were founded throughout the country.

Overshadowing the other new faiths that were springing up all over (faiths like New Thought, which took up where the Transcendentalists had stopped), was the rise of Christian Science in Boston, which soon had its own publications. Mary Baker Eddy and her new religion were attacked violently by the best magazines—Mark Twain in the *Cosmopolitan,* and a series of articles in the *North American Review,* which represented the consensus of its contemporaries in its view that Christian Science was reprehensible, although it did not go as far as

The Chautauquan's verdict that it was "a disgrace to the intelligence of the age." For its own defense, the church had a monthly *Christian Science Journal,* founded in 1883 by Mrs. Eddy, and fifteen years later a weekly newspaper, *The Christian Science Sentinel.*

Faith healing of different varieties produced magazines in other parts of the country as well, and there were also the theosophical journals, following the introduction of this Eastern philosophy to the country by Madame Helena Blavatsky.

In the denominational journals, toward the close of the century, there was less emphasis on more general news and greater attention paid to denominational news, supplemented by other kinds of religious reading. These periodicals, many of which had begun life looking like newspapers, were now uniformly magazines in size as well as in content. They were wise to make the change, and indeed had been forced to do so by the rapid rise of daily newspapers after the war, which made the periodicals seem both imitative and ineffective. The New York *Tribune* said in 1890: "Religious papers have found a formidable competitor in the secular press, which now treats religious questions and news with an ability and a fullness that no religious paper can hope to excel. This has compelled the religious papers . . . to develop new features of their own, in which the secular press cannot compete with them."

The net result of this change, however, was the beginning of a decline in the religious press during the nineties, one that is still going on today. The suspensions and consolidations began, at first slowly, and then more rapidly in this century. As *Zion's Herald* accurately forecast as early as 1904, "The old-time religious paper is gone."

That was true, but since there were so many different kinds of religious periodicals extant, at least a dozen categories, there was no danger the religious press would disappear, although it might diminish. Dr. Mott points out the variety of religious publications: general magazines with church backgrounds, like *The Outlook* and *The Independent,* liberal denominational journals, the denominational magazines themselves, the regional Protestant journals, the interdenominational magazines, publications of religious action groups, missionary society journals, quarterly monthly theological reviews, undenominational scholarly reviews, the Catholic press, the Jewish press, the foreign-language religious press, and a whole category of magazines on the periphery of the field.

In our own time, many of the old standards still remain, but the emphasis in religious publication has swung from magazines to books. All the major religions are served by their own publishing houses, and some of these have become large organizations in their own right, with retail outlets around the country. Religious book publishing has also become a highly profitable subdivision of large general publishing houses. In fact, at no other time in America, in spite of the "God is dead" era, have there been so many religious books published and read. But the great days of the religious periodicals are gone. The Catholic periodicals still carry some prestige, and the liberal ones of that faith are influential, but the other religious magazines no longer command national attention, even in their own faiths.

fifteen

Magazines Cover the Country

AS SOON AS THE WAR WAS OVER, a rapid nationalization process occurred. West and East were joined by the Union Pacific Railroad, and
a floodtide of settlers poured westward. The West Coast, already
booming before the war as the result of the gold rush, continued to
grow. The Middlewest had become the nation's breadbasket, as the
cliché went, and New England was being swiftly industrialized, not
entirely to its benefit. Only the South, devastated by the war, did not
participate in the general prosperity, and it would be years before it
could begin to recover.

Nationalization meant a greatly increased national audience for the
magazines. The great homogenization of the American people was beginning, and the periodical press was recording the process, helping
the rapid spread of magazines across the country. But the centers
of periodical publication continued to remain in the East, as they have
done to this day. Boston, Philadelphia, and New York were the centers, as they had been from the beginning, and of the three, New York
by 1865 had far outstripped its rivals. In that year there was more
magazine publishing in Manhattan than there was in both the other
cities together. The same was true of book publishing.

New York itself was a favorite topic in the magazines, sometimes
condemned, sometimes contemplated with awe. On the subject of
Broadway in 1866, *The Atlantic* asserted: "Despite its dead horses
and vehicular entanglements, its vile concert saloons, the alternate
meanness and magnificence of its architecture, the fragile character of
its theatrical structures and their limited, hazardous means of exit—

despite falling walls and the necessity of police guardianship at the crossings, the reckless driving of butcher-boys and the dexterity of pick-pockets—despite the slippery pavement and the chronic cry for 'relief'—Broadway is a spectacle and an experience worth patient study, and wonderfully prolific of life pictures."

The magazines patiently studied Broadway and the remainder of New York, deploring its rotten government, its bad transportation and its dangerous streets, clucking at its vice and crime. The stereotype of the country boy or innocent country girl wandering into a life of city vice and depravity in New York became a classic image of the day.

Boston still claimed intellectual ascendancy, and it was widely believed there and elsewhere that there was little literary life in New York despite its eminence as a publishing center. It was true that there were still excellent magazines and good publishing houses operating in Boston, but as a city it had slipped badly. Philadelphia was momentarily content with third place as a publishing center, but it was still the center for medical publishing, and the seat of the best ladies' periodicals.

Everywhere the quarterly magazine was in ill health. As one critic put it in 1873: "Men at the present date live too fast for the slow-going quarterlies. Questions that excite our utmost interest die away and are forgotten by the time the quarterly review is ready to discuss them."

Not so the monthlies. The weeklies might be livelier, but *Harper's* and *The Atlantic* and *Scribner's* and *The Galaxy* were living proof that a great deal of the intellectual excitement of the times resided in these prestigious magazines. Nevertheless, it was not an expanding field in the first decades after the war; few new ones were produced.

Along with the mass-market periodicals already described, a new kind of "story paper" rose after the war, and in an unlikely place, Augusta, Maine, where the *People's Literary Companion* first appeared in 1869. It was the child of a man named E. C. Allen, who sold a secret formula washing-powder recipe. He used an incredible merchandising technique, where the housewife was pledged to secrecy when she paid her dollar for the recipe. To carry his advertising for the product, Allen began the *Companion*. It was the forerunner of the free distribution magazines that are distributed so commonly today, and its formula was a kind of mixture of household helps and light reading. The *Companion*'s circulation was partly paid but mostly free (a mix that prevails now in a good many business magazines), and in its second year its circulation was 500,000.

Such prosperity was bound to produce imitators, and in Allen's own Augusta, P. O. Vickery in 1874 established *Vickery's Fireside Visitor,* a similar periodical, which had a comparatively long life of more than thirty years. Still another began in Augusta the following year, *Our Fireside Journal,* and these successes were soon being imitated in other cities, although Augusta remained the center for these "mail-order papers," as they were called. They lived by the advertising of companies that sold their products by direct mail, and prospered so greatly that most of them became weeklies. Story papers in general, no matter where they were published, came to depend at least in part on mail-order advertising.

The story papers were also an outlet for the dime-novel publishers, like George Munro and Beadle & Adams, whose magazines were spinoffs, as we would say today, from their highly profitable book businesses. Perhaps the most famous of them was *Beadle's Weekly,* begun in 1882, changing its name to *Banner Weekly* in 1886. Without the benefit of mail-order advertising, this magazine attracted generations of boys and men with the thrilling tales written by Captain Mayne Reid, "Ned Buntline," Albert W. Aiken, and Professor Edward S. Ellis. Frank Leslie was also in the field with *Frank Leslie's Chimney Corner,* first appearing in 1865 and outshining some of its rivals by Leslie's typical use of lurid pictures. There were, of course, dozens of others.

In the South after the war, when nothing much might have been expected from a region exhausted and still bleeding, there was nevertheless a renascence of literary magazines—twenty or more of them in the four years after Appomattox. Most of them did not live long, but the activity itself was remarkable. Southern publishing centered in New Orleans, Atlanta, Baltimore, Richmond, and Louisville. What the South was still not able to do for itself in the way of magazine comment, the North contributed through a generally sympathetic discussion of Reconstruction problems in all the important magazines. *Lippincott's* especially, as noted earlier, was particularly receptive to southern writers, and gave much other space to analysis and comment about the region.

To the frequently expressed astonishment of those in the East, the West was beginning to make itself felt as a place of spreading culture, not long after the war's end. As *The Atlantic* noted with some awe: "Civilization at a stride has moved a thousand miles, and taken possession of the home of the buffalo," to which the *Journal of the American Geographical Society* added, with remarkable perception in the light of later scholarship, "The recession of our frontier is the most important and the most interesting fact of our national history." The East viewed the Midwest, let alone the Far West, with all the excitement and wonder of Columbus contemplating the Indies for the first time.

Several cities drew attention to themselves with their magazines. St. Louis, by 1870 the third largest city in the country and the home of what came to be known as "the St. Louis movement," had as its chief ornament the *Journal of Speculative Philosophy,* which a critic in the *Educational Review* declared had "made St. Louis famous throughout the civilized world." Otherwise, the city was the home of a few good women's magazines and some specialized journals, particularly in the medical field.

Chicago, however, was the western city that posed the greatest threat to eastern superiority. Its astounding growth was the wonder of the nation, but most people thought of it simply as the great commercial center west of the Alleghenies, and they were truly surprised to find by 1870 that it was also the focal point of considerable literary activity. During the sixties and seventies, nearly a hundred magazines with at least some literary flavor were published in the city, and the Lakeside Publishing Company was printing no less than nineteen magazines in different fields.

One of the latter, the *Lakeside Monthly,* achieved distinction as the first really important magazine in Chicago. Begun in 1869 as the *Western Monthly,* it survived until 1874 as a literary magazine of high merit; its editor, F. F. Browne, attracted to his pages the best of the midwestern writers.

Of the purely literary magazines, the best was *Current*, the 1883 product of a noted journalist, Edgar L. Wakeman, in whose pages could be found writers like Joaquin Miller, E. P. Roe, John Burroughs, James Whitcomb Riley, and Opie Read. This magazine gave notice to the eastern literary establishment that the Midwest had its own school of writers who were developing rapidly.

There were also numerous story papers being printed, of varying quality.

Among the other midwestern cities, Cincinnati published a good many class (that is, quality) periodicals and story papers, while Toledo was the home of several others, especially the *Blade*, a weekly once edited by the eminent humorist "Petroleum V. Nasby."

San Francisco, ebullient, wild, growing, stood alone as the publishing center of the Far West. Its magazines were inclined to have the same characteristics as the city, especially the weekly and monthly miscellanies. The most famous of them was the *Overland Monthly*, made so because of the editorship of Bret Harte—or more properly, Harte's contributions, since he was no editor. While he worked only spasmodically at that job, he contributed some of his best writing to the magazine. After Harte left, the magazine was dead within five years.

Another San Francisco magazine to make its mark was *The Argonaut*, founded in 1877 by Frank M. Pixley, a rich California journalist who was often in the public eye, in one way or another. As with the *Overland*, one writer made it outstanding—Ambrose Bierce, who wrote a scintillating column called "Prattle." In his characteristic style, Bierce began his columnar chores with a solemn statement of intent: "It is my intention to purify journalism in this town by instructing such writers as it is worth while to instruct, and assassinating those that it is not."

Bierce and Pixley parted in 1879, in a blaze of bad feeling. The publisher lived to regret it because his prickly columnist then became editor of a rival journal, *The Wasp*, and for five years Bierce used the trenchant, vitriolic wit that made him famous on Pixley. He transfixed

Pixley at once with one of the mock epitaphs he wrote for the magazine's many enemies: "Here lies Frank Pixley, as usual." *The Wasp* also printed Bierce's famous work, *The Devil's Dictionary*. Together, *The Wasp* and *The Argonaut* put California on the literary map; there were certainly no weeklies in the East to match them for sheer color.

As the end of the century approached, the magazine trends that were evident soon after the end of the war were even more pronounced, particularly the continued concentration of both book and magazine publishing in New York. Periodicals were also becoming more and more national in character. The editor of *The Writer* stated the case clearly in 1899: "No one section of this country can or will support a magazine of general literature, and the country as a whole will not support such a magazine if it is published as the representative of any single section."

On the other hand, there was bound to be an increase of specialization, since it was obviously not possible for national magazines to serve every local and special interest. The medical and legal professions acquired new magazines by the dozen. Farm papers covered state or even regional areas, and there were religious and educational magazines that made no attempt to go beyond a particular region. New specialties were rising, too, like the more sophisticated comic magazines, the bicycling magazines that accompanied the great bicycle craze of the nineties, and a great many more.

One of the most unusual developments of the nineties was the urban weekly, which in a sense was the forerunner of today's *The New Yorker* with its blend of news, amusement, literary work, and politics. But these weeklies also carried a quantity of local society gossip, and the news was not likely to be very serious. *The New Yorker* is, of course, a national magazine, while the urban weeklies made no pretense of being anything but local. The tone of *The New Yorker*, however, has always been distinctively New York in its cartoons and "Notes and Comment" department.

Like *The Wasp* and *The Argonaut*, the urban weeklies tried to be distinctive, lively, local, and amusing, and like their western models, they succeeded best when they found a writer or editor who could do what Pixley and Bierce had done, or unearthed a literary figure of distinction like Harte. The St. Louis *Mirror,* for example, had William Marion Reedy's critical writing, and *M'lle New York* had Vance Thompson's. In a different vein, the tough attacks by George Creel on Boss Pendergast's political machine made the Kansas City *Independent* worth reading. Quite naturally, some of the weeklies veered off in the direction of scandal or even blackmail, but in general they were bright and interesting.

New York's best urban weekly, *Truth,* almost totally forgotten today, was one of the most brilliant periodicals of its time, and carried this kind of magazine to a peak of excellence. After a false start between 1881 and 1884, *Truth,* momentarily suspended, was born anew in January 1886, at ten cents for its twenty-four pages, and with a subtitle, "A Journal of Society, the Clubs, Sports, Drama and the Fine Arts." It struggled for a few years and had to be reorganized again in 1891, but at last it secured its resources, found its stride, and became a fascinating periodical of social satire, with news of high society as an added attraction. The best sophisticated writers of the day wrote for it, and there was handsome illustration, especially portraits in color lithography.

In the early nineties, it had an interesting specialty of actresses and bathing girls, and by the middle of that decade it had a circulation of 50,000. With various changes of ownership and editors, it went on for a while longer, for a time at five cents a copy; then in 1899 it became a monthly at twenty-five cents, complete with full-color portraits of actresses, suitable for framing (a portent of *Playboy*'s center fold). It leaned toward the women's market with some of its features, but it also carried some excellent literary work, including a serial by Henry James, and color illustrated articles on painters. By 1902 it was back to ten cents a copy, but now, in the sometimes inexplicable fashion of magazines, it was definitely on the downgrade, and soon died. Not even a final reduction to a five-cent monthly could help.

By the end of the century, every part of the country claimed at least one magazine of some distinction as its own. Urban centers everywhere, if they did not have an urban weekly, had other publications to boast about. The spread of magazines even extended to the Yukon, with the missionary paper *North Star* in 1887, and to Hawaii in 1888, with the founding of *Paradise of the Pacific,* a promotional monthly.

Understandably, the quality of magazine publishing and editing varied from superb to dismal, as it always has, but it was significant that by the end of the century magazines were operating everywhere, interpreting the times to a constantly growing number of readers who found in them what could be discovered in no other medium.

sixteen

New Faces, New Voices

INNOVATION WAS IN THE AIR as the magazine business gathered force in the late nineteenth century. Old patterns from the past still persisted, as we have seen, but there were those who were intent on pushing out the boundaries.

Ebenezer Butterick produced something new in 1863 when, in his tailor shop in Fitchburg, Massachusetts, he devised the tissue-paper dress pattern that soon became familiar to millions of American women. Butterick put his idea on the market at a most strategic moment, coincidental with the invention of the sewing machine, with which a whole new era of home dressmaking began. So successful were Butterick's patterns that he moved to New York the following year and in a short time headed a business that was growing so rapidly he could scarcely control it.

One of the offshoots of the enterprise in 1872 was a fashion magazine, designed to further E. Butterick & Co.'s pattern business. The magazine was officially launched in January 1873, and its long life did not end until 1937. Subtitled, "A Monthly Magazine Illustrating European and American Fashions," *The Delineator* sold for a dollar. In its forty-eight pages, readers found the styles departmentalized, arranged for the seasons, for "misses and girls" and "for little folks," as well as "hats and bonnets," "stylish lingerie," and similar subdivisions. The illustrations were woodcuts. Ebenezer pushed his main business by giving away patterns as subscription premiums.

Circulation increased steadily year after year, until by 1888 it reached 200,000, a remarkably high figure for those days. About that time the number of pages was increased to eighty, and various changes were made in the format to make it more attractive, and in the editorial department to increase the publication's scope. *The Delineator* now attempted to cover nearly everything that went on in a household. The result was another jump in circulation, to 500,000 in June 1892, and the number of pages shot up again, to 200 in 1894. Even by modern measurements, *The Delineator* at this point was a substantial magazine. Moreover, the Butterick company had established agencies to sell its patterns across the United States, and wherever a lady could buy a Butterick pattern she could also get *The Delineator*.

As time went on, the scope of the magazine became broader, including both fiction and articles, although most of it was light reading. Thus the form of the woman's magazine was established for decades to come—a mixture of hammock fiction, fashion, and articles and departments covering every home activity. In the trade, this kind of publication came to be known as a "cookie-and-pattern" magazine. It was based on the belief that these were the primary interests of women and that they either could not or did not care to think about anything outside the home. By following this formula, *The Delineator* and other magazines made fortunes for a long period, until changing times and the changing position of women in society caught up with them.

That did not happen to *The Delineator* until the 1920s. Meanwhile, the editorial quality of the magazine continued to improve. In the early years of the new century it was printing the fiction of such writers as Carolyn Wells, Richard Le Gallienne, Hamlin Garland, Anthony Hope, and Zona Gale. In 1907 no less a literary personage than Theodore Dreiser became editor. Those who thought or feared he might impart some of the realistic writing in his novels to the pages of *The Delineator* had nothing to worry about. Dreiser was too astute an editor to fall into such a trap. He understood his audience, and approached them conservatively. Charles Hanson Towne, the magazine's fiction editor who established his own reputation as a popular writer, wrote of Dreiser as editor: "Every department of the organization was under the control of Mr. Dreiser. Not a detail escaped his vigilant eye. He O.K.'d every manuscript that we accepted—read them all, in fact—and continually gave out ideas to the entire staff, and saw that they bore fruit."

It would have been unlike Dreiser, however, to adhere to *The Delineator* tradition of ignoring social problems. He was much too involved with them himself, and so the ladies were treated to articles about divorce, marriage problems, woman suffrage, the high cost of living, education, religion, and other problems of that or any other day. Dreiser also crusaded against the treatment of children in orphan asylums, and for better treatment of the underprivileged young.

He greatly improved the fiction department. There was much less hammock reading and many more big names, in the fashion of the popular magazines, who vied with each other to see how many names of noted authors they could cram on their covers every month. *The Delineator* had its share: Kipling, Conan Doyle, Woodrow Wilson, Jacob Riis, John Burroughs, Elbert Hubbard, Oscar Hammerstein, and F. Marion Crawford, among others.

In 1910 Dreiser went back to writing his own fiction, and the magazine tried to continue in the mold he set. But as always when the fire of genius was removed, the formula did not entertain as it had before, although *The Delineator* had some able editors. In common with most of the big magazines of the twenties, circulation went up during that delirious decade, well above the million mark. After another change of editors in 1926, the magazine moved away from its familiar formula and took on a more sophisticated air, both in its art work and text. After merging its sister Butterick publication, *The Designer,* in 1928, and after lowering its price to a dime, *The Delineator* reached its circulation peak, surprisingly, in the year after the Great Crash, with 2,450,000. At that point it stood in fifth place among the women's magazines, and one would have thought its position reasonably secure. Nevertheless, it was sold in May 1937 to Hearst, who merged it with his *Pictorial Review, The Delineator*'s closest rival.

An entirely new kind of trade magazine appeared in 1873 to chronicle the book trade, which was undergoing an explosion of its own. *Publishers' Weekly* had its origins in the trade promotion of Leypoldt & Holt, in the late 1860s, when Frederick Leypoldt, the firm's senior editor, got out a circular to the trade advertising the firm's foreign books. This circular became the *Literary Bulletin,* then the *Monthly Book Trade Circular.* Withdrawing from the book-publishing business so that he might serve it in another way, Leypoldt began the *Publishers' and Stationers' Weekly Trade Circular,* and within a month had added to it by purchasing its Philadelphia counterpart, the *American Literary Gazette and Publishers' Circular.* In 1873 Leypoldt changed the name of the *Circular* to *Publishers' Weekly,* and so it remains today, the "Bible of the book trade," as it has often been called. It is now one of several magazines published by the R. R. Bowker Co., which also publishes reference books for the trade.

One of the magazines published by Bowker is the *Library Journal,* also an offshoot of Leypoldt's tremendous bibliographic energy. This journal, devoted to the interests of libraries and librarians, was launched in September 1876. Both the *Journal* and *Publishers' Weekly* (PW, as it is known in the trade) were for many years under the general direction of Frederic G. Melcher, a beloved figure in the book trade, who was president of the Bowker Company.

No recounting of "new faces, new voices" in the late nineteenth century would be complete without recalling one of the freshest voices of all, *St. Nicholas,* beyond any doubt the best magazine for children ever published in America. It was the creation of Roswell Smith, who had been one of *Scribner's* founders, and its first editor was Mrs. Mary Mapes Dodge, whose *Hans Brinker and the Silver Skates* became a childhood classic. Another editor was the writer Frank R. Stockton, who had written for children and had also been a contributor to *Scribner's.*

In describing the kind of magazine she meant to edit, Mrs. Dodge made it clear that she did not intend "A milk-and-water variety of the periodical for adults." In fact, she went on, "it needs to be stronger, truer, bolder, more uncompromising than the other; its cheer must be the cheer of the bird-song; it must mean freshness and heartiness, life and joy. . . . Most children of the present day attend school. Their heads are strained and taxed with the day's lessons. They do not want to be bothered nor amused nor petted. They just want to have their own way over their own magazine. They want to enter one place where they can come and go as they please. . . . Of course, they expect to pick up odd bits and treasures. . . . A child's magazine is its playground."

This represented a refreshing change from the usual concept of children's magazines, most of which still retained the moralistic tone of the early models and were generally too innocuous to interest many young people. Beginning at an inauspicious time, during the Panic of 1873, the magazine was so beautiful physically and so warm and glowing inside that it captured an audience immediately—an audience that grew ever larger and more faithful. Its peak circulation was 70,000, under Mrs. Dodge's editorship. The contributors were the best writers for children available. Readers of that generation never forgot meeting in the pages of *St. Nicholas* such splendid company as *Little Lord Fauntleroy, The Hoosier School Boy,* and the *Recollections of a Drummer Boy*—along with *Two Little Confederates,* just to balance the Civil War scales.

Later on, *Tom Sawyer Abroad* ran serially, and Theodore Roosevelt contributed *Hero Tales from American History,* which was probably not as enthusiastically received as Howard Pyle's *Jack Ballister's Fortunes.* Kate Douglas Wiggin was a contributor, and so were Rupert Hughes, Brander Matthews, Robert Louis Stevenson, and G. A. Henty. Perhaps the most memorable of all *St. Nicholas*'s pages, however, were those that carried Rudyard Kipling's *The Jungle Book.*

When one considers contributors of this caliber, not to mention the noted nonfiction authors who wrote for *St. Nicholas,* and the famous illustrators of several generations who drew for it, it is easy to see why children who grew up with this magazine found it an experience they treasured all their lives. Like most magazines, however, when its great editor was gone, it began to wither. Mrs. Dodge died in 1905, and a succession of new editors and new owners could never restore the magazine to the glory it had enjoyed for the twenty-five years that she edited it. After so many changes that the original could scarcely be recognized, *St. Nicholas* was suspended in 1940, revived briefly in 1943, then disappeared.

While there were undoubtedly other reasons for its decline and demise, the chief villain appeared to be radio, which in the 1920s so altered children's tastes in entertainment that a magazine like *St. Nicholas* seemed old-fashioned to them.

One of the most remarkable magazine starts in the years around the turn of the century was the *American Magazine*. Originally one of Frank Leslie's progeny, beginning life as *Frank Leslie's Popular Monthly*, it became simply *Leslie's Monthly* in 1904, and did fairly well as a popular, rather light magazine, offering as its chief claim to fame in 1905 Ellis Parker Butler's *Pigs Is Pigs,* a minor classic of American humor. That year its name was changed to the *American Illustrated Magazine,* but later *Illustrated* was dropped.

In the following year, a group of well-known writers for *McClure's Magazine* deserted after a disagreement with its fiery publisher, Sam McClure, and bought a magazine of their own to run as they pleased. The magazine was the *American.* Its new owners were five of the biggest names in the business: Ida M. Tarbell, Lincoln Steffens, Ray Stannard Baker, Finley Peter Dunne, and William Allen White. Other members of the *McClure's* staff came with them.

At the beginning, the venture had all the air of a grand party, but then disillusionment set in. As Steffens tells it in his *Autobiography:* "The editing of the *American Magazine* by a group of fellow writers was a scattered control which was more cautious and interfering than S. S. McClure's dictatorship. . . . All the writers on the editorial board of our own magazine took an interest in what I was writing, and they had an appeal that *McClure's* lacked. I had—we all had—a financial interest in the *American*—stock. I was asked to 'go easy' at first, because we were just starting and needed friends. This I defied. . . ."

Steffens, as the leading "muckraker" of the day—in reality, one of the greatest investigative reporters of any era—could hardly "go easy" and remain true to himself. In a little more than two years he was gone; White and Dunne followed. But for a time Steffens and his fellow muckrakers had carried on some of the crusades begun, or suggested, in their days at *McClure's,* and they were joined by Upton Sinclair, whose attack on the idle rich, *The Metropolis,* appeared in the magazine.

Slowly, however, the pattern of the magazine changed, balancing civil reform with editorial material designed to satisfy broad middle-class interests. New writers appeared, like Edna Ferber, mingling with more established ones like O. Henry. Some of the best humorists of the day, like Stephen Leacock, Wallace Irwin, and Gelett Burgess, appeared in the pages of the *American*.

The magazine changed again in 1915, after it was sold to the Crowell Company, of Springfield, Ohio. The emphasis was now on human interest. Merle Crowell, the new editor, in time brought the magazine to a circulation peak of 2,300,000, with such writers as S. S. Van Dine and Clarence Budington Kelland. In the twenties the magazine also became celebrated for its success stories about American businessmen, and its general celebration of the middle-class American way of life. A new editor in 1929, Sumner Blossom, made it a family publication, emphasizing "togetherness," which was the *McCall's* formula. The magazine died at the end of 1956 with the collapse of the magazine division of the Crowell-Collier organization, which carried with it *Collier's* and *The Woman's Home Companion*.

Another fresh new voice in the waning years of the century was that of *Puck,* setting the tone for a kind of "golden age" of humorous magazines. Begun as a German-language comic magazine in New York, the work of a Viennese artist, Joseph Keppler, *Puck* began publishing in English in March 1877—a ten-cent quarto of sixteen pages. Keppler himself drew cartoons for it, and the remainder of the editorial content was bright satire, with some good critical writing. It was a welcome change from previous humor magazines, which had been rather sorry imitations of *Punch,* the London weekly.

In time the circulation of *Puck* reached 80,000, largely as the result of the astute business management of Keppler's partner, a printer named A. Schwarzmann, as well as Keppler's own contribution and the writing of his associate editor, H. C. Bunner. One magazine described Bunner's unique contribution: "To make the fine, violinlike tones of his 'comments' heard through all the trumpet-blast of Keppler's cartoons was no easy task, yet Bunner accomplished it." In the early years, Bunner sometimes wrote nearly half the issue. An incredibly varied and prolific writer, he could turn out either prose or verse in virtually any form, even supplying caption lines for the cartoons, short stories, and filler material. Bunner was no hack, however; he was a talented, endlessly amusing writer.

The motto of the magazine, running under the impish figure of Puck himself, was "What fools these mortals be!" and the kind of writing that went into the magazine was intended to prove this aphorism. *Puck*'s targets were primarily the political villains of the day and the corruption that followed in their wake. While the assault was carried partly in satiric pieces, it was the cartoons that constituted the main battery. "It is not refined humor that makes *Puck* a political power," said *The Critic* magazine, "it is the coarse strength of its cartoons, which thus far have been drawn almost uniformly in the interests of popular morality and political integrity." *Puck* also attacked the abuses of organized religion, and the social nonsense of the day. But its general offering was light humor.

As time went on, *Puck* benefited from other first-class editors, men like Harry Leon Wilson and John Kendrick Bangs, excellent writers themselves. Inevitably, however, as humor itself changed in America, the magazine declined a little and in 1917 it was sold to Hearst's International Magazine Company, and was soon discontinued, in September 1918. The bold, impudent figure of Puck, staff in hand, and the motto beneath, survived in, of all places, the masthead of Hearst's Sunday colored comic supplement. It was, indeed, a far cry from the *Puck* of H. C. Bunner to the Katzenjammer Kids.

As a result of *Puck*'s success, a rival, *Judge,* started appearing for the first time in October 1881. Like the *American Magazine,* it was founded by a dissident group from another periodical, in this case *Puck* itself. The dissenting artists began *Judge* (called at first *The Judge*) as a gesture toward their freedom, but what they created was remarkably like what they had left behind, and it was not until the magazine changed hands in 1884 that it began to find its own identity. At first it was meant to be the satiric organ of the Republican Party, but after further reorganizations it acquired a broader base, and by 1912 had a circulation of 100,000, well ahead of all its rivals.

Judge hit its peak in the 1920s, when it became perhaps the best humorous magazine ever published in America. Its editorials for a time were written by William Allen White, its book reviews by Walter Pritchard Eaton, its sports articles by Heywood Broun. The movie reviews were the work of Ruth Hale, and the theater critic was George Jean Nathan. Ring Lardner was a favorite contributor. John Held, Jr., headed a long list of outstanding artists while S. J. Perelman, Don Herold, and Milt Gross added their distinctive humor later in the decade. In the end, the Depression killed this excellent magazine. The pattern of American humor had shifted again from the giddy twenties, and the thirties produced a new kind of wry laughter in the midst of the Depression to which *Judge* could not adapt. It went bankrupt in 1932, and after further management changes, it died of slow strangulation in the late 1930s, much missed by the generation that had grown up with it.

The major rival of *Judge* was *Life*—not Henry Luce's picture magazine of the 1930s, but the only humor magazine to challenge *Judge* successfully. It followed its rival by two years, and few magazines could have had a less promising start. John Ames Mitchell, the young man whose idea it was, had no qualifications whatever for starting a magazine. A Harvard graduate in science, who had studied both architecture and painting in Paris, and settled down in New York to do illustrating, Mitchell had ten thousand dollars in the bank when he decided that he wanted to start a magazine that would reflect American life in art work—a satirical periodical that would employ both illustration and type, like the new *Judge,* but would do it better. For help he drew upon a Harvard friend, Edward Sanford Martin, who had been editor of the *Lampoon,* which he had hoped to make a national magazine. Still another Harvard man, Andrew Miller, became business manager. A printer was found—who insisted on a week's pay in advance—and the venture began.

Seldom has a successful magazine met more immediate discouragement. Writing about it later, Mitchell records that nearly all the third issue came back from the newsstands, and then, with the fourth and fifth returns, "the three anxious men who counted them made the blood-curdling discovery that the unsold copies outnumbered the edition printed! Six thousand had been issued, and there were six thousand two hundred returns. It seemed for a moment that miracles were being resorted to in order that *Life*'s defeat might be the quicker. A more careful examination, however, showed the extra copies were from previous editions."

After five months of this kind of discouragement, during which Mitchell went on pouring out his money to the printer, the magazine began to catch on with the public. It had started its existence in January; by September the magazine was breaking even, and as the second year got under way, it reached 20,000. About that time, Martin had to leave the firm because of poor health, but the others carried on.

Life was full of gentle social satire, most of it in pictures at first, as Mitchell had originally intended. Its standards for illustration were higher than those of *Judge,* and the level was carefully maintained. But it never reached a higher point than it did in 1887, when the drawings of Charles Dana Gibson, who was then not yet twenty-one, first appeared. His Gibson Girl became almost a symbol of the nineties—"this serene, self-reliant, beautiful American girl," as Dr. Mott calls her, noting that for nearly twenty years, while she flourished, she was accompanied by the Gibson Man—"square shouldered, firm-jawed, handsome, well groomed, self-possessed." They were unreal as people, but they epitomized the elegance of the Mauve Decade, and for girls the Gibson Girl was a model, while even the men tried to emulate the Gibson Man by shaving off their moustaches. As an artist, Gibson had the ability to tell a story in his single black-and-white frame, and thousands of Americans were so addicted to these pictures, usually a center spread in *Life,* that they framed them and hung them in their homes.

As the new century began, *Life* increased its advertising substantially, and advanced past 70,000 in circulation, helped by such features as Wallace Irwin's famous "Hashimura Togo" pieces and the drawings of lovely girls by Harrison Fisher and James Montgomery Flagg. By 1916 the magazine had 150,000 circulation, and was regarded as the most successful of the ten-cent magazines by an authority like Colonel George Harvey, who described it in *Harper's Weekly* as "crisp as a doughnut and as full of spice as a cooky." Its best work was anthologized annually, and its name was a synonym for smartness and wit.

When Mitchell died in 1918, followed by Miller a year later, Gibson became chief owner and president in 1920, with Martin as editor. The magazine also acquired a new drama critic, Robert Benchley, who was to add much to its luster. And now, in the twenties, *Life* presented in its pages the cream of the satirists who abounded in that decade and whose names have become legend: F. P. Adams, Corey Ford, Montague Glass, Rollin Kirby, Will Rogers, Dorothy Parker, Gluyas Williams, John Held, Jr., and Percy L. Crosby.

Robert E. Sherwood was the motion-picture critic, and he became editor in 1924, followed by Norman Anthony in 1929. Under Anthony, the magazine had changed character somewhat, becoming more "modern," until Gibson ordered Anthony to restore its traditional style, because some of the advertisers were complaining. This move proved to be the beginning of the end. Circulation began to decline, and the Crash nearly finished the job. By 1932, just five years from the time it was at its peak, *Life* became a fifteen-cent monthly. It was also under great pressure from *The New Yorker,* which represented a new kind of humor, as *Life* had represented the old, and from *Esquire.* Nevertheless, it was still making a little money in 1936 when Henry Luce bought it in order to give the name to his new picture magazine. The subscription list and other assets were sold to *Judge,* which did not live long enough to enjoy them.

Near the end of the nineteenth century, a new idea in eclectic magazines appeared that was to prove as successful as the idea behind *Life* in the field of humor. It was the *Literary Digest,* which first appeared on March 1, 1890, edited by Isaac Kauffman Funk, who had been a Lutheran preacher, a book and magazine publisher, a leader of the Prohibition Party, and a lexicographer of note. As a man who was even then in the process of producing a dictionary, Funk knew how to compile, and he understood the middle-class mind. These attributes helped him make the *Digest* a readable magazine, if not a distinguished one. It carried no pictures at first, only column after column of gray type. Yet these columns contained condensations of articles from American, English, Canadian, German, French, and Italian magazines. These were divided into sections, "political," "sociological," and four others. Two departments occupied the remainder of the magazine—"Books" and "The Press." Gradually "The Press" took over the magazine, in the sense that it became more and more a digest of newspapers rather than magazines. In 1904 a question-and-answer department, "The Lexicographer's Easy Chair," was begun, and added to the *Digest's* success.

The *Digest* reached its peak during the twenties, with a circulation of a million and a half by 1927. (Only the *Saturday Evening Post* surpassed it in circulation.) It carried so much advertising that some issues were more than 150 pages. It was acclaimed by *Time* later as "one of the greatest publishing successes in history." Editorially, its great attribute was its impartiality, balancing Republican with Democratic quotations equally. One observer of magazines, John E. Drewry, wrote in 1924: "No faction, whether political, religious, or intellectual, may honestly assert prejudice by the *Literary Digest* for or against its cause." It was a favorite in schools and colleges, where debating clubs and social-studies classes found it extremely useful.

Ironically, the *Digest's* most successful feature proved to be the cause of its downfall. Its straw polls in Presidential elections, beginning on a national basis in 1924, after earlier, smaller experimenting, were correct in predicting the winner in subsequent elections, although the percentage of error was far beyond the limits of modern public-opinion polling. In 1936, however, the *Digest's* ten million straw ballots (only a fourth of them were returned) incorrectly predicted a victory for Alfred M. Landon. While this spectacular failure (Landon carried only Maine and Vermont) was not the only cause of the *Digest's* sudden collapse, it was perhaps the major factor. Fickle public opinion somehow discredited the *Digest* in other ways as well as its political acumen, and this, combined with heavy advertising losses during the Depression, led to the sale of the magazine in July 1937 to the Review of Reviews Corporation, where it quickly lost its identity and finally suspended in February 1938. *Time* got its subscription list.

Still another landmark in magazine publishing begun before the nineteenth century ended was *Collier's,* which had a long career from 1888 to 1957. Peter Fenelon Collier, its founder, was an Irish-born young man who came to America at seventeen, and by the time he was twenty-four was already in the book-publishing business, directing his first lists toward Catholics but gradually expanding into the cheap reprint business, and then into the selling of "library sets" of standard authors, on the installment plan and by mail. Few men have been so successful in this field; Collier sold fifty million books by these methods in the last three decades of his life.

Branching out into the periodical business in 1888 with *Once a Week,* a popular magazine that attained a quarter-million circulation by 1892, Collier changed the name of the periodical in 1895 to *Collier's Weekly,* subtitled "An Illustrated Journal," and under that name it went on to great success. It was given fresh impetus by the founder's son, Robert J., who after graduating from Harvard in 1898, became its editor. The war with Spain gave him the opportunity to send James H. Hare, the best of the early news photographers and a pioneer in photojournalism, to Havana to cover the war. As young Collier wrote later, that act "involved me in more troubles and wars and libel suits than any one act in my life. It turned me from the quiet paths of a literary career into association with war correspondents, politicians, muckrakers, and advertising men."

Collier's coverage of the Spanish-American War, both in pictures and text, was outstanding. Money from the other Collier enterprises was injected liberally into the magazine, enabling it to buy the work of such illustrators as Harrison Fisher and Howard Chandler Christy, Frederic Remington, and others. Among the contributors were Rudyard Kipling, Robert W. Chambers, Frank Norris, and James Whitcomb Riley. One of the magazine's bright new ideas was the naming of All-America football teams by its sportswriter, Walter Camp.

With the editorship of Norman Hapgood in 1902, another era began. Hapgood, too, was a Harvard man, a graduate of the law school, and thirty-four years old when he arrived. His special responsibility was the editorial page. In other sections, *Collier's* was doing a remarkable job, with superb coverage of the Russo-Japanese War by Richard

Harding Davis and a large staff, and a sensational San Francisco earthquake issue, published two weeks later and featuring Jack London's story of the disaster, plus sixteen pages of pictures. But it was Hapgood's crusading editorials, tied to the magazine's articles on public affairs, that made *Collier's* one of the leading magazines. Hapgood wrote and fought against the patent-medicine racket, misleading claims in advertising, corruption in newspaper advertising, ineffective congressional leadership (a battle carried on by Mark Sullivan), and other governmental inadequacies. The editor also argued eloquently for such reforms as railroad rate regulation, child-labor laws, slum clearance, and woman suffrage. Few magazines have ever approached *Collier's* in the Hapgood years in terms of political influence.

Hapgood, however, fell out with Collier in the election of 1912, since he favored Wilson and the magazine was committed to Roosevelt. The editor was fired, and went over to *Harper's Weekly.* Collier took over the editorship himself for a few months until Mark Sullivan became editor in 1914; he was followed after three years by Peter Dunne. With Rob Collier's death in 1918 (his father had died in 1909), the magazine was sold by the heirs to the Crowell Publishing Co. In this transition period, the magazine nearly died, and once did not appear for four weeks. After an uncertain period in which it struggled to reestablish itself, an effective new editor, William L. Chenery, former managing editor of the New York *Sun,* was found in 1924. He assembled a first-rate staff, including a brilliant assemblage of sportswriters that included Grantland Rice, H. C. Witwer, Damon Runyon, and Quentin Reynolds. The associate editor was John T. Flynn.

Chenery harked back somewhat to *Collier's* crusading tradition by attacking prohibition, but he built the magazine chiefly through its fiction, which he regarded as "the backbone of mass circulations." Among the novelists and short-story writers he printed were Willa Cather, Kathleen Norris, Zane Grey, Peter B. Kyne, E. Phillips Oppenheim, Sinclair Lewis, and John Erskine. *Collier's* ran Sax Rohmer's "Fu Manchu" serials and Albert Payson Terhune's dog stories. Readers loved the short stories of Zona Gale, Samuel Hopkins Adams,

Sophie Kerr, Courtney Ryley Cooper, Stephen Vincent Benét, Joseph C. Lincoln, and Mary Roberts Rinehart. *Collier's* probably did more to make the American short story popular than any other magazine.

In five years, Chenery jumped *Collier's* circulation from one million to two million, and made the magazine strong enough to withstand the impact of the Depression. During the thirties, one of *Collier's* brightest stars was Winston Churchill, who began writing six articles a year at $1,500 each in 1930. He continued writing them until 1938, when he reentered the Cabinet.

By 1942 *Collier's* was over three million in circulation. Chenery retired the following year, and Charles Colebaugh succeeded him. Following the trend of the times, the magazine devoted more space to articles, especially war coverage, and less to fiction. There were further staff changes, culminating in 1949 with the ascendancy to the editor's chair of Louis Ruppel, a typical Hearst editor of the old school, who produced such circus stunts as a "World War III number" in October 1951, titled "Russia's Defeat and Occupation, 1952–1960: A Preview of the War We Do Not Want," in which an aggregation of writers, newspapermen, correspondents, editors, and others gazed into what turned out to be an extremely clouded crystal ball.

This kind of Hearstian acrobatics signaled coming disaster; in the continuing efforts to maintain its position in a highly competitive market, *Collier's* went farther and farther afield to shock readers into buying it. Sex, violence, and sensationalism in general had their inevitably stupefying effect, and the magazine was ripe for closure when the entire Crowell-Collier magazine group went out of existence in January 1957.

Lost with *Collier's* and the *American Magazine* in that debacle was the third Crowell-Collier onetime moneymaker, *The Woman's Home Companion.* Its origins lay in the wave of "home magazine" startings of the 1870s. Few of these had very long lives, but the one begun in Cleveland, Ohio, early in 1874, titled simply *The Home,* was luckier. Its founders were two brothers, S. L. and Frederick Thorpe, and their magazine was a thin eight pages, weak in everything except mail-order advertising.

After a good many vicissitudes and some changes in name and ownership, the magazine became *The Woman's Home Companion* in January 1897, a title that not only separated it from its rival, the *Ladies' Home Journal,* but reflected the editor's opinion that the word "lady" had been abused and that "the noblest ambition of our end-of-the-century femininity is to be a 'woman.' . . . The use of 'lady' as a synonym for 'woman' is vulgar."

Under the editorship of Arthur T. Vance, who took over in 1900, the *Companion* became more of a family than a woman's magazine. Fiction was emphasized, with names like Bret Harte, Rafael Sabatini, and Jack London appearing from time to time. While Vance was building the magazine, it passed into the hands of John S. Crowell, who had been a member of the firm's Springfield, Ohio, publishers: Mast, Crowell and Kirkpatrick. Crowell, as president and general manager, moved the periodical's offices to New York in 1901.

The strongest period for the magazine began in 1911, when Gertrude Battles Lane became editor. Hers was one of the most remarkable success stories in magazine-publishing history. Starting in the Crowell organization in 1903 at $18 a week, when she was only twenty, she was earning $50,000 a year and was a highly regarded editor before she died.

In a *Companion* promotion piece, Miss Lane told how she edited the magazine: "In editing the *Woman's Home Companion,* I keep constantly in mind a picture of the housewife of today as I see her. She is not the woman who wants to do *more* housework, but the woman who wants to do *less* housework so that she will have more time for other things. She is intelligent and clearheaded; I must tell her the truth. She is busy; I must not waste her time. She is forever seeking new ideas; I must keep her in touch with the best. Her horizon is ever extending, her interest broadening; the pages of the *Woman's Home Companion* must reflect the sanest and most constructive thought on the vital issues of the day."

That was the key to Miss Lane's success. She recognized that the days of the cookie-and-pattern formula were over and that to succeed, a woman's magazine must realize that women were thinking, sensitive human beings with many interests outside the home.

She edited the magazine for thirty years, through the First World War, the twenties, and the Depression—a severe test for any editor. She printed the popular writers of fiction for women, but she also bought the work of Willa Cather, Sherwood Anderson, Ellen Glasgow, Sinclair Lewis, John Galsworthy, and Arnold Bennett. She knew how to dress up her magazine with illustration, and she was enterprising. Her acquisition of unpublished correspondence by Robert and Elizabeth Barrett Browning for $25,000 in 1935 was a publishing coup.

Miss Lane's astute editing kept the *Companion* in the hammer-and-tongs race with its rivals in the field, *Pictorial Review, Ladies' Home Journal, McCall's Magazine,* and *Good Housekeeping.* In circulation and advertising it held its own, and had even gained during the later thirties when, in 1939, the magazine's management reorganized as the Crowell-Collier Publishing Company. Miss Lane died in 1941, and after a brief interval under Willa Roberts, who had been a staff writer, the magazine came under the direction of William A. H. Birnie in 1943. His articles editor was Roger Dakin, and these two men turned the *Companion* into something of a crusading organ—"a fighting lady." The crusades were in areas of special interest to women, like sex, marriage, and children. The circulation was up to four million by 1950, and by 1953 advertising had never been higher. But then the competition caught up with it, and the decline was rapid. When it folded with the issue of January 1957, it was losing several million dollars a year.

One of the rivals that helped push the *Companion* to the wall was *McCall's Magazine,* begun, like *The Delineator,* by a tailor. James McCall had learned his trade in his native Scotland, and came to America to succeed in it. Like Ebenezer Butterick, McCall built up a business in dressmaking patterns, known as James McCall & Co. Seeking to promote this enterprise he started *The Queen: Illustrating McCall's Bazar Glove-Fitting Patterns* in 1873. McCall died in 1884, and his widow headed the company for a time, until the wife of George Bladworth, another member of the organization, became editor and her husband, in 1890, was made president of what was now called the McCall Publishing Co.

For seven years, under the Bladworths, the magazine was called the *Queen of Fashion*. But in spite of its name, it became more of a general magazine for women than a fashion periodical. It was renamed *McCall's Magazine* in 1897.

For a long time *McCall's* remained a rather cheap periodical for women, undergoing various changes in editors and format, until it was sold in 1913 to White, Weld & Co., a banking firm, when it became the McCall Corporation. The new president was Edward Alfred Simmons, president of Simmons-Boardman Company, publishers of *Railway Age,* and later of other magazines and books.

The magazine did not really hit its stride until 1921, when Harry Payne Burton became editor, and brought to its pages a generous sampling of the day's best writers of popular fiction and articles, most of whom appeared in *McCall's* rivals as well. The emphasis was on making it a national magazine, which was done not only by concentrating on material with a nationwide appeal but also by the use of such promotional devices as referring to its national audience as "McCall Street," thus providing its readers with a sense of common identification.

Under Otis Wiese, who became editor in January 1928, the magazine hit an editorial peak. At twenty-three the youngest editor of a national magazine in America, Wiese, a difficult man but a great editor, introduced several new ideas into magazine publishing. One was a concept he called "three-way makeup," meaning the division of the magazine into three parts, each with its own cover page and content, giving readers the illusion of getting three magazines for the price of one. The three sections were "Fiction and News," "Home Making," and "Style and Beauty."

Wiese also revived the nineteenth-century idea of a complete novel in an issue, which no one but *Redbook* had attempted in the new century. He also reached out to a new audience with the "youth conference" series. These and other policies increased the circulation to 3,000,000 by 1940. Perhaps the best—certainly the most quoted—circulation device invented by Wiese was the idea of "togetherness," by which McCall's hoped to tie up the whole family in a shiny package. It seemed to work. In 1956, the year the idea was launched,

McCall's circulation reached 4,750,000. The later era of *McCall's* involves contemporary magazine history, which will be discussed later.

Clearly, the modern magazine had its roots solidly in the last two or three decades of the nineteenth century, when new forces rose in publishing that created different ways of interpreting the American scene than had been known before.

seventeen

The Ten-Cent-Magazine Revolution

PERHAPS THE MOST REMARKABLE PHENOMENON of the years just before and after the turn of the century was the rise and momentary triumph of the ten-cent magazine. The idea of pricing magazines at ten cents or lower was certainly not new, but the tremendous success of the ten-cent categories for a time dwarfed everything else that was happening in the magazine business.

Although not strictly a member of this genre, *The Ladies' Home Journal* showed the way to the others. Its first half million was achieved at a five-cent price; at ten cents, it was up to 700,000 by 1893. The *Journal* and others had been helped by cheap paper and printing prices, and the invention of the halftone, a newer and cheaper method of photoengraving. It replaced engraving on wood.

The heyday of the ten-cent magazine began with the founding of *McClure's* in June 1893, forcing its already established rivals, *Munsey's* and *Cosmopolitan,* to lower their prices to ten cents. *Peterson's* and *Godey's* also went down to ten cents. There followed a flood of ten-cent periodicals, until Frank Munsey estimated in 1903 that they comprised about 85 percent of the total circulation of magazines in America. Besides his own, Munsey estimated correctly, the biggest moneymakers were *Argosy, Cosmopolitan,* and *McClure's.* Other magazines tried a five-cent price, and some even went down to one or two cents, but only the *Saturday Evening Post* did really well at a nickel.

The basis of the ten-cent magazine's popular appeal was its liveliness and variety, its many and well-printed illustrations, its coverage of world events and progress at home—and most of all, its head-on confrontation with contemporary social problems.

The rise of the ten-cent magazine made the older and more expensive periodicals feel threatened. "The Revolution in the art of engraving, not to say its destruction, is threatening a change in the conduct of magazines," said *The Independent.* "What will be the effect on the high-priced illustrated magazines, like *Harper's,* the *Century,* and *Scribner's,* it may not be easy to foresee; but it seems probable that they will not find it wise to reduce their price to a like figure. . . . The reason is that they will wish to maintain that higher, purer literary standard which succeeds in securing the best but not the most numerous readers. . . . The fit audience in an educated country like ours is not few, but it is not yet unlimited; nevertheless, it is the only audience worth addressing, for it contains the thinking people. The rest may or may not be sturdy citizens, may count in the militia and the population and the lower schools; but they are not the ones who delight to seek the instruction they need most."

As Sam McClure pointed out in rebuttal, it would be hard to find a magazine with higher literary standards than his. *McClure's* contributors included Stevenson, Kipling, Howells, Gladstone, Conan Doyle, Edward Everett Hale, and others of the same caliber.

What the ten-cent magazine was doing, however—and the other editors were aware of it—was creating a huge new mass market for general magazines, particularly the monthlies. In 1885 there had been only four of these monthlies able to boast a circulation of 100,000 or more; their price ranged from twenty-five to thirty-five cents. In just two decades their number had grown to twenty, with a total circulation of more than five and a half million. Nearly all were priced at ten or fifteen cents. They were in more or less direct competition with that spreading phenomenon in the newspaper business, the Sunday paper, which Pulitzer and Hearst had established solidly. The *Saturday Evening Post* saw little difference between the two media. "A good magazine is a good newspaper in a dress suit," it asserted.

The success the ten-cent monthlies were having, particularly with their writings on social reform, compelled other magazines to direct more attention to politics, corruption, and contemporary problems. Even the old established quartet of quality periodicals, *The Atlantic, Century, Scribner's,* and *Harper's,* had to follow the others, at least to some extent. *Harper's* was the most reluctant, and made few concessions.

To understand the ten-cent magazines and their astonishing influence, it is necessary to examine the four cited by Munsey as the big moneymakers. The first of these to arrive was the *Argosy,* another offspring of Frank Munsey's fertile brain. To the newspaper business, Munsey was the "Grand High Executioner of Journalism," a man who bought and merged old and honorable papers ruthlessly, without regard for tradition or the ideals of the profession, or even the needs of the community. Munsey was first and always a businessman, with the morals of the countinghouse, as his biography, *Forty Years—Forty Millions,* makes clear. Yet he was also a resourceful innovator when it came to magazines, and at the beginning of his improbable career he was even something of an idealist.

He was ambitious even as a lonely boy in charge of the telegraph office in Augusta, Maine, home of the mail-order periodical. He studied the Augusta magazines with care, and began to dream about starting a magazine in New York, one for boys and girls that would outshine all its competitors by means of its enchanting covers in color and a great many woodcuts inside.

Like all successful entrepreneurs, Munsey was a superb salesman. He persuaded a broker in Augusta to lend him $2,500 to start his magazine, and added to it another thousand from a young Augusta friend who now lived in New York. Munsey himself tossed in $500, all he had. The remainder of his stock-in-trade was enthusiasm, and a keen but as yet untried business acumen. He used his $500 to buy manuscripts, and arrived in New York in the autumn of 1882, ready to begin. But the broker and his friend who had promised money under the hypnosis of Frank's persuasion had changed their minds when he was no longer present to shore up their inclinations, and reneged on their promises. That left Munsey with forty dollars in his pockets, a pile of manuscripts, and little else.

In true Horatio Alger style, he went around New York knocking on publishers' doors and trying to sell his idea. One of them, E. G. Rideout, publisher of his own magazine, *Rideout's Monthly,* and two others for women, listened. Rideout set Munsey up in business, and on December 2, 1882, the *Golden Argosy, Freighted with Treasures for Boys and Girls* appeared for the first time. Its eight pages, appropriately enough, carried the opening installment of an Alger serial, *Do and Dare, or, A Brave Boy's Fight for Fortune.* One of Alger's rivals in the field, Edward E. Ellis, was also represented with a serial, titled *Nick and Nellie, or God Helps Them That Help Themselves.* The remainder of the scanty pages had puzzles, short stories, and some amateur contributions.

Suddenly, Rideout went bankrupt after about twenty issues of *Golden Argosy.* But Munsey bought control of his magazine by applying what Rideout owed him on his salary. There followed a period of desperate struggle, with Munsey doing most of the work on the magazine himself, borrowing money, and trying to make ends meet. Unable to pay contributors, he began to write serials for the magazine himself. With all the money he could scrape together, he put on an advertising campaign for his publication, at a cost of $10,000, and distributed 100,000 copies free to stir up interest. It was enough to put the magazine in the black, but the effort plunged him into debt at the same time.

With nothing to lose, since he already owed a total of $15,000, he put on another campaign, doubled the size of *Golden Argosy,* and in five months distributed 11,500,000 free copies. Nothing like this had ever been seen before in the history of magazines. Munsey might have appeared to be a reckless fool to sober businessmen, some of whom thought he was insane, but he was applying methods well ahead of his time. With an instinctive understanding of distribution problems, he kept a crew of fifteen or twenty men on the road to see that his magazines got to where they were assigned. In the office, he was doing all the work himself, even the bookkeeping.

Again the campaign paid off, sending the circulation to 115,000 and giving him a profit of $15,000 weekly, but it had cost him $95,000, and again he was forced to borrow every dollar he could, write checks without funds in the bank, and resort to every financial trick he could devise to stay afloat. In the midst of his troubles, it occurred to him that publishing a magazine for juveniles was not the surest path to earning the millions he meant to have. The money was in the adult market, and that was where he turned, first with cheap books and then with a new adult magazine, *Munsey's Weekly,* which appeared in 1889. It soon became simply *Munsey's Magazine.* As the circulation declined for his original property, he converted that, too, to an adult publication. In 1888 it became the *Argosy,* an adventure-story magazine.

Even in its new form, *Argosy* might have disappeared; its circulation dropped steadily to 9,000 in 1894. But *Munsey's* turned out to be a success, and the proprietor used its profits to keep his first effort afloat, meanwhile changing it wholly to an adult monthly at ten cents. That helped, but *Argosy* still limped along after *Munsey's* until Munsey conceived the idea in 1896 of making it an all-fiction magazine, perhaps the first of its kind. By 1907 the circulation had reached half a million and annual profits were $300,000.

The new *Argosy* had no pictures, and it was printed on the kind of rough paper called "pulp," giving a name to a whole category of cheap magazines that thrived right through the twenties and early thirties. Its stories had little love interest; they were adventure and mystery tales, aimed at men and boys. There were popular authors like Terhune, William McLeod Raine, and Louis Joseph Vance, but there were also, surprisingly, writers like James Branch Cabell, Sidney Porter (he had not yet begun to use "O. Henry"), Susan Glaspell, and Mary Roberts Rinehart. One of the serial writers was a young man named Upton Sinclair.

Argosy became a weekly in 1917, and in 1920 it was merged with another Munsey magazine, the *All-Story Weekly,* the resulting hybrid being named the *Argosy All-Story Weekly.* Exercising the talents that made him the executioner of newspapers, Munsey also merged the failing *Peterson's* with his property. And still the adventure writers came on—Edison Marshall, Max Brand, and Zane Grey, among others.

After Munsey died in 1925, stipulating in his will that everything he owned must be converted to cash, *Argosy,* along with the other magazines and the New York *Sun,* were bought by William T. Dewart, Munsey's general manager and his executor. Dewart separated *Argosy* from *All-Story* in 1929, and it had another brief moment of glory. Readers of that generation delighted in the stories of H. Bedford-Jones, T. S. Stribling, Erle Stanley Gardner, C. S. Forester, Van Wyck Mason, Achmed Abdullah, and W. C. Tuttle. At this point its circulation was about 400,000, but the Depression crippled it again, as it did the other Munsey magazines, and all were sold in 1941 to Popular Publications. There was another revival after World War II, and under the editorship of Jerry Mason, the new *Argosy—The Complete Men's Magazine*—made a splendid comeback and established itself in the growing field of men's magazines. It reached a million circulation in 1951, and by 1955 had added 1,271,000 more.

Second of the great ten-cent magazines to enter the field was *Cosmopolitan Magazine,* which began life in Rochester, New York, designed to be a home monthly by its publishers, Schlicht & Field, who were printers and office-supply manufacturers. Shortly after its start in March 1886, however, it became a general literary magazine, and was successful enough in a year's time to move to New York. When the firm failed in 1888, there was a succession of owners—first Ulysses S. Grant, Jr., the General's son, then a California lawyer; and after him, Joseph Newton Hallock, publisher of *Christians at Work,* who placed a good editor, E. D. Walker in charge. Walker improved the magazine greatly, but not enough to make it popular, and once more it had to be snatched from the cliff's edge, this time by John Brisben Walker, a remarkable man, then forty-one, who had made successive fortunes in iron manufacturing and real estate, and had been a successful newspaperman as well. As one critic put it, Walker "introduced the newspaper ideas of timeliness and dignified sensationalism into periodical literature."

The new editor assembled a notable staff, topped in 1892 by the acquisition of William Dean Howells as co-editor. Howells's taste was literary; Walker's was popular. It was a co-editorship that had no prospect of success, and in fact it lasted only four months, but Howells left his mark with a notable first issue that led off with a poem by

Lowell, followed by a Henry James article, and carried stories by Hamlin Garland, Sarah Orne Jewett, and Frank R. Stockton, along with nonfiction by men of such stature as Brander Matthews and Theodore Roosevelt.

Actually, Walker could not have worked with anyone, because he was cast in the mold of all the great magazine editors: he was the czar, the man who made all the decisions, and the magazine was to be whatever he made it. Because of his efforts, by 1892 *Cosmopolitan* was among the best illustrated magazines in the country, with more emphasis on public affairs than on fiction. Under Walker's editorship, *Cosmopolitan*'s circulation jumped from 20,000 in 1889 to 300,000 by 1898. It was among the ten-cent revolutionists in 1895.

Cosmopolitan, under Walker, became one of the important magazines dealing with domestic and foreign affairs. Its coverage of the Spanish-American War ranked with the best magazine efforts, and its reports from abroad, by Julian Hawthorne and others, were often extraordinary. Walker was sometimes well ahead of his times; as early as 1902 he proposed a world congress of nations, and in 1897 he was hard at work trying to revise what he termed the "frozen curricula" of universities. It was Walker, too, who foresaw the eventual decline of the great American railways, and urged the government to nationalize them. Beginning in 1892, Walker also began pushing the idea of "aerial navigation"; *Cosmopolitan* was far ahead of every other magazine in its acceptance and sponsorship of air transportation. Similarly, Walker did everything he could to advance the cause of the horseless carriage as soon as it appeared.

As an editor, Walker was as ruthless and arbitrary as any of his nineteenth-century predecessors. When Tolstoi's *Resurrection* began to run in *Cosmopolitan* in 1899, Walker thought some of the Russian master's sexual descriptions were offensive, and deleted them. As the serial went on, Walker decided it would be impossible to make *Resurrection* chaste enough for his pages, and simply discontinued it. He much preferred writers like H. G. Wells, in any case, and was the first to print *War of the Worlds* and *The First Man on the Moon*. He was also one of the first editors to recognize Jack London as a major writer.

Walker's multiple talents could not be confined even to so absorbing an interest as *Cosmopolitan*. As automobile manufacturing increased, he found himself more and more involved with it, to the detriment of the magazine; and, losing interest in it, he sold it to Hearst in 1905 for $400,000. It was Hearst's second magazine acquisition; he already owned *Motor*. By 1912 he had added *Motor Boating* to his International Magazine Company, and his periodical empire was well on its way.

To Hearst, a magazine was simply an extension of the Sunday newspaper, except that more time could be spent on it to make it readable and "dressy." Under his direction, *Cosmopolitan* became more sensational. The magazine did its share of muckraking, although it joined the muckrakers rather late in the day, in 1905, when the wave was passing. Late it might have been, but its contribution was notable—one of the most penetrating and effective of all the muckraking series, written by David Graham Phillips and called *The Treason of the Senate*. The research for the series was done by Gustavus Myers, who had not yet written the searing analysis of the great American fortunes and the men who made them, which elevated him to fame.

This series, exposing the unholy alliance between big business and several of the most distinguished United States senators, led President Roosevelt to apply the word "muckraking," by which all such attacks on public men and institutions came to be known. It was only six years later that the Seventeenth Amendment, providing for the direct election of senators, was passed in Congress. Phillips and *Cosmopolitan* could claim at least part of the credit for this much-needed reform.

Another notable muckraking series in *Cosmopolitan* was called "The Owners of America," much of it written by Alfred Henry Lewis, but also including articles by Arthur Brisbane and Emerson Hough. Later in other articles, Lewis exposed election frauds in American cities, while Edwin Markham attacked the evils of child labor, and Poultney Bigelow unearthed corruption in the Panama Canal Zone.

In 1912 *Cosmopolitan* abruptly switched course, dropped muckraking, and turned to a fiction formula, to which it held for the next thirty years or so. The inspiration for this move was the astounding success of a fiction serial by Robert W. Chambers, *The Common Law,* for which Hearst paid $18,000, with another thousand added for illustrations by Gibson, after *Everybody's* had turned down the story as indecent. It proved to be a fantastic circulation builder; the figures showed a 70 percent gain while it was running, and the editor was justified in claiming, "It was a leading factor in making *Cosmopolitan* the best-selling magazine in the world."

Along with its slightly daring serials, *Cosmopolitan* also ran such outstanding features as George Ade's *Fables in Slang* and Booth Tarkington's *Penrod.* These, however, were somewhat overshadowed by the magazine's emphasis on sex.

In 1918 the magazine came into the hands of Ray Long, one of the great editors in magazine history. He was also one of the highest paid, reputedly getting $180,000 a year in salary and bonuses at his peak. Long described himself as an editor: "I happen to be an average American who has the opportunity to read a tremendous number of manuscripts. From these I select the stories I like, publish them within the covers of a magazine, and through the facilities of our circulation department put that magazine where people may see it; and there are enough other average Americans who like to read the same thing that I like to read to buy the magazine in sufficient quantities to make me worth my salary."

That was a fair estimate, and it would have applied to the other top-ranking editors like George Horace Lorimer, as will be seen. Long brought to the pages of *Cosmopolitan,* and to its familiar cover, where they were listed, the biggest names of the day: Wells, Blasco-Ibáñez, Philip Gibbs, Somerset Maugham, Michael Arlen, Robert Hichens, Sabatini, Tarkington, Edna Ferber, Sinclair Lewis, Fannie Hurst, Dreiser, Louis Bromfield, Frank Norris, Roark Bradford, James Oliver Curwood, Peter B. Kyne, Irvin Cobb, Ring Lardner, and Montague Glass, among many others.

In 1925 Hearst merged his *Hearst's International,* a monthly he had started in 1901, with *Cosmopolitan,* adding about 300,000 to the latter's circulation. Through the twenties the combined periodical continued in *Cosmopolitan*'s established pattern, although with increased emphasis on sex, until Ray Long resigned in 1931. He tried book publishing, failed, dabbled in the movies, and in 1935 committed suicide for reasons never disclosed.

During the Depression, *Cosmopolitan* slipped a little from the 1,700,000 it had when Long left it, but by 1942 it was up to 2,000,-000, and continued to increase a little more during the next decade. As the popularity of magazine fiction declined and nonfiction began replacing it as the chief fare in magazines, *Cosmopolitan* changed, too, through a succession of editors. Its contemporary revival with a new formula will be discussed later.

Munsey's Magazine, the third of the quartet of ten-cent money-makers, as mentioned earlier, was its publisher's first venture into adult magazines. It had started as a monthly, and in spite of everything Munsey could devise for it, did not catch on until he brought it out as a ten-cent periodical in 1893, distributing it through his own Red Star News Company when the American News Company failed to give him satisfactory terms.

With the new price, *Munsey's* was almost an instant success. Its first issue at ten cents in October 1893 sold 20,000 copies; by 1897 it was selling 700,000 a month. One of the things that sold it was sex. There were legitimate nudes displayed in the department titled "Artists and Their Work," which led the magazine every month, and less cultural undraped female figures in departments titled "The Stage" and "Types of Fair Women." Other magazines might be annoyed by *Munsey's* half-dressed women and undressed statuary, but the proprietor did not temper the wind to these shorn lambs until his circulation was secure at over half a million.

Otherwise, the magazine purveyed fiction, both serials and short stories. Hall Caine's famous novel, *The Christian,* gave it a good start in that division in 1896, and it was followed by serials by H. Rider Haggard, F. Marion Crawford, and Anthony Hope. Other writers of both fiction and nonfiction were attracted to *Munsey's* by the good rates paid to contributors.

In general, however, the pictures contributed most to *Munsey's* success. Also a principal attraction were the magazine's dozen departments, covering the stage, literature, music, and Munsey's own reflections in "The Publisher's Desk."

The magazine did not muckrake when most of the other popular ten-centers were doing it. Munsey was quite firm: *"Munsey's Magazine has never been committed to the muck-raking theory, and never will be. Muck-raking is one thing, and progress is quite another."*

After 1906 the magazine's circulation began to decline slowly but consistently, descending to 400,000 in 1912, when the price was raised to fifteen cents. Munsey had less time than ever to devote to it; he was up to his editorial ears in his other magazines and newspapers, not to mention his immersion in politics. Still the magazine staggered on, falling back to ten cents in 1916, advancing once more to twenty cents in 1918, meanwhile gathering in enough advertising to make some issues of 260 pages. By 1920, however, it was back to about 130,000, and its advertising pages down to twenty.

In another frantic effort at revival, the policy of running a complete novel in every issue was instituted once more, and there were contributions by P. G. Wodehouse, George Barr McCutcheon, Joseph Conrad, Arnold Bennett, and Rupert Hughes, among others—names big enough to keep the magazine alive for a while longer. Then there was an injection of leading pulp-magazine writers—T. S. Stribling, Charles Francis Coe, Max Brand, Homer Croy, Edgar Rice Burroughs—but the magazine was nevertheless on the edge of ruin when Munsey died in 1925; its circulation had been only 64,000 the year before. The merger with *Argosy* in 1929 was the inevitable result. *Munsey's* was never as good a magazine as *McClure's* or *Cosmopolitan*; its level was nearer the mediocre, and often it was distinguished more for quality than quantity. Nevertheless, it made its own unique contribution to the ten-cent revolution.

McClure's, the last of the four to be started, proved to be in many ways the most sensational of the ten-cent magazines. No doubt that was inevitable, considering the personality of its founder, Samuel Sidney McClure—S. S. McClure, as he was known—who was one of the great showmen of his time. Like so many other nineteenth-century publishing figures, McClure came from a background of poverty, and clawed his way to the top. Irish-born, he came to this country, got an education at Knox College, and afterward went into the business of syndicating fiction and other feature material to newspapers. His partner was John Sanburn Phillips, a Midwesterner who had gone to school at Harvard and Leipzig.

When they decided to start a magazine in 1893, Phillips had $4,500, McClure only $2,800. But Sam McClure had something else more valuable, a natural flair for magazine-making and the kind of personality that virtually ensures success. The original plan was extremely modest—to make a cheap magazine filled with material from the syndicate operation and paid for out of its profits. The first issue, consequently, was priced at fifteen cents, and while it was bulky enough with nearly a hundred pages, illustrated with as many pictures, it was hardly distinguished. Not surprisingly the newsstands returned 14,000 of the 20,000 copies distributed.

At the same time, unfortunately, the financial collapse of 1893 began to depress the economic structure so severely that the syndicate could not collect its own bills, much less pay *McClure's*. Surprisingly, contributors and friends came to the rescue. Henry Drummond, the scientist-theologian who had contributed to the new magazine, lent $3,000 out of his lecture receipts, and Conan Doyle followed suit with $5,000 from the same source. Colonel A. A. Pope, the bicycle maker for whom Sam had once worked, gave a thousand dollars which he said he would take out in advertising. In this way, *McClure's* contrived to get through its first year.

It took a writer and a subject, as so often happens, to bring the magazine to public attention. The writer in this case was Ida M. Tarbell, soon to be the queen of the muckrakers, and her subject was "Napoleon," illustrated with pictures from the Hubbard collection. This serial alone more than doubled *McClure's* circulation, which had been a limping 40,000.

Hiring Miss Tarbell as a staff writer, McClure put her to work immediately on a new project out of his active brain. Lincoln had been dead thirty years, but Sam's editorial instincts told him that people would never get tired of reading about him—and how right he was, as the tide of Lincoln books still continues to flow. There were, moreover, many people living who could talk about him from personal knowledge. "Look, see, report," McClure instructed his new writer. The result was Miss Tarbell's *Early Life of Lincoln,* begun in 1895 in the magazine; it meant the addition of 75,000 new readers. The series was full of unpublished material, and it was illustrated with many Lincoln portraits never in print before.

McClure backed up this kind of enterprise with fiction by Stevenson, Anthony Hope, and Kipling's *Captains Courageous* and *Stalky and Co.* His short-story contributors included Thomas Hardy, Conan Doyle, Stephen Crane, and Joel Chandler Harris. Kipling's *Jungle Tales* also ran in *McClure's* as a series of short stories. Some of these authors were still obscure, but none more so than O. Henry, whose first printed story was submitted from a jail cell in the Federal penitentiary at Columbus.

McClure provided his readers with a good deal about scientific discoveries of the day, railroads, wild animals, explorations, and public personalities.

Steffens, in his *Autobiography,* provides a picture of McClure at work in those days. "The wild editor," as Steffens labeled him, was "blond, smiling, enthusiastic, unreliable, he was the receiver of the ideas of his day. . . . He was rarely in the office. 'I can't sit still' he shouted. 'That's your job, and I don't see how you do it!'" Returning from a trip abroad or from some far part of America, McClure would "come straight from the ship to the office, call us together, and tell us what he had seen and heard, said and done. With his valise full of clippings, papers, books, and letters to prove it, he showed us that he had the greatest features any editor had ever had—the most marvelous, really world-stunning ideas and stories." When it came to judging manuscripts, the editor told Steffens, "I go mostly by myself, for if I like a thing, then I know that millions will like it. My mind and my taste are so common that I'm the best editor."

That, indeed, was the hallmark of the "best editor," but McClure was fortunate to have his friend John Phillips in the business office. Phillips not only kept the circulation and advertising departments running smoothly, but he performed the functions of a modern managing editor in keeping the editorial department on an even, efficient keel. He was a first-rate editor, as well as businessman. His actual title was general manager and supervising editor, although titles were never very clear at *McClure's*. No matter what they were hired to do, most of those who came turned out to be contributors. Among them were Ray Stannard Baker, John H. Finley, and Steffens briefly.

McClure's glowed with vitality. Its coverage of the Spanish-American War was mostly the work of eyewitnesses, and at the end of the conflict the magazine published Admiral Mahan's *The War on the Sea and Its Lessons,* which future generations were to mull over. By 1900 *McClure's* was larger, at 370,000, than any of its competitors except *Munsey's.*

What finally made *McClure's* preeminent, however, was its plunge into muckraking in 1902. In its January 1903 issue, the magazine declared: "We did not plan it so; it is a coincidence that this number contains three arraignments of American character such as should make every one of us stop and think. 'The Shame of Minneapolis'— the current chapter of the history of Standard Oil by Miss Tarbell, Mr. Ray Stannard Baker's 'The Right to Work'—they might all have been called 'The American Contempt of Law.' Capitalists, workingmen, politicians, citizens—all breaking the law or letting it be broken. Who is there left to uphold it? . . . There is no one left—none but all of us."

All the stories mentioned in this editorial note were landmarks in the turbulent history of muckraking. The Minneapolis article was one in a celebrated series by Steffens called *The Shame of the Cities.* Baker's assault on the leaders of labor unions was his opening gun; he went on to attack the misconduct of the railroads. These series attracted so much public attention that by the time the Panic of 1907 arrived, *McClure's* was approaching half a million.

Then, at the peak of his success, McClure conceived a plan vast enough to rival the trusts he was attacking—adding to an expanded magazine a great book-publishing company, his own life insurance company designed to finance the other parts of the scheme, and his own bank to provide the immediate financing. Out of the enormous profits he visualized, he would set up large foundations to dispense charity, establish settlements for the poor, and put up magnificent housing projects. This grandiose plan gripped McClure as though he had been a convert to a new faith, and no one could talk him out of it.

As a result McClure and Phillips ended their long association. McClure bought out his partner. With Phillips, however, went the better part of the staff, including Steffens, Baker, and Miss Tarbell. (As mentioned, this group, along with Finley Peter Dunne and William Allen White, bought the *American Magazine*.)

After building a huge new plant in Long Island City, as a first step in his master plan, McClure was convinced by declining circulation and advertising figures that he would not be able to implement his ideas, at least for the moment. He turned his attention again to the magazine, hired a new set of muckrakers, and went back to the old stand. A new staff was recruited, but not many stayed long. Will Irwin lasted a year; Willa Cather survived longer, and contributed her first nationally published stories. Witter Bynner was in residence for a time as poetry and features editor.

Despite these changes, and the continued publication of outstanding work, the magazine declined steadily. McClure himself was not well, and his financial affairs were a jungle. His son-in-law, Cameron Mackenzie, was really running the magazine in 1911 when McClure decided to sell it to Mackenzie and a partner, Frederick Lewis Collins, both twenty-nine, and ambitious. Collins had been editor of *The Woman's Home Companion*.

The new organization was known as McClure Publications. Slowly, and with some pain, the magazine abandoned its old pattern, deserted muckraking for the most part, and followed the trend toward more fiction; the usual assemblage of big names decorated the cover every month. During World War I it hit its highest circulation, an annual average of 563,000. That, however, was not a substantial figure in a period when many magazines were soaring over a million, and *McClure's* was therefore at a distinct disadvantage in competing for advertising. It lost 20,000 circulation soon after reaching its peak, and Collins sold it in 1919 to Herbert Kaufman, an advertising man.

But it was too late; the magazine went into bankruptcy in 1921, and *The Nation* wrote its obituary: "The soul of *McClure's* had long since fled. It was a good magazine when it had one." The soul of *McClure's* was, of course, McClure. The magazine was revived briefly in 1922, with McClure himself recalled as editor, under the ownership of a publisher named Moody B. Gates, but in 1924 Gates turned the magazine back to McClure, having lost all the money he cared to.

It was hard to kill *McClure's*; few magazines have died so lingering a death. McClure had to suspend again after four months; then he succeeded in getting new financing, and began once more in May 1925. For a while it looked as though the old days might return, as McClure attacked the editorship with something of his old vigor and wild enthusiasm. But the publisher, like the magazine, was past his prime, and he gave up at last with the January 1926 issue. McClure himself outlived all his enterprises, dying at ninety-two.

When he gave up the magazine, a decent burial might have been expected, but Hearst made a third attempt to revive it, adding "The Magazine of Romance" to its illustrious name. Under the new management, said *The Independent,* it was "distinguished by an almost incredibly even vulgarity and ineptitude." A new editor improved matters for a time, adding names like Carl Sandburg and Konrad Bercovici, but then Hearst, despairing of a profit, sold it again to the Magus Magazine Corporation, headed by James R. Quirk, publisher of *Smart Set* and *Photoplay.*

Now it was billed as "A Man's Magazine!", and *The Saturday Review of Literature* called it "the greatest mess of shrieking type and bad illustration" on the stands. Its virtues were writers like Herbert Asbury, Donald Ogden Stewart, and Irvin S. Cobb. In this incarnation, it lasted only until March 1929, when it was decently interred by merger with *Smart Set,* which itself had only two years more to live.

The muckraking pioneered by *McClure's* was widely imitated in other magazines, and the net effect was to give periodicals a social dimension they had not been able to boast before. They were not simply mirrors of national life now, but critics. Naturally, there were abuses, and not all muckraking was backed by the careful research Miss Tarbell and Steffens brought to their work. In the end, of course, the movement wore itself out by shouting. Nevertheless, magazines would never be quite the same innocuous medium they had been before the turn of the century.

eighteen

Curtis, Bok, and Lorimer

CYRUS HERMANN KOTZSCHMAR CURTIS, like Frank Munsey, was a
Maine boy, but there the resemblance ended. Munsey's contributions
to magazine history and to American culture were transitory, and designed solely with the idea of creating Munsey's forty-million-dollar
fortune. Curtis, too, was a businessman, and a shrewd one, but he had
a vision that extended well beyond the countinghouse, and the publishing empire he created made a lasting impression on the nation's cultural life, an impression that only now is beginning to fade.

Unlike most of his publishing contemporaries, Curtis made no pretense of being an editor. His particular genius lay in knowing how to
establish magazine properties, and in finding the editors to edit them.
He had the consummate good sense to leave these editors alone, and
they rewarded him by giving him, in the *Ladies' Home Journal* and
the *Saturday Evening Post,* two of the most successful magazines ever
produced in America, and, in the *Post,* one of the most beloved.

His life story was solidly in the nineteenth-century rags-to-riches
tradition. Born in Portland, Maine, in 1850, his first job was carrying
newspapers on a route, but at thirteen he was publishing his own
newspaper, *Young America,* on a $2.50 press. Sixty years later, he
owned printing plants worth more than $8 million. When the great
Portland fire of 1866 destroyed his family's home, Curtis had to leave
high school after only a year and go to work, first as errand boy in a
dry-goods store, then as salesman in a Boston department store. From
there it was a short step into newspaper advertising on Boston papers.

He started his own paper, *The People's Ledger,* in 1872 and carried it on for six years, moving to Philadelphia in order to get cheaper printing. He sold the paper there, became advertising manager of a weekly, then in 1879 founded a new paper, the *Tribune and Farmer,* whose subscription price was fifty cents a year. His wife, Louisa Knapp, was editor of the woman's supplement he added to the *Tribune,* and this supplement was so successful it became clear to Curtis that he would do well to sell the parent publication and keep the supplement. This supplement came under his direction and sole ownership in December 1883 as the *Ladies' Home Journal.*

Starting at 20,000, Curtis built up the *Journal's* circulation by various devices. The first was to offer four subscriptions for a dollar in a "club," thus making one subscriber a salesman in obtaining the other three. Curtis was a master at this kind of list building; in his first attempt the *Journal's* circulation doubled in six months. To this he added a newspaper advertising campaign, costing him only $400, that doubled his circulation again in the succeeding six months.

Demonstrating the kind of sensitivity that made him so successful, Curtis now began to improve his magazine, knowing that something more than circulation devices and advertising would be required. A magazine needed a big name to sell it, and Curtis went up to Massachusetts to get one—a writer named Marion Harland, who was then one of the best-known writers for women in America. For $90 he got a short story from her, and spent some more money to advertise her presence in the *Journal.* As he had hoped, she attracted many new readers, and the circulation reached 270,000 by early 1886.

It was not easy to get writers, however. The best ones did not want to write for a woman's magazine that was regarded as scarcely above the level of a household-hints organ. Curtis persuaded Louisa May Alcott into adding her name to his "List of Famous Contributors" by promising to contribute $100 to her favorite charity if she would do one piece for the *Journal.* There were not many other noteworthy names, however, except perhaps for Marietta Holley, whose "Samantha Allen" byline had made her well known, and Mary Jane Holmes, the popular novelist.   → NT. PG

Nevertheless, circulation climbed steadily, even at a fifty-cent

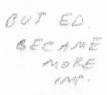
BUT ED.
BECAME
MORE
IMP.

annual price. Curtis declared in 1887 that he meant to have a million subscribers soon, and to achieve this he devised new circulation schemes, along with his cleverly written advertising. In 1889, taking a large gamble, the publisher jumped his subscription price to $1 a year, increasing the size of the magazine to thirty-two pages and adding a cover. Fortunately, he was able to get $200,000 in advertising credit from F. Wayland Ayer, one of the founders of N. W. Ayer & Son, the noted advertising agency, who also endorsed Curtis's notes in the amount of $100,000 so that he could get the paper he needed.

With such backing, Curtis was able to launch the broad, bold advertising campaign he envisaged, but it still required careful financing for a few years until, in 1891, he established a stock company, capitalized at $500,000, and the Curtis Publishing Company was truly launched.

With circulation somewhat over 400,000 in 1889, Curtis made the move that elevated the *Journal* to preeminence. His wife had been editing the magazine since its days as a supplement, but now she wanted to leave to spend more time with her children, and Curtis had to find a new editor. No one knows what kind of second sight led him to Edward William Bok. Certainly Bok was a most unlikely candidate. A Dutch immigrant at the age of seven, he had been in book publishing and had edited the *Brooklyn Magazine* briefly before going into the newspaper syndicate business.

Aside from that, what made his selection as editor of a woman's magazine so remarkable was that Bok had no particular fondness for women except his mother, whom he adored. A bachelor, he seemed to have little feeling for the other sex except a kind of idealization. His ideas about them were odd, to say the least. Moreover, he had a truly staggering egocentricity, and in the manner of similarly self-absorbed men, he often referred to himself in the third person. His autobiography, *The Americanization of Edward Bok,* for many years on every high school reading list, was written in that mode.

Yet, somehow, Curtis divined that Bok would know how to talk to women in a magazine. Perhaps, as Mott suggests, he made the magazine in the image of what women wanted to be instead of what they were. Or it may be that he simply had a sixth sense about his audience, as so many of the best editors seem to have, and knew, by that same "instinct" with which he credited the ladies, what they wanted to read.

In any case, the other magazines viewed his assumption of the editor's chair as a hilarious event, and he was the victim of a good deal of lampooning in the newspapers and other magazines. Some of it was cruel, and occasionally verged on the libelous. Eugene Field, nominally Bok's friend, solemnly announced the editor's engagement in his Chicago *Daily News* column, first to "Miss Lavinia Pinkham, the favorite granddaughter of Mrs. Lydia Pinkham, the famous philanthropist," and then, in an even more unlikely event, to Mrs. Frank Leslie.

Meanwhile, Bok quietly went about his own courtship of Curtis's daughter, whom he married. Even then he suffered abuse and ridicule as long as he was editor, but more of it was inspired by Bok's success than by his peculiar nature. Somehow he managed to make his readers feel that the magazine was their intimate friend. They told it their problems and were answered in the department "Side Talks with Girls," written for many years by Isabel A. Mallon under the pseudonym "Ruth Ashmore," and in "Heart to Heart Talks," edited by Mrs. Margaret Bottome. There was even a "Side Talk with Boys" department. In articles, readers were given views of the private lives of great men, all the way from P. T. Barnum's "How I Have Grown Old" to Benjamin Harrison's description of family life in the White House. Bok refused to take patent-medicine advertising, and with the help of Mark Sullivan, who joined his staff, carried on a crusade against the manufacturers. This exposé was a factor in the passing of the Federal Food and Drug Act in 1906.

As time went on, Bok began to fill the pages of the *Journal* with the best writers of the day, foreign and domestic. By this time he was vice-president of the company, the magazine was highly profitable, and he was visiting England and France in search of new work. Kipling became a friend and contributor, but Bok did not hesitate to edit what he thought might offend his ladies—for instance, he eliminated a drinking scene from Kipling's first contribution to the *Journal*. Bok edited Twain, too, and in his sublimely arrogant way, declared that the author had admitted he was right, which hardly seems consistent with Twain's character.

One of the unique features of the *Journal* was its publication of music—everything from Sousa marches to Paderewski, Strauss, Mascagni, and Josef Hofmann, who edited a music department in the magazine for a time.

Bok's editorial genius was expanding the magazine in new directions constantly, pushing back the frontiers of women's periodicals. He began publishing house plans in 1895, and held contests for best homes. "I firmly believe," said Stanford White, probably the best-known architect of his day, "that Edward Bok has more completely influenced American domestic architecture for the better than any other man in this generation." Bok also wanted to improve interior decoration, Pullman cars, the appearance of cities, and he was one of the first, if not the first, to protest and fight against outdoor advertising.

Under Bok's administration, the *Journal* had surpassed every other magazine in circulation by the turn of the century. It was 800,000 in 1900, 900,000 two years later, and finally passed Curtis's long-sought million mark in 1903. To the publisher's talent for thinking up new circulation devices, Bok added one of his own—the awarding of scholarships in colleges and conservatories to the most successful subscription solicitors.

There were classics in the *Journal*'s pages: Kipling's *Just So Stories* and *Puck of Pook's Hill,* Jean Webster's *Daddy Long Legs,* and the work of Kate Douglas Wiggin. Bok even persuaded Roosevelt to dictate a column to a newspaperman, in two sessions every month while he was shaving, for a department titled "The President." Later, Roosevelt wrote another column, but anonymously, a department called "Men." His authorship was a closely guarded secret.

Bok kept the *Journal* in the forefront of its field by bold and imaginative editing, often ahead of his time and sometimes ahead of his audience. It took real editorial courage, as well as foresight, to come out in behalf of sex education. He lost thousands of subscribers by permitting the *Journal* to talk about syphilis, the first time the word had appeared in an American popular magazine.

Bok brought to the editing of women's magazines the concept of service, which later came to dominate all of them. As Bok described the process in his autobiography: "Step by step, the editor built up this service behind the magazine until he had a staff of thirty-five editors on the monthly payroll; in each issue he proclaimed the willingness of these editors to answer immediately any questions by mail; he encouraged and cajoled his readers to form the habit of looking upon his magazine as a great clearing-house of information. Before long, the letters streamed in by the tens of thousands during a year. The editor still encouraged, and the total ran into the hundreds of thousands, until during the last year, before the service was finally stopped by the Great War of 1917–18, the yearly correspondence totalled nearly a million letters."

In line with this policy of service, Bok instituted the Curtis Advertising Code, which protected readers from fraudulent or extravagant claims in advertising, and specifically banned financial, tobacco, playing cards or liquor advertising. The prohibition on liquor was absolute; not even wineglasses or steins could be shown.

Circulation of the magazine was beginning to approach two million by 1912, and reached that point in the fall of 1919. It sometimes carried more than a million dollars' worth of advertising in a single issue, and often ran to more than two hundred pages. As editor of the most valuable magazine property in the world, whose prosperity he had personally created, Bok earned his salary of $100,000 a year.

At the end of World War I, during which the *Journal* astonished the business by ranking third among the magazines most demanded by soldiers, Bok resigned his editorship. He had created a great magazine and he was rich. Now he wanted to write and pursue his philanthropic interests. His characteristic farewell did not run in the *Journal* but in its companion publication, the *Post*. There, in 1919, he reviewed his life in the United States since he landed as a penniless immigrant, and titled it, with total egocentricity, "Where America Fell Short with Me." Nonetheless, he had made magazine history, not only as an editor who had created an entirely new kind of magazine but as an advertising genius who joined his extraordinary talents with Curtis's to promote it.

Meanwhile, Curtis had been equally fortunate in finding an editor for his other publication, the *Saturday Evening Post*. The *Post* had passed through a good many ownerships and vicissitudes since its founding. In 1897, however, it was near expiration, and its owner, Andrew E. Smythe, virtually begged Curtis to buy it from him, although the subscription list contained no more than 2,000 names. Curtis offered a thousand dollars for the property, and Smythe took it.

Once in possession, Curtis did not quite know what to do with his property. Temporarily he put an editor from the *Journal's* staff, William George Jordan, in charge of the magazine until he could find a permanent editor. The news of his purchase had gone out on the news-service wires, however, and the announcement was read in the city room of the Boston *Herald* by a restless young reporter named George Horace Lorimer, who had recently come over to the paper from the rival *Post,* where he had been refused a two-dollar raise. The wire-service story had said that Curtis was hoping to find an outstanding editor who could make his new property successful, and within an hour Lorimer had wired him, asking for the job. Curtis wired back that he would be in Boston the following week, and would be delighted to talk with him. As Lorimer recalled it later: "I expected to go to Philadelphia. Mr. Curtis, however, replied that I should meet him at the Hotel Touraine in Boston. There, on a divan in the lobby, we talked one morning for about ten minutes." Before they shook hands and parted, Lorimer had been hired as the first—and last—literary editor of the *Saturday Evening Post.*

Lorimer was not at all what Curtis had been looking for. He was anything but literary; he was obscure, and he had no magazine experience. Curtis wanted the exact opposite, and for the moment did not think of him as editor in chief. Nevertheless, something about Lorimer must have reached Curtis's sixth sense; his hiring could hardly be explained otherwise.

Lorimer's father, George Claude, was one of the nation's most powerful evangelical ministers, who had preached in Boston's Tremont Temple before he was called to Chicago, where Lorimer grew up. Young George went to Yale, to please his father, but he dropped out after his freshman year to go to work for one of the Reverend Mr. Lorimer's richest parishioners, P. D. Armour, the eminent packer. Working a fourteen-hour day for $10 a week, Lorimer discovered that he loved business, and it remained a lifelong passion with him. He rose steadily in the ranks, married the daughter of a Chicago judge five years after he joined Armour, and three years later was about to be made head of the canning department when he suddenly made an uncharacteristic quixotic gesture. He quit to go into the wholesale grocery business, which proved to be a disaster.

Looking about for a new occupation, Lorimer deliberately chose writing. "I went into newspaper work," he explained years later, "with the same spirit that a medical student enters a hospital as an interne —for practical experience and training. I hoped to be both an editor and a writer. . . ." He had become an omnivorous reader, and already had some ideas about magazines. Newspaper work, he believed, would be the best preparation for a career on periodicals, so that was why he returned to Boston (he had been born in Louisville on October 6, 1867, but he always thought of Boston as his home town, having arrived there when he was less than a year old) and went to work first for the *Standard,* and then, after a year's study as a special student at Colby College, Maine, for the Boston *Post.*

When he arrived in Philadelphia to begin his new job, he found Curtis and his temporary editor, Jordan, already at odds. Curtis wanted to make the *Post* a five-cent quality periodical that would get away from the newspaper competition he believed was inspired by the close attention magazines like *Leslie's* and *Collier's* paid to the news. But Jordan did not quite understand his employer's objectives. As a man trained in the *Journal's* (meaning Bok's) methods, he could only make the *Post* a rather drab imitation of its sister publication, but without the emphasis on feminine affairs.

Curtis fired Jordan early in 1899 and went abroad to look for a successor—a man of eminence, if possible—to take the job. While he was gone, he put Lorimer in charge as managing editor. Lorimer knew he had only a short time to prove himself, and as he said later, "I had little money to spend and the paper had no reputation."

Lorimer made two immediate policy changes that revolutionized the whole magazine business. He promised to pay for manuscripts on acceptance, and to give yes-or-no answers on submitted articles and

stories within seventy-two hours. Nothing could have been better designed to attract writers; the common practice was to hold submissions
for weeks, months, or longer, at the editor's convenience, and to pay
on publication, which might be a month away, but more likely a year.
He began, too, the practice of making regular trips to New York in
search of writers, another policy that soon bore fruit.

When Curtis returned from Europe, having searched in vain for an
editor, he saw what Lorimer was doing and was pleased. Lorimer explained it simply: "When Mr. Curtis returned to Philadelphia he liked
the way things were going so well that he made me editor in chief of
the periodical." That was on St. Patrick's Day, 1899. Lorimer was
now editor of what was still, as Irvin Cobb put it, "an elderly and in-
disposed magazine." When he left the editor's chair, nearly thirty-nine
years later, on the last day of 1936, the *Post* had been for three decades one of the most successful and significant magazines in the history of periodicals.

Lorimer left an indelible mark on his times. He was the articulate
voice of millions, the purveyor of entertainment, advice, and political
sentiment to a considerable body of Americans—yet he was almost
unknown to the *Post*'s readers. Of the more than three million people
who bought the magazine at the peak of its circulation under his editorship, only a few knew the editor as more than a name on the masthead. He remained an anonymous figure until the final issue of the
Post under his editorship, when for the first time he signed an editorial. Nevertheless he was a man whom nine Presidents of the United
States recognized as the potent spokesman for a sizable bloc of voters,
and whom thousands of writers, both famous and unknown, looked
upon as a god. Lorimer was the *Post*, and the *Post* was Lorimer.

His rise to the top was rapid, but the beginning was not easy,
and only Curtis's unqualified support made it possible. His early policies improved the *Post*, but it still lost a staggering amount every
week. Lorimer knew that he had to do two things to save it: get more
advertising, and give the magazine an identity. His business experience
helped him to accomplish the first objective, and in a sense led to
achievement of the second. For Lorimer ardently believed, as Calvin

Coolidge remarked later, that the business of America was business, and if that were true, a magazine that dealt with business, both in fiction and nonfiction, must necessarily appeal to large masses of Americans.

Lorimer struggled to devise some way to accomplish this. He was poor, often hungry, worked day and night, and his job was at stake every day. Already, at the office, there had developed between Lorimer and Bok what was to be a long, silent feud. The two men could hardly have been more different; they had nothing in common except their genius for editing magazines. Bok wanted the *Post,* which he called "the *Journal's* little brother," discontinued, and it seemed as though he might win when the company treasurer reported to Curtis that the magazine was $750,000 in the red.

"Well," Curtis replied mildly, "Mr. Lorimer's got two hundred and fifty thousand to go before he touches a million. I like round numbers." At somewhere near the million mark, Lorimer's policies began to work. The *Post* made back its losses at an astounding rate as circulation and advertising shot up together. It was never in trouble again, while Lorimer lived.

Lorimer knew exactly what he wanted to make of the *Post*. It was to be a magazine without class, clique, or sectional interest, intended for every adult in America's population of 75,000,000. He meant to edit it for the whole United States—a truly mass magazine. As a later editor, Wesley Stout, said: "He set out to interpret America to itself, always readably, but constructively."

The accent at first was on business. When Lorimer was unable to find any writers who were willing to write on that subject, he concluded that he would have to do the job himself. In vain he had argued that every business day was full of comedy, tragedy, farce, romance—all the ingredients of successful fiction. In the summer of 1901, Lorimer began to write, nights and weekends, his *Letters from a Self-Made Merchant to His Son,* which began to run serially in the *Post*. The merchant was modeled after P. D. Armour, and his salty comments had a powerful effect on circulation. Reader response to the first installments was tremendous; Lorimer had received 5,000 letters before the end of 1901. Published as a book in 1902, the *Letters* became a simultaneous best seller in the United States, England, and

Germany; it was later translated into a dozen languages, and survived for more than forty years, more generally circulated in all parts of the world than any book of American authorship since *Uncle Tom's Cabin*. It was followed by another best seller, *Old Gorgon Graham*.

Naturally, everyone wanted to write about business after this spectacular success. Lorimer was now overwhelmed with manuscripts on the subject, among them Frank Norris's novel *The Pit,* which the *Post* ran serially. There was even a cycle of Broadway plays on business themes. To cover business in articles, Lorimer hired two outstanding reporters, Sam Blythe and Isaac Marcosson, whose names were soon household words. Beginning with the first interview ever given by John Archbold, president of Standard Oil, Marcosson went on to become the greatest interviewer of his time, writing about celebrities of every variety all over the world. Blythe became equally celebrated as a political correspondent, and for years made the *Post*'s coverage of domestic politics the best any magazine could boast.

So swiftly and thoroughly had Lorimer created his product that by 1909 the *Post* had taken on, although still in rough form, the distinctive character it would retain for the next quarter century. It was already the nation's leading magazine, and was rapidly becoming an American institution as well. Curtis was content to let Lorimer take the credit. He was fond of repeating what he once told Frank Stockbridge: "I take down some of the profits, but the *Post* really belongs to Lorimer. I would no more think of telling him how to run it, what to print and what not to print, than I would think of telling Commodore Bennett how to run the New York *Herald*."

That, in sum, was the secret of the *Post*'s subsequent amazing success. Lorimer had total control of the magazine, and he possessed the genius to take full advantage of it. He personally read and okayed every line of editorial matter and advertising that went into the magazine. Many, if not most, of the editorial ideas came from him, and writers were loyal to him, personally. When the *Post* became the largest carrier of advertising in the business, Lorimer's monumental integrity led him to throw out of his office one day an advertiser who suggested that his space be tied in with an article. Lorimer insisted that there be absolutely no influence on editorial content by advertisers, and in time that became a novelty in itself in the magazine business. Yet Lorimer remained the thorough businessman, and directed the business operations of the magazine himself.

Lorimer, in effect, interpreted middle-class America to itself, as Stout said. No ivory-tower editor, he drove out to the Grand Canyon (his private and public passion) every summer, dawdling along the way to talk to the people in the small towns and cities—his readers. Since his own interests and attitudes were primarily theirs, he had no difficulty editing a magazine for them: he simply put in it what he himself liked. He could sense the national mood with the accuracy of the keenest political leaders. In the twenties, for example, when sports were a national passion, the *Post* carried the life stories of Babe Ruth, Jack Dempsey, Bobby Jones, and other contemporary heroes.

In politics, Lorimer was a firm Republican, and after the Wilson administrations, when the *Post* was really in its stride, the mood of the country was Republican, and the *Post* rode that wave, too. It even found something good to say about Harding, whom Lorimer believed was too much maligned. The President's wife, in fact, was reading Sam Blythe's piece, "A Calm View of a Calm Man" to him when he said to her, "Go on," turned over on his side, and died not long after.

Lorimer was probably the first to recognize Herbert Hoover as a man who could be President, and he and William Allen White did as much as any others behind the scenes to get him elected. By the mid-twenties, Lorimer's *Post* editorials were probably more influential than any carried by the newspapers, and they played an important part in pushing public opinion in the direction of Hoover. Once he was in the White House, Mr. Hoover lost the approval of both Lorimer and White, leaving intact Lorimer's record of dissatisfaction with every President he knew.

It is easy to see why Lorimer came to cherish the dangerous illusion that he knew the American people better than anyone. This big, bluff man, who looked the epitome of the business entrepreneur, was speaking for millions of people, as the success of his magazine and his voluminous mail constantly told him. The famous *Post* covers, by Norman Rockwell and others, mirrored the idealized, apple-pie middle-class population of America. The fiction and articles in the *Post* were, year after year, a record of their tastes, interests, and aspirations.

It was all the more shocking, then, to Lorimer when in 1932 Franklin D. Roosevelt, a man who represented everything he despised, except his wealth, became President. Lorimer felt personally betrayed by this event. The people whom he had loved and trusted and served with all his might had turned on him and made an even worse mistake than electing Wilson. Lorimer could not understand it. He was profoundly shaken, and both he and the *Post* began to decline. The magazine fought Mr. Roosevelt hard for four years, both in editorials and articles, and when he was reelected in 1936, it was the end for Lorimer. He resigned at the close of the year, making it public in the only signed editorial he ever wrote for the *Post,* in the issue of December 26, 1936.

When Wesley Stout, the new editor, asked readers in his first editorial to join a staff petition seeking to persuade Lorimer to continue writing editorials, it provoked one of the most remarkable outpourings of mail any periodical ever received, and certainly the most heartfelt tribute paid to any editor. The hundreds of thousands of letters represented a cross section of the *Post* readership, most of them from people who had just learned who Lorimer was. Many of the letters were as much outpourings of affection for the magazine as they were tributes to Lorimer. However, already ill, he refused to write again for the *Post*.

Less than a year later, on October 27, 1937, Lorimer was dead, the victim of throat cancer; he had been a heavy smoker all his life.

The man whom everyone called affectionately "The Boss" had created a magazine in his own image. It was not, of course, without critics. Intellectuals generally despised it, although many of them wrote for it. Lorimer himself was regarded as hopelessly "square," long before the word was common slang, and indeed he was. There were those who thought him ruthless, in the manner of the business tycoons he admired, but others considered him just, and certainly many of his values were at odds with those of the tycoons.

To Lorimer, publishing was "the business of buying and selling brains; of having ideas and finding men to carry them out." He believed correctly that there was a plebiscite on every issue of a periodical, to determine its worthiness, and no business could so quickly succumb to apathy or contentment on the part of its director. "Drugs may be prepared by formula, steel made true by process, and other commodities standardized," he wrote, "but so long as the word counts for more than the type in which it is fixed, so long as the story counts for more than the picture which draws the eye to it, and so long as literature becomes a lifeless thing in the very act of conforming, the periodical will never be standardized and sold indefinitely on the strength of its pretty package and the uniformity of its contents. Publishing is and always will be a contest of ideas—the last stronghold of unrestricted competition free to all comers."

With Bok's retirement and Lorimer's death, the first installment of the Curtis Publishing Company's serial came to an end.

nineteen

Magazines Become a Business

NONE OF THE CHANGES in the magazine business at the turn of the century was more significant than the conversion of magazines from purely personal enterprises to business institutions. A similar change occurred at the same time in newspapers, as the personal journalism of the nineteenth century began to be replaced by the corporate structures of large business enterprises.

In both cases, the change was the result of a tremendous growth in advertising, so that these media no longer depended on circulation for the greater part of their income. It was not an overnight transition, by any means, and its effects were uneven, but generally speaking it was advertising—national in the magazines, local and national in the newspapers—that came to dominate the media.

For the most part, urban newspapers successfully resisted the natural inclination of advertisers to attempt to influence or control editorial content. Flagrant exceptions could always be cited (and could still be named today), but most of the press, especially the dailies, remained independent of advertising influence, in spite of the popular myth to the contrary. The influence and control that existed in so much of the small town and rural press rose from the economic facts of the situation—the total dependence on advertisers for a paper's existence. In urban centers, circulation remained essential but secondary, and there was at least a degree of mutual dependence between advertisers and newspapers.

In magazines, on the other hand, because the advertising was national and not local, the advertisers were in a far stronger position. A magazine's circulation became not so much a primary source of income (since in time it cost more to service subscriptions than they were really worth) as a bargaining force in the competitive struggle for the advertising dollar, which had to be spread around among all the media. This situation, in time, became much more intense and difficult with the arrival of radio and television.

The ultimate result was a relationship between advertising and editorial content that virtually ended editorial independence in all but a relatively few magazines. A magazine struggling to retain its share of a soap account, for example, when the manufacturer was already pouring the bulk of his advertising money into competing media, would not be likely to undertake an exposé of the soap industry, if one were demanded. On a more commonplace level, magazines had good reason not to risk offending advertisers in any respect whatever if they wanted to survive, and when public relations dictated a particular working arrangement between advertising and editorial matter, no one was likely to question it.

Some magazines, to be sure, clung to their independence, but they were likely to be either the rich and powerful periodicals, which could afford to lose a little, or the small and radical, which either had little to lose or were subsidized. But on the great middle ground, a gradual homogenization occurred as the twentieth century wore on. Most magazines came to reflect the conservative business interests of their advertisers. In brief, they became business institutions themselves—extremely large ones, in the case of group publishing—and behaved like it.

But the tidal wave of advertising, with accompanying huge revenues, transformed magazines from relatively drab productions to works of graphic art. The income made it possible for publishers and editors to buy anything that would make a magazine better to look at and more readable. Graphic arts craftsmanship in illustration and design was matched by craftsmanship in the advertising itself, as the agencies developed their skills. In time readers found the advertising in a magazine as attractive to look at and as interesting to read as the editorial matter, at least in some periodicals.

Advertising not only provided the lifeblood that made magazines advance, and greatly improved their appearance and content, but it also (as the publishers and advertisers constantly reminded critics) helped to raise the material quality of living in an increasingly affluent America because magazine readers found laid out before them, weekly and monthly, a giant smorgasbord of consumer goods from which to choose. Consumers were helped in their choice by numerous home-service departments in the magazines, and by departmental attention to virtually every aspect of daily living—all reflected in the advertising columns.

The beginnings of this mass movement toward institutionalization in magazines began inauspiciously in the period between 1885 and 1892, when the growth of national advertising and the consequent influx of large revenues encouraged publishers to take unwise risks in starting new ventures. As a result, millions were lost. Bok, a cautious man himself, wrote in the magazine *Epoch* in 1891: "I should think a man would weigh carefully the chances before putting any money into new magazine schemes. It is not so much a survival of the fittest as the survival of the largest capital."

National advertising also had the effect of making circulation figures important, and before the advent of auditing procedures by the Audit Bureau of Circulations in 1914, there was little honesty in making circulation claims. The *Western Plowman* offered perhaps the most penetrating comment on this situation when it reported, under the heading "Circulations": "The editor was dying, but when the doctor placed his ear to the patient's heart and muttered sadly, 'Poor fellow —circulation almost gone!' he raised himself up and gasped, ' 'Tis false! We have the largest circulation in the country!' Then he sank back on his pillow and died, consistent to the end—lying about his circulation."

Not only did the publishers lie about their circulations, but when attempts at auditing began, some of the more conservative magazines took the position that their circulation figures were no one's business. The Harpers indignantly refused to give any such information. Eventually it was the advertisers themselves, as well as the agencies, who insisted on accurate information; they refused to believe what the publishers chose to tell them unless it was backed up by certifiable figures.

These pressures compelled magazines to submit to auditing by the ABC, and, later, by similar organizations.

The first magazine to boast of a million circulation was one of the Augusta mail-order products, *Comfort,* which claimed to have achieved the figure in 1895. By 1905 there were about a dozen sworn statements from periodicals (most of them mail-order) claiming a million, and by that time *Comfort* and the *Woman's Magazine,* in St. Louis, said they were well past that mark. In 1906 *The Delineator* claimed a million and a half. From that time onward, the trend of circulations was steadily upward.

They were boosted, as has been noted, by the premium method, inspired by the success of *The Youth's Companion,* but competition ran the premium business into the ground, carrying some magazines with it. The only other method that resulted in real success was the carrier boy plan. Carriers solicited while they delivered in the hope of earning bicycles, scholarships, and hundreds of lesser rewards. The Curtis Publishing Company, and especially the *Saturday Evening Post,* made the magazine carrier boy an American institution. When Lorimer retired and the letters poured in, many of those who wrote spoke with nostalgic affection of their old magazine routes.

Newsstand circulation had existed since the founding of the American News Company in the 1860s, and this organization had monopolized that method of distribution until the Railroad News Company and the Union News Company came together in 1872, thus uniting the principal retail and the sole wholesale periodical businesses in the country. Frank Munsey fought the monopoly through direct-mail and newspaper advertising, then with his own agency, but he was the only one able to defy it successfully.

The result of this competition was a gradual swing from annual subscriptions to newsstand sales, and before the turn of the century the magazines were providing posters for the stands to advertise their wares, some of them by artists like Gibson. Distribution of magazines had also been helped considerably by a new postal law in 1885 that reduced the rate to a cent a pound for second-class matter, and by the creation of the rural free delivery system in 1897.

However circulations were obtained and magazines distributed, the impressive new figures at the turn of the century spurred the onrush of advertising. By 1905 total advertising revenues had passed $145 million, double what they had been in 1890. The seasonal pattern, too, had been established—slimmer in summer, fattest before Christmas. *Collier's* led all the other magazines in advertising by 1905, carrying more than thirteen pages a week, but the *Post* surpassed it before long, and led the field for years.

The rise of advertising was linked directly to the great change in marketing and distribution that was taking place in America about the turn of the century, as selling by this method shifted from retailer to manufacturer as far as the magazines were concerned, through the rise of national advertising. Newspapers began to carry most of the burden of retail advertising, which had always been their function, while the periodicals, reaching a national audience, were ideally designed to carry the manufacturer's message.

Familiar figures and slogans began to appear, and to become part of the national culture: "The W. L. Douglas $3 Shoe for Gentlemen," Mrs. Pinkham's Vegetable Compound for Female Complaints, the "Absolutely Pure" motto of Royal Baking Powder, Baker's Breakfast Cocoa; Durkee's Salad Dressing, "Unequalled for Excellence"; Armour's Extract of Beef, producing "That feeling of contentment"; the country scenes advertising the Columbia wheel. These were advertisements of the eighties. In the nineties, came another flood: the Eastman Kodak Company, with its memorable "You press the button; we do the rest"; Postum Cereal and Grape Nuts, with its slogan "There's a Reason"; the enduring Victrola ad, with the patient dog listening to "His Master's Voice"; Procter & Gamble, boasting two immortal slogans, "99 44/100 per cent pure" and "It Floats"; Castoria, with its promise, "Children Cry for It," and hundreds of others familiar to some of us, but merely quaint or ludicrous to those brought up on television.

Yet the rhymes that began to accompany advertising in the nineties were not so far removed from the radio and television commercials of today. The cleaning powder Sapolio, with its sparkling "Spotless

Town" glittering in its advertisements, was the predecessor of today's Mr. Clean, using jingles like this:

> "I am the Mayor of Spotless Town,
> The brightest man for miles around.
> The shining light of wisdom can
> Reflect from such a polished man,
> And so I say to high and low:
> The brightest use Sapolio."

Modern advertising, as well as public relations, begins to appear in the jingle written by the advertising manager of the Lackawanna Railroad. After switching from bituminous coal, the railroad, exploiting its new slogan, "The Road of Anthracite," advertised:

> "Says Phoebe Snow,
> About to go
> Upon a trip to Buffalo:
> My gown stays white
> From morn to night
> Upon the Road of Anthracite."

There were still no restraints on advertising, and for a time the abuses were many. In a period when extreme reticence about sex was still the mode, it is astonishing to see advertisements for bust developers, manhood restorers, and dubious contraceptives. Patent medicines were said not only to cure coughs and colds but also to cure cancer and tuberculosis—or "consumption," as it was called then. Fraudulent stocks, before the passage of "blue sky laws," were freely and enthusiastically sold.

The publishers were aware that such abuses would hurt circulation, and before things got entirely out of hand the leading magazines not only restricted their own advertising but fought against fraudulent claims. There were those who thought testimonial advertising was a fraud, although a harmless one, but it continued to flourish and, in fact, has never died. Even so respected a figure as Henry Ward Beecher testified to his intense satisfaction with Pears' Soap.

Various forays were also made against makers of corsets and underwear for ladies, who advertised their products in a way that frequently offended public prudery. Bok, with rare discrimination, announced in 1898 that the *Journal* would no longer discuss such matters as women's underwear in its articles and departments, but he did not mention that advertising for it would continue.

It was the familiar trademarks, however, with their pictures and slogans, that did the most for national advertising. As *Printer's Ink* observed in 1905, "The trade-mark has offered a method of disposing of a product so broad, and individual trade-marks have in many instances become so valuable, that all manufacturers are interested, big and little. They now realize that this is a golden age in trademarks. . . ."

If advertising was the major factor in transforming magazines into a business, the rapid development in graphic arts that began at the turn of the century was equally important in making them a handsome product the business could sell. The Kodak advertisements heralded a new day in photography, but the change to photography had already begun to take place in periodicals before the Kodak was in general use—in fact, as soon as the rapid dry plate process was invented in the eighties. Magazines and newspapers in their coverage of the Spanish-American War took as much advantage of the new art as possible. Taking pictures became a popular pastime, and photography magazines sprang up by the dozen until there were hundreds of them by 1905, although few of them had circulations of much more than a thousand.

It would be a time, though, before photography substantially replaced illustration in the periodical press; meanwhile, there were first-rate artists doing work for the best monthlies and weeklies—men of the caliber of John La Farge, Joseph Pennell, Howard Pyle, Gibson, Christy, Fisher, Flagg, Remington, Arthur B. Frost, and Edward W. Kemble, among many others. The wave of poster art, which became a fad in the nineties, overflowed into advertising and editorial pages alike. Portraits were also in public demand. *McClure's* publication of Napoleon pictures was a great success, and its Lincoln portraits were even more enthusiastically received.

There was also, surprisingly, a great deal of nude or seminude art.

When critics complained that the editors of Henry Luce's *Life* in its earlier years had used every known device to display the nude female figure without printing pictures of unabashedly naked women, they were only echoing those who viewed with dismay the parade of actresses in tights or low-cut gowns, bathing girls in what we would think of as awkwardly provocative poses, and "living pictures," in which girls were posed like statuary to represent classic scenes or masterpieces of painting.

Photography, however, was the most exciting new dimension added to magazines as they emerged into the twentieth century. By 1893, halftone reproductions accounted for a third of the *Century's* illustrations, half of *Harper's,* two-thirds of *Scribner's* and virtually all of those in *Cosmopolitan.* In *Brush and Pencil* for November 1901, the epitaph for nineteenth-century art was written by William C. Whittam, who lamented: "Steel engraving, the glory of a former generation, is today an art of the past, and wood-engraving has but few representatives." Not long after, woodcuts, too, disappeared. A few magazines were surprisingly slow to use photography—the *Post* did not do so until about 1919—but as early as 1905 it was clearly the wave of the future.

PART FOUR

MAGAZINES OF THE TWENTIETH CENTURY

(1905 –   )

twenty

The Postwar Struggle
for Survival

WHILE INDIVIDUAL MAGAZINES had to struggle to stay alive from the time the magazine business began, periodicals were not threatened in large numbers until after World War I, and the enemy was none of the expected sources of trouble.

It had been said, for example, that magazines, having survived the violent financial swings of the economy after the Civil War, would not be able to withstand the great bicycle craze of the nineties, when it seemed that all America was on wheels, and it was freely predicted that both books and magazines faced possible extinction, since the bicycle had liberated the footbound pedestrian.

Nothing of the kind happened, however; in fact, magazines used the bicycle fad in articles and stories, and in periodicals devoted to cycling. But no sooner had this fear subsided than the automobile replaced the bicycle in the public fancy, and the early years of the century were filled with gloomy predictions that the horseless carriage would do what the bicycle had failed to do and end reading in the home. Again, the net result of the new transportation was a whole category of magazines dealing with automobiles, including many businesses and industrial periodicals reflecting the multiple interests of the auto industry.

In the decade after World War I, there appeared to be much more cause for concern. The fresh threat was radio. It was a different kind of menace because the bicycle and the automobile had taken people out of their houses, and so had the burgeoning motion-picture business, another dark cloud on the horizon. But radio was competition *within* the home for the reader's time.

Adding to the gloom was the undeniable fact that many of the old, established magazines that had dominated the business for so long were on their way out or had already died. The melancholy roll of the fallen cut across every category, from the established quality magazines like the *Century* to *St. Nicholas, Judge,* and *The Delineator.* It was shocking to older readers to see such pillars as the *North American Review, Living Age, Forum,* and the *Independent* beginning to crumble.

A prime example in the debacle of the old leaders was the fate of two long established popular magazines, *The Outlook* and *The Independent.* The younger of the two, *The Outlook,* had begun in 1867 as a Baptist paper, *The Church Union,* and was on the point of expiration after only a few years when Henry Ward Beecher's publishers, J. B. Ford and Company, bought it, changed the name to *The Christian Union,* and made Beecher the editor. By converting this rather drab specialized religious periodical into a general family weekly, the new management succeeded in making it, at 30,000, the most successful religious magazine ever printed by 1873. After that, its fortunes declined again until, in July 1873, after several ownership changes, it emerged as *The Outlook,* a journal of opinion.

Within a few years, the magazine was one of the most respected and best read in America. President Theodore Roosevelt was its contributing editor for a time after he left the White House, and the weekly carried such outstanding work as Booker T. Washington's *Up from Slavery* and Jacob A. Riis's *The Making of an American.* In the first two decades of the twentieth century, circulation reached 125,000 under the direction of an outstanding editor, Lyman Abbott. But when Abbott died in 1923, after forty-seven years of editing the magazine (he owned it for thirty-two), within a year *The Outlook's* circulation had slipped as low as 84,000. It gained only 10,000 later in 1924 by absorbing the *International Interpreter,* and in 1928 was forced to merge with *The Independent.*

The Independent was even older, having been founded in December 1848 to further the cause of the Congregationalists and to fight slavery. Beecher was editor of this paper, too, for a time, and used it as a platform to exhort President Lincoln into issuing the Emancipation Proclamation. Under various ownerships after the Civil War, it led an up-and-down existence as a magazine of opinion, crusading for good causes. It exerted its greatest influence, perhaps, in the fight to establish the League of Nations. By 1924, however, it was in serious difficulty, and an involuntary petition in bankruptcy was filed. An attempted reorganization failed, leading to the merger with *The Outlook*. The new publication was called *The Outlook and Independent,* and it seemed to many a natural marriage of old established properties that had followed similar paths. The union was too late and not enough, however. With the Depression, the magazine suspended in May 1932. It was bought by Frank A. Tichenor, who owned five other specialized and trade magazines. Under the new management, and with Alfred E. Smith at least nominally sitting in the editor's chair, it endured until June 1935.

In this postwar struggle for survival, several different factors were responsible for the death of magazines. Perhaps most important was the inability of publishers to alter old formulas in an era of dramatic change. Several periodicals that tried to adapt to the new age failed to do so rapidly enough, and died while they were in transition for lack of capital to keep operating until new formulas could be established.

Another major reason for failure was the competition from innovators in the field like De Witt Wallace, Henry Luce, and Harold Ross. They were introducing magazines of a kind never seen before, and winning audiences attracted by these fresh formulas. The newcomers were closer to changing tastes than the old-line entrepreneurs.

Nevertheless, some of the former leaders managed to survive after the war, and although they were often troubled, they shared leadership in the industry with recent arrivals like Time, Inc., and the Reader's Digest Association. These survivors were the Curtis Publishing Co., Crowell-Collier, the McCall organization, and the Hearst group.

Curtis's two major magazines had been in quite different positions during the twenties. The *Saturday Evening Post,* as noted earlier, was at its peak, establishing new circulation and advertising records under Lorimer's firm and still knowledgeable hand. The *Ladies' Home Journal,* on the other hand, was undergoing its worst trials since Curtis had bought it. After Bok's departure, a succession of editors had failed to keep it from a steady decline.

In addition, the strong hand at the top of the organization had faltered. In the old days, Curtis would have been able to find another Bok. Now, an old man, overly confident that his properties were in good hands, he sailed on the Atlantic on his yacht, summered in Maine, and took less and less interest in the business. A year before he died in 1933, Lorimer succeeded him as president of the company, and faced four years of ordeal. The *Post* began to slip, too, as a result of its editor's fierce opposition to the New Deal.

A year before he resigned, however, Lorimer did for the *Journal* what he could no longer do for his own magazine. In 1935 he gave the editorship of Bok's masterpiece to a husband-and-wife team, Bruce and Beatrice Blackmar Gould—something that had not been seen in the business since Frank Leslie and his wife had turned things upside down after the Civil War. The Goulds rescued the *Journal* from the service-and-fiction rut into which it had fallen and restored much of the luster Bok had given it by using some of Bok's ideas—chiefly the argument that women might have interests other than their homes. They picked up once more the fight against venereal disease that Bok had begun, and in the vein of the new morality they dared to talk about birth control, the sex problems of the young, divorce, mental illness, alcoholism, slum clearance—all the ills beginning to beset an urbanized America. One of the most effective series they ran was "How America Lives," in which American families were examined in detail for the benefit of other readers. Some of these families had their homes redecorated and their lives reorganized by the *Journal's* assiduous editors. The series was an extremely long one, and once, in an attempt to get away from the parade of "typical" families, the *Journal* ventured to depict life at home with Hollywood's happiest married couple, Jennifer Jones and David O. Selznick. That issue appeared on the stands just as the couple announced the breakup of their marriage.

But such minor mishaps did not impair the vitality the Goulds had brought to the *Journal*. It climbed steadily, and by 1955 it was leading all the other women's magazines in both circulation and advertising. At one point, in 1947, its advertising gross was greater than that of its two competitors, *Good Housekeeping* and *McCall's*, combined, and some readers were complaining that the thick magazine was so heavy they had trouble reading it in bed.

Flush with this income, Curtis Publishing launched some new publications, first *Jack and Jill*, for children under ten. Begun rather tentatively in November 1938, it grew rapidly from an initial run of 40,000 to 726,000 by 1955. The second venture was *Holiday*, launched in March 1946. It faltered in the first few months, primarily because of poor design and art work, but then the company brought in a new editor, Ted Patrick, who proved to be the kind of editorial genius Curtis himself used to be so adept at finding. Under his direction, the magazine became a successful property.

Along with the new, Curtis improved its position by casting off some of the old, notably *The Country Gentleman,* which with *Farm Journal* had been one of the two leading national farm magazines for years. But the rural scene was changing rapidly as the urbanization process went on in America, and by 1955 there was no longer room for so many farm magazines. In the face of declining advertising revenues, Curtis changed the name of *The Country Gentleman* to *Better Farming,* and five months later sold it to its chief rival, the *Farm Journal.*

Crowell-Collier, like Curtis, survived in the postwar scramble because its properties, while not without their troubles, were basically strong, and because the company disposed of its lesser magazines. In 1919 it owned, besides its big three, *American, Collier's,* and *The Woman's Home Companion,* another periodical called *Farm and Fireside.* This was renamed *Country Home* in 1929, but suspended ten years later. In 1920 the company bought *Mentor,* a magazine devoted to one subject in each issue, and designed to provide detailed information on that subject from specialists. The specialists covered a wide range of knowledge, from Luther Burbank to Roger Babson, and Dan

Beard to Fritz Kreisler. Obviously, it was not a mass magazine nor would it ever become one, and since that was Crowell-Collier's business, *Mentor* was sold in 1930.

One of the first publishing companies to diversify, if not the first, Crowell-Collier did not depend on its magazines for its entire income. Its publishing and distribution of books, particularly *Collier's Encyclopedia,* was a highly profitable part of its business, and so was its Sunday newspaper supplement, *This Week.* In time, too, the company acquired some valuable broadcasting properties. These other divisions looked particularly good to management in 1953, when all the magazines were losing money, producing nearly a $5 million deficit in the company that year.

This situation led to the hiring of Paul C. Smith, who had been general manager of the San Francisco *Chronicle* for seventeen years, and highly touted as a boy wonder. Smith, by tight management practices, brought the company into the black within two years, but then a new group of twenty-six investors gained control in the summer of 1955, and the handwriting was on the wall. When it came time to make a corporate decision about strengthening the company's profit position, it was clear that by eliminating the magazine division Crowell-Collier would eliminate its primary problem. In the new climate of the fifties and sixties, there was no sentiment involved in killing old and honorable magazines.

Among the other survivors, the McCall Corporation fared somewhat better. *McCall's* itself had a difficult time after Wiese's editorship ended, and its vicissitudes in the fiercely competitive women's magazine field were not mitigated until the company hired away Herbert Mayes from the editor's chair at *Good Housekeeping.* Mayes was another of the great individualists, like Bok, Lorimer, Long, and the others, who was always the star of his own show. He had made *Good Housekeeping* one of the most valuable magazine properties in the world, and himself foremost among editors in the women's field. Brought to *McCall's,* he revived the magazine with fresh art work and new approaches, and restored it to former glories.

The company's other major property, *Redbook,* had been edited for many years by Edwin Balmer, and had successfully reached, as Balmer himself once put it, "the little old ladies in Kokomo." But the little old ladies were now reading other magazines, it appeared, and Balmer was replaced by Wade Nichols, a young fireball, who turned the magazine around and aimed it at young marrieds, or "The Magazine for Young Adults," as the official subtitle put it in 1951. *Redbook,* under this new banner, attacked social problems and exposed controversial issues until it had won itself an audience of two million.

The McCall Corporation had also inherited *Bluebook* from a 1929 acquisition of properties owned by the Consolidated Magazines Corporation, but this largely fiction pulp magazine, which many older readers remembered for its serials by Mary Roberts Rinehart, James Oliver Curwood, H. Rider Haggard, and others, could not survive in the changing times after World War II, and it was suspended in 1956.

Later, the McCall Corporation acquired the *Saturday Review,* a respected but nearly moribund book-reviewing medium, and made it into an exciting review of the arts, also carrying articles of general intellectual interest. The corporation itself in time became one of the wholly owned subsidiaries of Hunt Foods, in California, the agglomerate controlled by Norton Simon, a West Coast financier.

As for the Hearst Corporation, the other major survivor of World War I, it suffered, perhaps, less than the others because so many of its magazines were in specialized rather than general fields. By 1955 it was publishing *Motor, Motor Boating, American Druggist, Harper's Bazaar, House Beautiful, Town and Country, Good Housekeeping, Cosmopolitan,* and *Sports Afield.* All were profitable properties, although their values varied considerably, and all were edited according to Hearst's own formula: "Find out what your readers want and give it to them. And give it to them regularly." This almost simple-minded dictum was faithfully carried out by a corps of able editors. When *Cosmopolitan* showed signs of seriously faltering, old formulas were thrown aside, and under a new editor, Helen Gurley Brown, it achieved a new success as a kind of *Playboy* for girls.

The secret of the Hearst Corporation's financial vitality was its diversification. Besides the Hearst newspapers and the magazines, it owned newspaper supplements, a newsreel company, a book-publishing house, radio and television stations, subscription agencies, paper mills, and real estate. Its annual gross was about $350,000,000 in 1955, and the magazines accounted for only a seventh of that total. Long before the wave of mergers in the communications business started, the Hearst Corporation was showing how to stay alive and prosper in a changing economic climate.

For the economy was expanding in an unprecedented way as the twentieth century unfolded. Interrupted by the Crash and the Depression, artificially stimulated by World War II, it burst into a new age after 1945. The magazine market expanded with the economy, and in spite of damaging competition from television, the magazine business entered into another Golden Age.

twenty-one

The Little Magazines

A PHENOMENON IN MAGAZINE PUBLISHING that deserves much more attention than it has received has been the so-called "little magazine," a kind of periodical that began about 1912 and is still a force, although a diminished one, today.

The little magazines offered an important and unique service—an opportunity for young writers to be read who could not hope to appear in the other magazines. In the nineteenth century this had not been a problem, because the quality monthlies and the literary weeklies, extant in substantial numbers, were eager to print anything "literary." After the turn of the century, however, two factors began to change this situation.

One was the diminishing number of magazines willing to print "literary" work, as consumer magazines and large audience interests began to predominate. The other was the split between the new realism and the established ways of writing fiction. No such division had existed in the previous century, but now the work of writers like Frank Norris and Gertrude Atherton signaled a naturalism not palatable to most Establishment magazines, although both Norris and Mrs. Atherton experienced little difficulty. When the intellectual ferment in Europe began to reach American writers, as well as artists, those who wanted to experiment and to experience the freedom of new forms in fiction found they had nowhere to go in the established market.

Hence the rise of little magazines, often badly printed and nearly always in financial difficulty, but offering in their pages the first work of writers like Sherwood Anderson, Ernest Hemingway, William Faulkner, Erskine Caldwell, T. S. Eliot, and a host of others. It has been estimated that nearly 80 percent of the most important critics, novelists, poets, and storytellers who emerged after 1912 first appeared in the little magazines.

Since 1912, there have probably been nearly a thousand little magazines published in English. Many had brief lives. Some could hardly be described as bold carriers of the *avant-garde* banner. Probably no more than a hundred were important in the struggle for a mature literature in America. They paid their contributors little or nothing (usually nothing), and existed on little themselves, but this fact alone made the union between publisher and writer a truly creative effort, relatively selfless and dedicated.

To quote from the definitive work in this field, *The Little Magazine,* by Frederick J. Hoffman, Charles Allen, and Carolyn F. Ulrich, the little magazine is "a magazine designed to print artistic work which for reasons of commercial expedience is not acceptable to the money-minded periodicals or presses." Thus it is a noncommercial venture. But serious quarterlies like the *Sewanee Review,* the *Southern Review,* the *Kenyon Review,* the *Yale Review,* and the *Virginia Quarterly Magazine* are not little magazines, these authors point out, even though they are not profit making, because they do not have the freedom to experiment or to look for unknowns, as the true little magazine does.

These noncommercial periodicals, then, became proving grounds for authors. Once established, many writers moved on to commercial publication, in commercial magazines and in books. Editors in book-publishing houses, for many years, have scanned the pages of the little magazines, looking hopefully for new talent, and so have magazine editors. It is no particular credit to the Establishment that it has insisted on this trying-out process, letting someone else take the risks in printing new talent. In doing so, it has discovered on its own relatively few new authors and has done little to stimulate American literature at the grass roots. It has, instead, accepted authors who have succeeded in getting themselves printed and talked about elsewhere. This old-line rigidity has changed in recent years, but it is no longer important because magazines are not the primary outlets for fiction they once were; the book business has taken over what magazines used to do in that respect.

The history of little magazines is essentially a history of personalities, whether of editors or contributors—so many of them that only a broad idea of their variety can be offered here. From the beginning, the little magazines were individualistic and *avant-garde*, and no doubt the first one, filling both qualifications, was *The Dial*, whose editors, Margaret Fuller and Emerson, were considered to be in the literary vanguard. Other nineteenth-century little magazines have been mentioned earlier, periodicals like the *Saturday Press*, which flourished between 1858 and 1866, and *M'lle New York*, a literary publication of the nineties, a period that also produced the *Chap Book*, in Chicago, and *Lark*.

These were all preliminary ventures. The little magazine of our time properly began in 1912 with Harriet Monroe's *Poetry: A Magazine of Verse*, closely followed in the same year by the *Masses*, edited by Floyd Dell and Max Eastman; and the *Poetry Journal*, in Boston. Still more came out: *Glebe, The Little Review, Others*, and in their pages appeared, often for the first time anywhere, such writers as Carl Sandburg, Vachel Lindsay, T. S. Eliot, Wallace Stevens, Marianne Moore, John Reed, John Gould Fletcher, Maxwell Bodenheim, and Robert Frost. Among those already published but whose reputations the little magazines helped to establish were Edgar Lee Masters, Amy Lowell, Edwin Arlington Robinson, and Sara Teasdale.

The authors of *The Little Magazine* separate their subject into six major classes: poetry, leftist, regional, experimental, critical and eclectic, although they point out that there is considerable overlapping.

To consider the poetry magazines first, most of the best American poets after 1912 were published for the first time in their pages, and indeed were sustained by them after their names were known. Harriet Monroe's *Poetry* was the most famous, perhaps, but it was rivaled in reputation by *Voices*, begun in 1921, and *Smoke*, which published between 1931 and 1937.

Sometimes the little magazines' influence went beyond the purely literary, as in the case of the *Masses*, which is generally credited with being the fountainhead of the proletarian literary revolution of the thirties, although it functioned only between 1912 and 1917 under the direction of its two great editors, Dell and Eastman. It also inspired the starting of other Left-wing magazines, the most noted of which, the *Partisan Review,* is still a leader among the critical periodicals. Those with shorter lives in this category included the *Anvil, Blast,* the *Little Magazine,* and a half dozen others not so well known.

Regional publishing of little magazines was particularly important to the developing literary culture of this century because it enabled the Midwest, particularly, to break away from eastern dominance and give its new writers a showcase, while to the Southwest and in the Far West it meant an opportunity for publication virtually denied to the writers of those regions. The best of the regional periodicals may have been John T. Frederick's *Midland,* published in Iowa City between 1915 and 1933; but others as noted were the *Southwest Review,* begun in 1924, and the *Prairie Schooner,* appearing in 1927, along with the *New Mexico Quarterly Review,* initiated in 1931.

Of all the six major types enumerated earlier, the largest category was the experimental magazine, and it is their names that are probably most familiar to contemporary readers. *The Little Review,* the first of them, beginning in 1914 and continuing until the Crash, was probably the most famous; but *Broom* (1921–24), the *Double Dealer* (1921–26), the first twentieth-century reincarnation of *The Dial* (1920–29), and *transition* (1927–38) were among the notables.

As for the critical magazines, the *Hound and Horn* (1927–34) and the *Symposium* (1930-33), along with *The Dial,* were among those that presented the work of T. S. Eliot, John Crowe Ransom, and R. P. Blackmur, among others.

In the sixth category, the eclectic magazines often originated on university campuses, although the *Seven Arts* (1916–17) and Whit Burnett's *Story,* which has passed through so many transitions to survive today, were independent of university life or connection. But *Accent,* published at the University of Illinois beginning in 1940; and the *University Review,* of the University of Kansas City, beginning in 1935, were typical of the genre. Some, like *Chimera* and *Furioso,* originating in 1942 and 1939, began life at the universities but in time moved off-campus.

In their prime, the best of the little magazines carried an astonishing amount of work by writers who would shortly be recognized as among the best in America. In the twenties, for example, *Double Dealer* printed Hart Crane, Edmund Wilson, Malcolm Cowley, John Crowe Ransom, Robert Penn Warren, Allen Tate, and Ernest Hemingway. The magazine specialized in new poetry and fiction, although it also carried criticism and book reviews, and it is credited with discovering both Hemingway and Faulkner. Although it cost only $300 an issue to produce, it ran a perennial deficit, which was made up through the generosity of about forty people who supported it on an informal basis. Unlike many other little magazines, *Double Dealer* began by paying for contributions—a cent a word for prose, fifty cents a line for verse—but had to stop after six issues for lack of funds, and never did so again. Its circulation was never much above 1,500.

Actual discoveries of writers, oddly enough, were made largely by the smallest of the little magazines, rather than the better-known periodicals already cited. About 80 percent of the writers who appeared for the first time in this kind of publication were printed in ephemeral and far-out organs like *Blues,* the discoverer of James Farrell and Erskine Caldwell, or *Bruno's Bohemia,* where Hart Crane first saw literary daylight.

The most substantial benefit the little magazines gave their contributors was the encouragement of seeing their work in print. As Stephen Vincent Benét put it, "The little magazines, of course, are absolutely indispensable. They give the beginning writer his first important step—a chance to see how the thing looks in print. And there's nothing as salutary."

Of course, not all that appeared in these magazines was the work of genius. Some of it was literary junk, much was only mildly interesting, and a good deal of it was worthy enough but not first rate. Editors had their own predilections and passions, and sometimes they were utterly wrong about a writer. But out of the immense variety they printed, the discovery of pearls was inevitable. And because the little magazines were innovators, they constantly refreshed the literary stream. As encouragers of young writers, their importance can hardly be exaggerated.

If one speaks of the little magazines in the past tense, it is not because they have disappeared, by any means, but because their function is no longer so much discovering new fiction talent as offering an outlet for *avant-garde* writings of all kinds. Soaring production costs of producing anything in print has accounted for many of them. A few, like *Partisan Review,* have become members of the literary Establishment themselves. Contemporary rivals, like the *New York Review of Books* (which is, of course, not a "little magazine"), have taken a new form that is somewhere between a magazine and a newspaper.

As the New Criticism developed after World War II, some of the little magazines emulated their bigger brothers, the quarterlies, by devoting more space to criticism than they did to new fiction and poetry. New writers, too, seemed better able to establish themselves with novels than with magazine short stories, although the books themselves were sometimes collections of short works.

Today the little magazines are still the *avant-garde,* concentrated in centers like San Francisco, Chicago, and New York. While they have produced some poets like Allen Ginsberg, and a few of the old generation of "beat" writers, most of the work they have printed has been too experimental to be translated into magazines of wider circulation, as in the early days. Some of it, however, has led to the publication of books. New Left philosophy has appeared, too, but not usually for the first time, since there are many other outlets for it.

There is also a kind of semiunderground little-magazine business operating today, often under four-letter titles that bar them from most newsstands, containing much from the cult of the obscene, as well as writing from the nihilist hard core of the Far Left. Again, the line between newspaper and magazine is so hard to define in many of these cases that it is difficult to say in which category they belong.

While the little magazines may actually be more numerous today than they ever were, the days of their greatest usefulness and brilliance are in the past. There will always be fringe publications of every kind in the magazine business, and some of the best of the old little magazines are still with us, but the rapid rise of specialized magazine publication has just about finished the little magazine as a well-defined and important kind of publication.

twenty-two

New Ideas of the Twenties and Thirties

AS ADVERTISING VOLUME FLUCTUATES with the general movements of the economy, the fortunes of magazines rise and fall, too. Consequently, there are periodic predictions that the industry is in dire trouble. Sometimes these predictions seem to be borne out by the death of established magazines or by the severe sinking spells experienced by properties considered virtually invulnerable.

The loss of advertising pages over a year's time in an established periodical may be a signal of serious trouble. But it may only reflect the general state of the economy, and hence of advertising. Nor do the expirations of noted magazines portend the ultimate collapse of the industry. Whatever the immediate cause of the disaster may have been, it is a good bet that the basic reason was the magazine's inability to meet the demands of a constantly changing public taste.

One thing we can learn from the history of magazines in America is that people who appear with new ideas acceptable to large numbers of readers will be successful in establishing new magazines, everything else being equal, whether times are good or bad, and regardless of the industry's current condition.

No better illustration could be given than the history of the twenties and thirties, when some of the most notable magazines and magazine empires of our time were launched. The ideas behind them were new. Many of them were begun in the affluent twenties, but others appeared for the first time in the bleakest days of the Depression. In both instances, they succeeded equally well.

In spite of its affluence, the twenties was a period when old and honorable magazines were dying. Yet it was also the time when Henry Luce and De Witt Wallace were founding their empires, and when Harold Ross began his phenomenally successful *The New Yorker*. In the thirties, while the nation was undergoing the worst depression of the century, Luce had the courage to start *Fortune Magazine,* directed to an audience for whom the very title was largely a memory, and, moreover, to charge them an unprecedented one dollar a copy. Meanwhile, David Smart was putting on the market, in one of the period's worst years, a new magazine, *Esquire,* to sell for fifty cents, double the price of the ordinary periodical. Luce began publishing *Life* in 1936 against the advice of experts who assured him it was not only the wrong time but the wrong formula.

Like Luce, De Witt Wallace revolutionized the magazine business. Wallace, however, in creating the *Reader's Digest* did so not by introducing a new idea, but by taking an old one, improving it, and making it the most successful single magazine ever published.

The Wallace story never ceases to amaze; indeed it amazes Wallace himself. Born in St. Paul, the son of an eminent father who was president of Macalester College, besides being a Greek and Latin scholar and a Presbyterian minister, Wallace graduated from Macalester and the University of California, worked briefly for the Webb Publishing Company, of St. Paul, who were in the textbook and farm magazine business, then went to work for Brown and Bigelow as a salesman for their line of calendars and advertising specialties. The idea of the *Digest* had already occurred to him. It was the oldest idea of them all in America—the eclectic magazine, with which the business had begun. But Wallace had a variation in mind. He would edit the articles he clipped and offer the shortened version as a time-saver for busy people. Editors had always shortened copy, but Wallace made an art of the practice, preserving the essential meaning while trimming away the nonessential ornamentation. He hoped to make as much as five thousand dollars a year from his idea.

While he was recuperating from wounds incurred during World

War I, Wallace practiced his art, and as soon as he came home to St. Paul, he made up a dummy which included thirty-one articles clipped from old magazines he found in the public library, and shortened by his method. The New York publishers and possible financial backers who saw this dummy returned a unanimous verdict against it. Meanwhile, Wallace was fired from his job in the Westinghouse Company's publicity department, which in a sense was the turning point, since he then worked full time on starting his magazine.

His marriage to Lila Bell Acheson provided him not only a bride but a full working partner in his venture. With a borrowed capital of $5,000, they put together the first issue of the *Reader's Digest* in a Greenwich Village basement. On the day he married Lila Bell, Wallace sent out a mailing of several thousand circulars to solicit subscriptions. That was October 1921, while the postwar slump still lingered. Back from their honeymoon, the enterprising couple found 1,500 charter subscriptions waiting for them. On the strength of this response, the *Digest* published its first issue in February 1922.

Wallace had definite ideas about what his magazine should be. Articles would not be selected simply according to the editor's personal predilections, as in the old days of the eclectics. What was chosen for reprinting would have to meet three criteria he laid down: applicability, lasting interest, and constructiveness. The first two were largely rhetoric, since the idea of giving readers articles that were applicable to their lives was a commonplace notion, widely practiced for years; and the concept of "lasting interest," by which Wallace meant that the articles should be worth reading a year later, was very much a matter of subjective opinion. But in the third criterion, Wallace had hit upon a prime ingredient, one that had much to do with making the *Digest* America's favorite magazine.

For "constructiveness," translated as perennial optimism, was the key element in the philosophy of the American middle class, to whom the magazine was primarily directed. The *Digest* saw "sermons in trees, books in the running brooks and good in everything." It was designed, as Wallace himself put it, "to promote a Better America, with capital letters, with a fuller life for all, and with a place for the United States of increasing influence and respect in world affairs."

Again, translated, this meant giving the middle class exactly what it wanted to believe about itself and the world.

Another element in the *Digest*'s success, not often mentioned, was the bargain it offered. Looking down the table of contents on the front page, readers saw articles condensed from magazines large and small, prominent and obscure. Wallace was offering his readers the "best" from the periodical press, shortened to an easy length that could be read in bathroom or bedroom, and for a bargain price.

The *Digest*'s success far exceeded Wallace's expectations. The office was moved first to Pleasantville, a small town in Westchester County, north of New York, where it functioned first in a garage, with the addition of an adjacent pony shed, then in a house the Wallaces built for themselves with early profits. In 1939, the *Digest* moved again, to nearby Chappaqua, on a hill overlooking the Saw Mill River Parkway. Mrs. Wallace designed the building herself, and eventually filled it with the formidable gallery of contemporary art she and her husband collected. The editorial executive offices were done in different periods; Mrs. Wallace redecorated her husband's office periodically.

Knowledgeable visitors were awed as they sat in the small reception room off the lobby and gazed upon the walls from which hung not the usual office art, but genuine Utrillos, Cézannes, and Renoirs. The building cost $1,500,000 originally, and in time was surrounded by a colony of *Digest* personnel, living comfortably if incestuously together, in rural luxury. No one was more conscious than the proprietor of how far this was from a Greenwich Village basement. "Sometimes I don't believe it myself," he remarked to a visitor one day, as he walked from his private dining room to his office, which at that moment resembled a Hollywood setting for an executive-suite drama, with a wall-filling Chagall as backdrop.

A magazine so powerful was bound to become controversial, and so the *Digest* proved to be. Its basic system of buying stories and then "planting" them in selected magazines to be reprinted later was the underlying basis of most of the controversy. The *Digest* paid the magazine for this privilege, which theoretically put the recipient in a subsidized position. To a small magazine like the old *American Mercury,* struggling along in the early forties in its post-Mencken days, the subsidy represented a substantial part of total income. If the *Mercury,* or any magazine under contract, refused an article sent down from Chappaqua, there was no difficulty; the *Digest* simply sent another one. The only real problem involved was a technical one: if the recipient magazine shortened a *Digest*-submitted article to fit its own space, the new version had to be read on the telephone to a *Digest* editor to be certain that what the *Digest* "reprinted" had appeared originally.

Among those who objected to this system was Harold Ross, *The New Yorker's* acerbic editor, who denounced it roundly one day in public and declared that his magazine would have no more of it. Most other periodicals declined to follow Ross's lead. Either they needed the money or wanted the added publicity given a magazine when the *Digest* reprinted an article. Many others saw nothing wrong with the practice. Those who did argued that the system gave the *Digest* the power to propagandize its political viewpoint across a broad spectrum of the periodical press. This criticism grew stronger as the *Digest's* staff came to include more and more hard-line conservatives and it was clear that the magazine used its own columns and those of other periodicals to promote its view on everything from sex to communism.

Individual characteristics of the magazine also came into public question. One was the *Digest's* medical articles, known as "New Hope" stories because they were usually titled "New Hope for" whatever human ailment was under discussion. Many times the hope lay in some drug or other treatment still in the laboratory stage, and unproved, but publication of the articles produced waves of anguished telephone calls from afflicted individuals and their families to local doctors, pleading for the "new treatment" or the "new medicine." Occasionally the articles were so unsound as to be actually dangerous. There was considerable outrage expressed from time to time in the medical profession about the "New Hope" pieces, but the *Digest* blandly persisted, and as recently as 1968 carried one of the worst examples of this kind of journalism. (It is an office joke at the *Digest* that this series will not end until it arrives at its final, logical title: "New Hope for the Dead.")

The *Digest* had begun as an adless magazine, and proved the exception to the rule that such periodicals never succeed. Having proved the point, the magazine reversed itself in 1955 and announced it would accept advertising, restricting itself to the kinds it chose to carry, and prohibiting large categories, like liquor. The pressures from agencies to place ads in the magazine with the world's highest circulation was the greatest ever known in periodical history. The *Digest* could—and did—set the highest rates. As a result, the magazine became even richer and more impregnable.

As time went on, too, the proportion of reprints—"pickups," as the *Digest* called them—decreased steadily until by mid-1969 about 65 percent of the material used was original. Thus the initial idea had been sharply modified, and some *Digest* executives believed the pickups would be given up entirely in time.

There continues to be apprehension in many quarters about the *Digest,* and its satellite empire of record clubs, condensed-book clubs, record distribution services, and other agglomerate assets. The power of a magazine whose total circulation is well over 15,000,000 is obviously great. Moreover, the *Digest's* international editions circulate in many languages all over the globe, spreading whatever word the magazine wants to spread. Some believe it is spreading the word of the CIA. Others regard it as a high-level propaganda agent for ultraconservative political groups. The *Digest* itself continues to insist it is not selling anything except entertainment and information.

Unquestionably, however, it has a political point of view, and a social one as well, and both are reflected in what the various editions of the *Digest* print. Since each international edition has its own editors, these viewpoints can be pinpointed toward specific nations and areas of the world. In sum, the fear of most critics is that a great deal of power has been placed in the hands of a tiny group of men, who are free to use it in any way they wish.

The only other comparable power in the magazine business today is the empire the late Henry Luce began building in 1922 in conjunction with his partner Briton Hadden. Like Wallace, these men were amateurs in the magazine business, and were even more so, since they were only twenty-four years old, and just out of Yale. Hadden had some experience on the New York *World,* and Luce had been a legman and researcher for the formidable Ben Hecht, then a Chicago *News* columnist. Both Hadden and Luce meant to use these jobs as stepping-stones to the project they had conceived at Yale, nursed through World War I, and begun to develop while both were employed by Frank Munsey's Baltimore *News,* where they had come together again after their Chicago and New York tours of duty.

Resigning in 1922, they raised $86,000 from various sources, primarily friends, and founded *Facts,* which became *Time* when it finally appeared in March 1923. The staff was small and young, and its work was often amateurish, but the basic idea that inspired the magazine was as certain to succeed as Wallace's. Unlike the *Literary Digest,* which merely quoted from the press and commented on the quotes, *Time* intended actually to present the news itself, subdivided into topics for the benefit of the busy reader. Thus the mass-market reader who was quite willing to permit Wallace to predigest the nation's magazines for him presumably would be equally willing to let Luce digest the world's news and regurgitate it in a form that would be the most entertaining and least taxing on his intellect.

The primary means by which Luce chose to do this was a style of writing that has probably been more imitated, praised, denounced, and discussed than that of any other periodical in the world. It enriched (or degraded, depending on the viewpoint) the American language by coining new words, such as "tycoon." It produced sentences that were the delight of satirists. Wolcott Gibbs's *New Yorker* profile of Luce employed a memorable description: "Backward ran sentences until reeled the mind," and "Where it all will end, knows God."

The newsmagazine method originated by Luce was a successful experiment in mass journalism. For the first time, a magazine was not produced by people working apart, but by teams of writers and editors and researchers. Preserved from the past, however, was the dominant figure of the publisher himself (Hadden died in 1929), Henry Luce who decided all policy matters, in the traditional way, and whose own views, particularly his strong ones on China (he had been born there, the son of a Presbyterian missionary), were plainly evident to those who knew something of the magazine's inner workings.

Time's method was to assign writers to one or more stories as a week's work. These assignments were made by a departmental editor, who was in turn responsible to a senior editorial executive responsible only to Luce. The senior executives decided what stories to cover out of the week's grist, and what prominence to give each one. Stories were put together by a writer-researcher team, using wire-service copy, books, other magazines, daily newspapers, and the information supplied in a constant flow from *Time*'s correspondents and their bureaus established in all the principal cities of the world.

Sometimes the public got a glimpse of how this method could go awry, as when the originally unsympathetic stories about the Chiang Kai-shek regime filed from Chungking during World War II by Theodore H. White, *Time*'s correspondent there, were drastically revised in the home office, presumably at the instigation of Luce, one of Chiang's strongest supporters. White's resignation over this caused a brief flurry in the press.

In 1940 some subscribers were given another view of what was happening to the Luce method when those who wrote in to complain about *Time*'s highly biased coverage of the 1940 Presidential campaign, in which Wendell Willkie was viewed as the savior of middle- and upper-class America, were told that the magazine had decided it could no longer be politically impartial.

No doubt this was Luce's honest conviction, but it created the first wave of discontent about *Time* in the intellectual community. Until then *Time* had maintained a reasonably impartial point of view toward the news. It was often wry and ironic but never really unfair; knives were seldom deliberately pulled. But as Luce and the magazine became rich and powerful, the temptation to slant and sell (a natural consequence of *Time*'s method of writing stories) became irresistible. Every story was written to a predetermined point of view, decided by the departmental editor and the senior editorial executives, and the facts were made to fit the viewpoint, whatever it might be. Often the results were harmless enough, even amusing, and frequently informative to those whose other reading was relatively limited.

The trouble came when *Time* concluded that its viewpoints were right, and the newsmagazine became a vehicle, not for reporting and interpreting the news, but for selling attitudes about the news. Since the ordinary reader was quite unable to distinguish one from the other, he regarded the news in *Time* as just as credible as what he read in newspapers that were making an attempt to be fair and impartial— and perhaps *Time* was even more believable, because it continued to speak as an omniscient authority, an approach that often verged on pure arrogance.

Today it is safe to say that the intellectual community does not believe much of what it reads in *Time*. That is a small matter to the magazine, since it is not addressed to intellectuals but to an affluent audience (attractive to advertisers) that wants what Henry Luce knew from the beginning it wanted—a painless way to get the news.

Time's chief competitor, *Newsweek,* was begun in 1933 by Luce's first foreign-news editor, Thomas J. C. Martyn, who called the publication *News-Week* and devoted it simply to digesting the news. After running through several million dollars without making any headway against *Time, News-Week* merged with Raymond Moley's *Today* in February 1937, Vincent Astor became president, and a few months later the name was slightly altered to *Newsweek*. These changes meant that Moley, a former brain truster, was to supply the overall direction and Astor was to supply the money.

There began a long period in which *Newsweek* sought some kind of identity. Its organization and its method of putting stories together was the same as *Time*'s, but in leaning over backward in the effort to avoid imitating its rival's distinctive style, it was often dull. One departure from the *Time* format was *Newsweek*'s use of the signed column, although everything else remained anonymous. Moley, as a disgruntled New Dealer, gave the magazine its political direction, and for a while Astor continued to write rescue checks whenever it showed signs of financial collapse.

In the end, *Newsweek* survived largely on the strength of those readers who liked the newsmagazine idea but were repelled by *Time*'s style or its more blatant biases. Not until the 1960s, in fact, did *Newsweek* succeed in finding itself completely as a magazine of news interpretation, and then, with the further impetus of fresh capital provided by its sale to the Washington *Post,* and the new editorial impetus given to it by the *Post*'s publisher, Katharine Graham, it began to overhaul its rival and show signs of surpassing it. Editorially, most observers agreed, it was now a better product than *Time*.

A third newsmagazine was begun almost at the same time *Newsweek* appeared in 1933. *United States News* was a by-product of the syndicated columnist David Lawrence, and editorially quite different from the other two periodicals in the field. It was much simpler and briefer stylistically, and it intended to do more forecasting of the news, in the omniscient manner of the columnist himself. It appeared to be addressed to an audience more conservative and somewhat farther down in the social, economic, and intellectual scale than *Time* and *Newsweek* readers. The self-image *United States News* had of itself was, of course, quite different, and this image became more apparent after 1948, when Lawrence merged his unsuccessful companion publication, *World Report*, begun in 1946, with the original magazine, as *United States News & World Report*. Since then it has made a successful place for itself in the newsmagazine field by carefully avoiding any physical resemblance to its rivals, concentrating on its special fields of forecasting and analysis, and appealing directly to the conservative audience that follows Lawrence's column.

Meanwhile, having precipitated a whole new category of magazines with *Time*, Henry Luce turned his money and talents elsewhere. If his partner, Hadden, had supplied the editorial genius that made *Time* so successful, Luce, as the executive head of Time, Inc., demonstrated that he had, like Curtis, the ability to innovate and to assemble talented people to execute his ideas. *Fortune Magazine* was his own idea, rising from *Time*'s obvious inability to cope with the flood that regularly inundated its department devoted to business news. Like Lorimer, Luce saw clearly that business was the preoccupation of a great many people, but cannily he chose the upper managerial level as the one audience that had not yet been exploited by publishers.

Luce began to experiment with the idea for *Fortune* in 1928, and produced a trial dummy at just about the time business was devastated by the Crash of 1929. Reason dictated that the project be abandoned. *Fortune*, after all, was to be a luxury magazine in format and presentation, to sell at a dollar a copy, and directed to an audience knocked out and clinging to the Depression ropes. Nevertheless, in the mistaken belief that the slump would last no longer than a year, it was decided to go ahead with publication. The first issue was dated February 1930.

Fortune became one of the miracles of publishing history. Against all logic, it continued to gain in circulation and advertising as the Depression deepened and crisis followed crisis. The magazine has never had any serious reverses since it began. It was a quality publication, a handsome magazine physically, filled with high-level advertising for expensive consumer products and institutional declarations. Editorially, its product was unique, offering the first in-depth examination of the business world, in all its phases, ever to appear in a magazine. *Fortune* was also unique in being a business magazine, supported by business advertisers, which successfully resisted being influenced by these advertisers, and avoided casting a rosy light on the community it served. Thus it has become a valuable and respected source of information both inside and outside the business community, while making its inevitable enemies. (It might be added that the *Wall Street Journal,* the newspaper equivalent of *Fortune,* has exhibited the same honesty and produced the same successful result.)

In 1932 Luce bought a magazine already in existence, *Architectural Forum,* intending to make it a more general magazine for the building industry. In time, it was enlarged to cover the entire construction industry, and therefore changed its name in 1950 to *The Magazine of Building.* But even this roof was not large enough to shelter the broad interests represented in the magazine. Two years later *The Magazine of Building* split into two publications, *Architectural Forum,* directed to the heavy building industry; and *House and Home,* for residential home builders, architects, and mortgage lenders.

The next and probably most spectacular brick in the Luce structure was *Life* magazine, the inspiration of a Luce editor, Ralph Ingersoll, who persuaded his boss to publish it against the advice of numerous experts who predicted failure. Appearing in November 1936, it offered ninety-six pages of photographs, with a minimum amount of text—and the modern picture magazine came into being, a late descendant of Frank Leslie, who started it all.

In addition to representing a new relationship between pictures and text, *Life* had the highest professional standards of photography a magazine had ever offered. Its superb photographers came to be known everywhere in the world, and the pages of *Life* offered an unexampled display of their work, illuminating America and the world.

The magazine also did much to further the cause of art appreciation for a mass audience, offering the work of artists past and contemporary, with accompanying texts. It also used the picture-text combination to explain scientific developments to its lay audience, and to teach graphically such subjects as history and architecture. On its editorial page, *Life* propagated the conservative and sometimes idiosyncratic views of its publisher, but readers paid little attention to this page; it was lost in the wealth of illustration.

In the 1960s, *Life* began to slip, partly because of the competition from its rival, *Look,* and partly because of the developing collapse of the general mass magazine market, which will be discussed later. Promotion and subscription devices of every type failed to stem the slow descent. Changes in format, chiefly in the direction of more text and more departmentalization, seemed only to discourage old customers.

But the Luce touch was apparently infallible, even in the later years of the publisher's life. When he launched *Sports Illustrated* in August 1954, it was against the considered advice of experts who pointed out that no general sports magazine had ever succeeded. Moreover, it was said, the Golden Age of reading about sports, which had flourished in the twenties, was over with the advent of television.

Again Luce confounded the experts. *Sports Illustrated* combined the photographic excellence of *Life* with the work of the best sportswriters available. The result was the kind of in-depth examination of the sporting scene that *Fortune* had provided for the business world. It was not an instant success, and it has had its struggles, but the magazine has survived them and, presently, its continued existence is not in doubt.

Before Luce died in 1967, his empire included not only the magazines described above, but real estate, radio and television stations, a thriving magazine export business, a subsidiary devoted to selling technical developments to the printing trades and its allies, part ownerships in paper mills, and preeminently its book-publishing division, which by the mid-sixties had become Time, Inc.'s largest moneymaker, accounting for 8 percent of its gross profits. First (1950) in the field of creating and selling books by mail, Time-Life Books by 1966 had seven different "libraries" or series in operation.

As *Newsweek* rose to challenge *Time* successfully, after a long search to find its own formula, so *Look* went through the same process to establish itself against *Life*. There were at least fifteen imitations of *Life* in the wake of its successful launching, but only *Look* survived to become formidable competition. Historically at least, *Look* was not an imitator, since it preceded *Life* by some ten years in experimenting with the picture-text idea in the Sunday rotogravure section of the Des Moines *Register-Tribune,* owned by John Cowles and his family. One of the family, a son, Gardner Cowles, Jr., planned to develop the ideas he was testing in the roto section, and create a picture magazine from them. He even traded ideas with the Luce organization as the planning for both magazines moved along at the same time. *Look* followed *Life* on the stands by two months, appearing in January 1937 as a monthly (*Life* was a weekly from the start), later as a biweekly. Although there were many other dissimilarities—for instance, *Look* was printed at first on cheap paper, by rotogravure, and dealt with general magazine ideas rather than the news—nevertheless, in the public eye the two were rivals from the beginning.

The later history of *Look* was remarkably similar to *Newsweek's.* Like *Life,* it was a picture-text magazine, and kept reworking this basic formula through several transformations in an effort to find its own identity. While never unsuccessful, it came into its own in the sixties by offering more text, including a kind of investigative reporting of life in America reminiscent of Leslie's early explorations of New York. As of this writing, it is solidly established as one of the most succesful of American magazines.

Among the notable new starts of the twenties and thirties, none was more remarkable than that of *The New Yorker.* Harold Ross, its creator, has been the despair of his biographers—an improbable man not susceptible to definition. As one of his writers, Russell Maloney, put it: "No man . . . has been the subject of so much analysis, interpretation, and explanation with so little concrete results." But his biographers inside and outside the organization, down to and including the most recent one, his widow, would agree on one thing—that Ross, without question, was the most unusual editor the magazine business had ever known.

An Aspen, Colorado, boy who grew up in Salt Lake City, a high-school dropout after two years, a wandering newspaperman from Salt Lake City to Sacramento, Atlanta, Panama City, New Orleans, and San Francisco, this large, rough man was an unlikely candidate to be the originator of a sophisticated magazine. As editor of the Army newspaper, *Stars and Stripes,* during World War I, he directed a staff that included Alexander Woollcott, Franklin P. Adams, John Winterich, and Grantland Rice. It was Woollcott, according to most accounts, with whom he talked about his ideas for starting a new magazine, and began to develop them in long conversations. After a brief postwar job as editor of *Judge,* Ross found a financial sponsor in Raoul Fleischmann, heir to the yeast fortune, who was one of his poker partners in the gathering of wits that comprised the Algonquin Hotel's Round Table.

Ross's prospectus for *The New Yorker* was one of the most accurate any prospective publisher ever produced. It described the proposed magazine as follows:

"The *New Yorker* will be a reflection in word and pictures of metropolitan life. It will be human. Its general tenor will be one of gaiety, wit and satire, but it will be more than a jester. It will not be what is commonly called sophisticated, in that it will assume a reasonable degree of enlightenment on the part of its readers. It will hate bunk.

"As compared to the newspaper, the *New Yorker* will be interpretive rather than stenographic. It will print facts that it will have to go behind the scenes to get, but it will not deal in scandal for the sake of scandal nor sensation for the sake of sensation. Its integrity will be above suspicion. It hopes to be so entertaining and informative as to be a necessity for the person who knows his way about or wants to.

"The *New Yorker* will be the magazine which is not edited for the old lady in Dubuque. [This became the most often quoted line from the prospectus.] It will not be concerned in what she is thinking about. This is not meant in disrespect, but the *New Yorker* is a magazine avowedly published for a metropolitan audience and thereby will escape an influence which hampers most national publications. It expects a considerable national circulation, but this will come from persons who have a metropolitan interest."

That remained an excellent description of *The New Yorker* a quarter of a century after the magazine first appeared on February 19, 1925, and indeed in the years after, because, following Ross's death in 1951, the magazine did not change. In fact, *The New Yorker* was the least changed of all the older American magazines that survived through the decade of the sixties, and some observers thought this the primary reason for the magazine's decline in advertising during the later years of the decade. Its circulation had always been deliberately limited to the neighborhood of 500,000. Ross did not want it to become a mass magazine, even if the masses should turn out to want it.

As an editor, Ross was a perfectionist who tortured himself and those who worked for him in an impossible effort to match his ideals. One of his noted writers, E. B. White, described him as "restless, noisy, consumed by curiosity, driven by a passion for clarity and perfection. . . ." He was never satisfied with what he or others accomplished. People either loved him or hated him; there was no room for middle ground with Ross. Those who loved him (and no doubt hated him on occasion) formed a cult of writers and editors who worked for *The New Yorker*, and deeply resented any criticism of either Ross or the magazine. They took themselves and the periodical with extreme seriousness, and firmly believed that Ross had revolutionized magazine publishing, if not journalism itself.

A more objective observer would assess *The New Yorker* as a twentieth-century version of the great literary magazines of the nineteenth century, with the addition of features, like its cartoons, that were the product of its own times. Like all great editors, Ross left his stamp firmly and indelibly on the magazine; it was as much his as the *Post* had been Lorimer's. Even his personal idiosyncrasies were reflected in its pages, as in his prudishness about sex, which left *The New Yorker* immaculately chaste in an age of realism, until recently.

Ross gathered around him perhaps the most brilliant staff of writers and artists ever assembled on a magazine, and the list of contributors was no less notable. E. B. White became one of the leading essayists of his time. James Thurber was admired almost equally for his prose and his distinctive cartoons. Wolcott Gibbs was distinguished as much for his critical writing as for his profiles and fiction. Much of John O'Hara's work in the short story first appeared in *The New Yorker*. S. J. Perelman, among the greatest of twentieth-century humorists, was a steady contributor. Ogden Nash's wry and much quoted poetry appeared regularly. Helen Hokinson's drawings of ample, behatted club ladies became a national institution. Otto Soglow, Peter Arno, Whitney Darrow, Jr., Charles Saxon, and a long list of others were the best cartoonists of their time.

The New Yorker contributed some original ideas of its own to magazine journalism. Its plotless short stories were so characteristic of the magazine that they became known as a type, although the magazine's editors always denied that they were anything of the kind. The interview article that Isaac Marcosson established in the *Post* became in Ross's hands the Profile, a name the magazine registered but which passed into the language as a lower-case noun. Many of them were outstanding examples of biographical writing. The magazine's filler material—typographical and other lapses clipped from newspapers and other periodicals—was not a new idea, but Ross made the fragments original by adding the magazine's own ironic comments either below them or in headings above. Some of these—Social Notes from All Over, Letters We Never Finished Reading, Ho-Hum Department, Department of Utter Confusion, among others—became a part of the language.

For a long time *The New Yorker* was also read for its critical departments, whose writers included Robert Benchley, Dorothy Parker, Clifton Fadiman, and Edmund Wilson, but as time went on, the magazine became less noteworthy in this respect, drifting into the fashionable coterie writing of the postwar period. Its leadoff feature, Talk of the Town, short and long paragraphs reporting aspects of contemporary society, was another nineteenth-century idea raised to a high level of contemporary excellence by the hard work of its staff writers. Ross's belief that all copy required endless, meticulous editing resulted in what critics came to call *The New Yorker* style, although once more the magazine denied that such a thing existed. But there was, in fact, a certain homogenization produced by overediting that raised the readability of lesser writers while it reduced the individuality of some of the better ones.

Nevertheless, there was no lack of individuality in *The New Yorker*'s pages, as proved by the long list of books based on material that had first appeared in the magazine—more than any other magazine had ever produced. Some of them, like Ruth McKenney's *My Sister Eileen* and John O'Hara's *Pal Joey* became famous Broadway musicals as well. The magazine also ran John Hersey's *Hiroshima,* which occupied an entire issue in 1946, and Truman Capote's *In Cold Blood.*

Less apparent to the lay public, the magazine also made a substantial contribution to the art of interpretive reporting, of which *Hiroshima* was probably the best-known example. But others contributed to this field too—Rebecca West, Alva Johnston, Joseph Mitchell, Richard Rovere, Lillian Ross, A. J. Liebling, E. J. Kahn, Jr., and St. Clair McKelway, among others.

No assessment of *The New Yorker* would be complete without noting that its advertising was the first in magazine history to be read with as much attention, and in some cases as much pleasure, as the editorial content. In the sixties, when serious criticism of the magazine began to be heard for the first time, one critic referred to the "gray rivers of type flowing endlessly between the columns of advertising." Certainly advertising craftsmanship reached a peak in *The New Yorker,* and its volume became so great in the fat issues between October and Christmas that advertisers fought for contracts, and column after column was refused. Near the close of the sixties, however, this was reported to be down as much as 500 pages in a single year, 1968.

There were other criticisms. Chief among them was the charge that *The New Yorker* was a mausoleum dedicated to Ross, and carefully preserved by those who had worked for him. Certainly there was little change in the magazine, and nothing that was fundamental. Occasionally the work of new, young, innovative writers like Donald Barthelme appeared, but there were few other concessions to changing times. While *The New Yorker,* at this moment, has an extremely long way to go before it can be considered in danger of extinction, nevertheless it appears (in 1969) to be facing the problem, so common in

magazine history, of having a formula that has been successful for a
long period of time but that cannot or will not be changed.

Change itself, of course, would not guarantee security. Habit is
often the solid rock on which a magazine's readership is based, and
The New Yorker has become a national habit, although it is now
common to hear faithful readers say they read little beyond the advertisements and the cartoons. But *The New Yorker* in 1969 is still
unique. It is as Ross had created it, reaching metropolitan-minded
people from coast to coast, whether they live in cities or not. The urbanization of America, beginning in the twenties, has unquestionably
done much to ensure the success of Ross's idea. Nearly twenty years
after his death, his magazine still has no rivals.

The remainder of the new leaders in magazine publishing during
the twenties and thirties were less colorful, with the exception of Ber-
narr Macfadden, whose parlay of physical culture and sex made him
a millionaire. It would be futile to try to convey the peculiar flavor
of Macfadden's life and works in a few paragraphs. He became a familiar figure in American life during his later years; his white-maned
head, with its sharp, aggressive features was seen often in the pages of
newspapers, recording his many marriages (the last occurred when he
was eighty); his bizarre exploits, like his parachute jump into the Hud-
son River when he was in his eighties; his exhibitions of physical fit-
ness at all ages, and his views on every subject from international
relations to happy marriages.

Macfadden introduced to the magazine business the confession and
true-detective periodical. *True Story* became the prototype of the numerous publications in that field, including a whole series of "True"
magazines published by Macfadden himself. His *Physical Culture*
magazine, a later venture launched in 1943, was, similarly, the prototype of all the large-muscle magazines devoted to the interests of
those weaklings who were weary of having beach sand kicked in their
faces, and (unintentionally) of homosexuals who delighted in the pictures of muscular men in loincloths. Then there was Macfadden's no-
torious excursion into newspaper journalism, the New York *Graphic,*
known affectionately in its day (the twenties) as the *Porno-Graphic,*
and later as "the world's zaniest newspaper." Its famous "cosmo-

graphs," which were sketches of courtroom scenes with photographic heads of the participants pasted in, made newspaper history.

Perhaps some of the flavor of Macfadden's publishing life can be conveyed by recalling the days when the *Graphic* and the magazines both were being published out of the same Manhattan loft. Macfadden would stride into the *Graphic*'s city room in the morning, clad only in his familiar leopard-skin loincloth, leap on the city desk, summon his entire staff of scandal-chasers to rise to their uncertain feet, instruct other minions to open all the windows wide, even if it was the heart of winter, and lead the assembled multitude in calisthenics.

Some of Macfadden's other excursions into publishing included his purchase in 1931 of *Liberty* magazine, which he used first as a platform to advocate the election of Roosevelt. It then became a popular, cheap magazine one of whose features was a "reading time" note preceding each contribution, guaranteeing that it would take no more than "10 minutes, 30 seconds," or whatever it might be, to absorb what was in a particular segment of type. In 1932, after the election, Macfadden established *Babies: Just Babies,* for young parents, with Mrs. Roosevelt and her daughter listed as editors, thus providing fuel for the early Roosevelt-haters. It was short-lived.

Nevertheless, there was no denying that Macfadden had the popular touch, the ability to reach millions with material that required little if any cerebration. At their peak, his magazines had a combined circulation in 1935 of more than 7 million, larger than that of any other group. Three years later, Macfadden Publications, Inc., was in the red, and two years after that, under the pressure of stockholders' suits, Macfadden himself had to retire as president. He died in 1955, at eighty-seven. His empire, in other hands, managed to get itself into the black once more, but it was never the same again, at least as far as magazines were concerned.

A characteristic of magazine publishing in the twenties, carried over into the thirties, was the increase in specialization, forecasting the decisive trend that is taking place today. Publishers who could visualize a particular audience for a magazine to fill a special need were able to create durable properties. For example, there was *Photoplay,* if not the first, the best of the movie fan magazines, which satisfied the public curiosity about what was happening during the golden age of Hollywood. In one respect, *Photoplay* was unique. While other fan magazines featured reviews of new movies that were merely extensions of the advertising columns, or puffs exchanged for expected favors, *Photoplay,* particularly when it was under the direction of James R. Quirk, was honestly critical of the new pictures. Its reviews, running under a still from the picture, were a reliable guide to what Hollywood was producing, and were much appreciated by its readers.

Reminiscent of *The Nation,* and its national influence despite a miniscule circulation, was the *American Mercury,* founded by H. L. Mencken and George Jean Nathan in December 1923, and first published by Alfred A. Knopf. This magazine, whose green cover protruded from the coat pockets of young reporters all over the country, was the organ of iconoclasm in an era of Babbitry. Besides Mencken's attacks on the activities of what he called the "booboisie" of the nation, and Nathan's superb theatrical criticism, the magazine printed the work of the sharpest satiric minds extant. Its fiction and articles were first rate.

Viewed in retrospect, however, Mencken was not exactly what he seemed to be at the time. The *Mercury* delighted the social rebels of the day because it pilloried the Establishment, the stuffed shirts who had made a religion out of Wall Street and exalted Rotarianism to the level of a national philosophy. It was against organized religion, organized politics, and organized-everything-else. This, together with Mencken's masterful, erudite prose, which made him one of the century's finest stylists, obscured the fact that much of what Mencken wrote and what the *Mercury* advocated, in its reverse way, was not only nonsense but essentially conservative.

There was something authoritarian about Mencken's iconoclasm, something of the savagery of the revolutionary just before he has enough power to raise his own guillotines. All this became somewhat clearer, to the vast disillusionment of Mencken's followers, by that time grown older and wiser, when he appeared on Alf Landon's campaign train in 1936, wearing a large Kansas sunflower in his buttonhole and exhorting to follow him the same booboisie he had scorned only a decade before.

Mencken sold his magazine in the late twenties. Its next editor was Paul Palmer, who gave the magazine an extreme right-wing tone before he went on to the *Reader's Digest*. Lawrence Spivak, who followed as publisher, chose as editor Eugene Lyons, a disenchanted wire-service correspondent who had once gone to Moscow with high hopes, and returned to write the book that made him famous, *Assignment in Utopia*. Lyons assembled a stable of the similarly disenchanted and disenfranchised, and the magazine became professionally anti-communist. Its great distinction under Lyons's editorship, however, was its dramatic fight for air power at the beginning of World War II. Using the writings of Major Alexander Seversky and General (then Colonel) Hugh J. Knerr, among others, as a spearhead in the attack, the magazine was responsible for generating most of the pressure that persuaded Congress to vote appropriations for heavy bombers against the die-hard opposition of the Navy admirals.

In the late forties, Spivak sold the *Mercury* and went on to greater fame as the owner and chief interrogator of "Meet the Press," an idea he originated. The *Mercury* drifted gradually into the hands of the hate merchants, like the *North American Review* and *Scribner's*. It ended ignominiously as an organ of the far, far right in Texas. One of the survivals of the Spivak regime was *Ellery Queen's Mystery Magazine,* which he began as a subsidiary and highly successful venture, along with a line of paperback mysteries.

There were, of course, many other magazines begun in the twenties and thirties, and it is painful in a short history to be compelled to omit their stories. But the point has been made that this was a period of innovation, a time when new leaders came on to replace the old leaders, some of whom were still far from dead. It was a time of ferment, leading directly to the successes and failures of the postwar era.

twenty-three

The Triumph of the
Business Press

THE MAGAZINES INTENDED FOR GENERAL AUDIENCES, known in the trade as consumer magazines, dominate the newsstands, make the headlines, and provide a highly diversified source of information and entertainment. But they are only the most visible part of periodical publishing. There are more than 16,000 magazines of every kind published in the United States, and fully 10,000 of them are involved with the business world. About 8,000 of these are company magazines, known also as industrial publications and house organs, and as of 1967, nearly 2,400 were business publications, with a total circulation of more than 61 million.

More and more in this century, the publications that are intended either to reach the business world or describe its activities not only completely dominate publishing but also constitute what is probably the greatest reservoir of printed information in the world.

The American Business Press, the industry trade association to which most of the larger publishing houses belong, defines its members as "specialized business publications serving specific industrial business, service, or professional business audiences, not including general business or business news magazines." ABP's membership includes only 14 percent of American business publications, but its 353 members account for nearly 50 percent of the total advertising volume.

That volume is impressive indeed; in 1967, business publications carried an estimated 1,273,000 pages of advertising—figured in dollars, a volume amounting to $772.1 million. Moreover, since 1950, these magazines have grown more in terms of national advertising than any other medium except television, whose phenomenal 1,519 percent rise in that period—the time of TV's greatest growth—far exceeded the otherwise spectacular 215 percent growth recorded by the business papers. (On this scale, direct mail comes next with 206 percent; then other magazines, with 144 percent; and newspapers, with 135 percent.)

If one compares business-publication growth with that of the American economy during the same period, its 215 percent rise is substantially ahead of all other national advertising, including television—at 190 percent, compared with a 160 percent rise in gross national product and 152 percent in national income.

Statistics alone do not define the dimensions or measure the importance of the business press. What is most formidable about it is the sheer volume of information in every conceivable field of human activity that pours from its presses every day, not only in the United States but around the world. Except for the developing countries, few nations are without a business press of some kind, and some Western European countries match the United States in quality if not in volume.

Nearly half the business magazines are industrial, followed, in order, by merchandising, medical, export and import and international, financial, educational, government, and religious. As in so many other fields, they tend to be published in groups. McGraw-Hill, for example, had thirty-eight publications in 1968, and was the largest, followed by Cahners Publishing, of Boston, whose merger in 1968 with Conover-Mast gave it thirty-three publications. Other leaders are Chilton, and Ojibway Press, both with twenty-two; and Miller Publishing, with sixteen.

The Canadian groups are even larger; MacLean-Hunter Publishing has fifty-five monthlies and fifteen annuals; and Southam Business Publications, thirty-six. And far surpassing any of these are the giant British publishing combines of the International Publishing Corporation, whose 200 business publications are scattered all over the world;

and the Thomson Organization's 136 magazines of various kinds, most of them in the trade and technical category. IPC also owns a 40 percent interest in the Cahners group.

The primary function of these magazines is to provide information about events in whatever segment of the business world each one covers, and at the same time anticipate changes and advise how to meet them. Thus they are first of all newsmagazines. Secondarily, they provide how-to information. But they also are opinion organs, analyzing the news and evaluating its impact.

The largest combines have assembled staffs comprehensive enough to cover the world in carrying out these functions. McGraw-Hill, for example, has a full-time correspondent in the Soviet Union—only one of its 800 full-time reporters and editors who annually make more than 80,000 visits to plants and offices in pursuit of the news. McGraw-Hill publishes about 50,000 editorial pages in its magazines every year. All told, the business press puts out more than 800,000 editorial pages per year, the work of 14,000 full-time editors. As a class, business magazines enjoy a far greater longevity than consumer publications, of which only a handful now date before the beginning of the twentieth century. Scores of business periodicals have observed their centennials.

Businessmen absorb their magazines with an intensity unmatched by consumer periodical readers. "Survival reading," one steel executive has called it—which sums up the motivation of a large part of the readership. Moreover, the business magazines offer a merchandise mart through their advertising pages that is comparable to the kind of smorgasbord laid out before the general public by the mail-order catalogs in their prime.

As the technological revolution progresses, the business press moves with it. Some of the newer entries in the field are *Data Processing Magazine, Electronic Design 29, Electronic Products,* and *Micro-Waves.* No area is neglected. *Ice Cream Field* is just as important to its readers as *UnderSea Technology* is to its readers. The worldwide growth of the business press is seen in *Business Automation,* which has an international edition.

Those who imagine that the business periodical is the kept woman of its particular organization or industry are unaware that it is often a crusading organ, and sometimes is the conscience of the people it serves. It was an editor-publisher serving the vending industry, for example, who broke the Bobby Baker story, piecing together random bits of evidence until an anonymous early-morning telephone call led him to the Maryland official records that disclosed Baker's control of vending-machine companies, hotels, and other real estate. Again, it was a business editor who led a campaign against the high-voltage swimming pool lighting fixtures that were electrocuting unsuspecting swimmers at the rate of one a month, on the average, in 1960. The achievements of business-paper editors in public health and safety alone have been remarkable.

Nor have the editors been content with simple exposés. Examining the causes of hospital-acquired infections, one publication conducted its own original research to trace some infections to mops and mop bucket water, then developed tests that would help hospitals to evaluate disinfectants and set labeling standards. It was a business magazine, too—one serving the advertising industry—that helped to bring about the Better Business Bureau; and certainly the automotive service magazine that trained 40,000 mechanics by correspondence course in the interest of road safety deserves some kind of special commendation. No other medium, it may be added, has done more to spread scientific knowledge.

Few editors work as hard as those in the business press, or, as a group, go to greater lengths to get the news. They travel more than 50,000,000 miles annually, and one company's editors made 231 trips abroad in a single year. Several publishers have European offices, and maintain correspondents in Asia and Europe.

Oddly enough, however, business editors tend to downgrade themselves, and for years this has been a serious psychological problem in the industry, although some publishers scoff at the idea. But it can hardly be denied that for a good many decades "trade publishing," as it was disparagingly called, was the Siberia of the magazine business. It attracted primarily older men who had never made it on the consumer magazines, or young people who could not find jobs elsewhere and still yearned to get into print. Appallingly low salary scales discouraged bright beginners, who soon went elsewhere, and caused a steady turnover in the upper echelons as those who had the talent to escape did so.

This has changed, slowly but steadily. Wage scales have increased until on the better magazines they compare favorably with consumer publications. Working conditions are incomparably better, especially among the larger groups, and little by little more able men and women have come to work for business periodicals. The change is evident in today's magazines, the best of which are written and edited with as much professional skill as the leading consumer publications. From a production standpoint, there are some that would rank with the finest, regardless of source. In fact, there is more originality and sheer skill in layout and design demonstrated in the business press as a whole than in consumer publications.

The business editor and those who work for him no longer have any reason to denigrate themselves or their area of journalism. On the other hand, the business press has not reached a millennium by any means. There are still many unaudited publications of dubious value, edited with a sharp eye directed toward advertising, and essentially superficial in content. Some magazines, too, have not yet shaken off the lazy mediocrity of the old days, and the editorial sweatshop has far from disappeared.

A major reason that the business press is not even better than it is appears to be the existence of publishers who neither appreciate nor understand the editorial product they are selling. Usually they are men who have come up through the advertising or sales departments and who exhibit a kind of contempt for the writer and editor. This is based on the familiar conviction, held by so many people, that they, too, could write if they had the time. "Are you still working, or do you just write?" a hometown friend asked the returned successful writer in the British movie *Charlie Bubbles*. It is this attitude that leads some publishers to observe that writers and editors are a dime a dozen, but it is difficult to get a good advertising man or a salesman. That conviction is invariably reflected in the magazine's quality.

People in the business press, however, no longer think of themselves as second-class citizens in the communications world. They know they

are doing highly important work that will become even more important as technology and knowledge proliferate. Already the immense
store of information existing in the world as the result of their labors
has created a gigantic problem of storage and retrieval. Publishers
like Norman Cahners, whose group alone turns out a mountain of information, are exploring ways to organize factual material on a worldwide basis. Some experts believe this will never be done by the
business press on an industry-wide scale. Others say it is possible and
desirable, but more likely to be done on an individual basis—that is,
memory banks for chemists, engineers, doctors, and so on.

Whatever the solutions, no one doubts that the business press is
today, more than ever in the history of magazine publishing, one of
the world's prime sources of information about the interdependent
activities that unite people everywhere.

twenty-four

Magazines Today

IF THE PUBLIC IS SOMETIMES GIVEN THE IMPRESSION by the disappearance of national institutions like the *Saturday Evening Post* that the magazine business is dying, they could not be more misled. At the beginning of 1969, circulation and advertising revenues in the magazine industry had reached an all-time high. In the decade of the sixties, 676 new magazines appeared, and only 162 of all periodicals disappeared through sale, merger, or suspension. In 1968 alone, 94 magazines were started, while only nine were merged and sold and a dozen others suspended. During that year, there was a 3.2 percent jump in revenues to an impressive $1.09 billion for the top fifty magazines during the first eleven months, while circulation was up 3.3 percent during the first six months of 1968.

Nevertheless, the industry is not without problems. Its biggest is television—not so much in the competition for attention as in the race for the advertiser's dollar. To sell products successfully, magazines must be strong in circulation and advertising as well as in editorial content; these factors are interdependent. Loss of advertising is usually the direct cause of a magazine's death, but this is brought on most often by weakness in the other areas.

There is no denying the fact that television has hurt magazines in a way that other competition has not. Periodicals have competed successfully with bicycles, motion pictures, the automobile, and radio, each one of which was predicted to be their assassin. But television is different, simply because its advertisements reach a mass audience that is often larger than any single magazine can reach. Color television has increased the threat, since color in advertising was once the magazine's exclusive province. Moreover, the cost of television advertising is so high that the agency stretching its client's money over the competing media often finds a disproportionate amount of it going to the tube.

This situation has affected mass magazines the most. In recent years many of these periodicals have reported losses in advertising pages. *Reader's Digest* and *Time* have slipped every year since 1965; *Life* has declined every year since 1966; *The New Yorker,* as noted before, lost 500 pages in one year (it is a mass magazine in advertising terms, if not in circulation).

A few mass magazines have operated against the trend, notably *Newsweek,* for reasons cited earlier; and *TV Guide,* whose service to the competing medium causes it to prosper. Paradoxically, advertising revenue is not necessarily related to circulation, even within the same company. Thus *McCall's* in 1968 led both its rivals, *Ladies' Home Journal* and *Good Housekeeping,* with 8.5 million, and it had the highest page rate at $45,900, but it lost more than the others, which were also down in both pages and revenue.

Yet the McCall Corporation's two other magazines, *Redbook* and *Saturday Review,* prospered. The former went up from 813 to 910 advertising pages, with 4.5 circulation, while the latter, at the beginning of 1969, was delivering a circulation of 600,000 to advertisers, and growing steadily, with advertising revenue that had increased fourfold in five years. Their success represented the two major trends in magazine publication today. *Redbook* was reaching a specific market: young mothers. *Saturday Review* was typical of the rapid growth achieved in the past decade by the specialized magazines.

Begun in the twenties as a book-reviewing medium titled *The Saturday Review of Literature,* and attaining distinction under the editorship of Henry Seidel Canby, its circulation and advertising revenues were negligible, in a class with *Harper's* and *The Atlantic.* Later it came under the editorship of Norman Cousins, one of the most noted liberal editors of his time, who changed the character of the magazine, developing it into a diversified periodical. In 1968 the McCall Corporation became a part of the Hunt Foods conglomerate put together by the West Coast industrialist Norton Simon, and today the *Saturday Review* is the leading general review of the arts.

Within the larger intellectual, specialized audiences it had aimed at before, it carved out smaller audiences interested in its weekly supplements—communications, education, science, and recordings—and by putting all these together, plus travel, it could offer multiple specialized audiences to its advertisers. Circulation and advertising jumped accordingly. As the general mass magazines began to decline in the sixties, periodicals like the *Saturday Review* experienced an astonishing regeneration. No one would have believed a decade earlier that an intellectual magazine primarily devoted to the arts could achieve a 600,000 circulation in America.

The key to magazine success in the sixties was the ability of a publication to deliver to advertisers a specific market that could not be reached so specifically by any other medium. Television and mass magazines cannot compete in this kind of selling, except to a limited degree. Perhaps the outstanding example of such pinpoint delivery is *Playboy,* the magazine its young proprietor ran up from a simple idea to an empire grossing nearly $50 million a year from its multiple parts. The publication itself earned nearly $8 million in 1968.

The magazine's success may have been based on Hefner's shrewd understanding of the American male's attitude toward sex—someone once remarked that the Playboy Clubs were the only whorehouses in the world where there was no overt sex and the customers were not permitted to touch the merchandise—but that may or may not be true. If one judged by the "Playboy Philosophy," enunciated at length by the Chief Playboy, the formula is simply based on Hefner's feeling that there ought to be complete freedom for everybody in everything, including sex. There is little doubt, however, about what *Playboy* actually does to earn its phenomenal success: it delivers the extremely large young male market in the United States to its advertisers—something television, which is generally considered a female medium, cannot do.

It must be pointed out, too, that media buyers in the advertising agencies are concerned not only with paid circulation but also with something they call CPM, or how much it costs to reach every thousand readers of a magazine. Thus, when *Life* printed its first 8.5-million-copy issue in January 1969, it could point to a total readership (these figures are compiled by firms specializing in magazine research) of 48 million, based on the number of people who see each copy. No regular TV program commands such an audience, but it costs an advertiser a great deal to reach it. At $64,200 a black-and-white page, *Life* had the highest rate of any mass magazine, which probably accounts for its financial troubles while sitting perched on such a dizzy pinnacle. If an advertiser also wants to be on television, he may not be able to afford the periodical.

Other page rates based on paid circulation, for purposes of comparison, are: *TV Guide,* 12.5 million circulation, $35,400; *Reader's Digest,* 17 million circulation, $56,000; *Time,* 4 million, $33,000; *Newsweek,* 2.4 million, $20,700. Despite its losses, *The New Yorker* in 1968 was still carrying more advertisements than any other magazine, with 5,252 and a circulation of 478,000. Its net profit that year was over $2 million.

An important factor that helps magazines reach increasingly specialized markets, and thus combat television competition, is the growing practice of printing split run, or regional, editions. Computers and zip codes have aided this endeavor substantially, as well as the tremendous research carried on by the Magazine Publishers Association and other industry organizations, as well as by the magazines themselves. With these tools, publications can reach with split runs a city, a metropolitan area, a region, or subscribers who live in affluent sections, pinpointed by the zip codes. In 1968, 235 magazines were printing such editions, and regional advertising accounted for 17 percent of the total.

In helping advertisers to reach their markets, magazines have developed nearly a score of ideas. The gatefold ad has been increasingly popular, and so has the use of three or more pages running together. Sometimes these multipage units become small magazines within the larger one, as the Celanese Corporation's 100-page advertisement in the October 1967 issue of *Harper's Bazaar,* and Uniroyal, Inc.'s 40-page full-color pages in the May 1968 issue of *Reader's Digest.*

Other devices are the inserted catalog, guide, or recipe booklet, the extension of the old-fashioned coupon to be clipped from the bottom of ads, inserted reply coupons and postcards, and redeemable coupons. Some companies have used actual product samples in their ads, and others have given the smell of their product to their advertising by the use of perfumed inks. Perfume is only the easiest application of this technique. Baker's Coconut has used it, and so has Vicks' Sinex Nasal Spray. A new technique employs what are called "scratch and sniff" strips embodied in the ad, a technique known as "microencapsulation." This has been used for cologne, perfume, and mint-scented soap.

Among other advertiser gadgets are illustrated pop-ups, used effectively by Wrigley gum in Curtis's children's magazine, *Jack & Jill*, but also to produce a three-dimensional pop-up of a prefab building in *Nation's Business* and *Better Buildings*. Thin-vinyl recordings have been used as inserts, rotogravure and offset sections are now common, and metallic ink is in use. One of the most recent devices, with much promise for the future, is three-dimensional printing of pictures, developed and introduced by *Look*. It has been used by advertisers in several magazines, and regularly on the cover of American Express's new travel magazine, *Venture*, which has had a spectacular rise in its field.

The post office is opposed to some of these devices, particularly the smaller-than-page-size units that magazines sometimes carry as subscription cards, and that ordinarily would go at a higher postal rate. In any case, second-class rates, under which magazines travel, were due to go up by 8 percent in January 1970, adding more to the already high cost of producing periodicals. Further increases are likely. Since 1958, second-class postage has risen 89 percent, labor 50 percent, and printing costs 25 percent, while advertising revenues were up to 73 percent, advertising pages up only 16 percent, and circulation up 31 percent.

There is only one way a magazine can mitigate its dependence on display advertising, in the opinion of John Mack Carter, editor and publisher of the *Ladies' Home Journal,* and that is by "the development and maintenance of a mass loyal audience."

The later history of the *Saturday Evening Post* shows what can happen when that audience is not maintained. Lorimer's *Post* commanded the intense loyalty of its readers, perhaps more so than any other magazine at any time. Loyalty was so great that the magazine survived the rough years after Lorimer's departure, until it could be stimulated once more by the editorship of the laconic Kansan Ben Hibbs, who held the editorial reins from 1942 to 1961, until he went to the *Reader's Digest*. Once that strong hand was removed, it was difficult for readers, particularly in changing times, to be loyal to any one of a succession of editors who followed, although some of them were very able men. It is also difficult to maintain loyalty when a magazine is increasing its price from ten to fifty cents, changing the nature of its content periodically, and even removing itself physically from one city to another, in this case from Philadelphia, where it had always been, to New York.

In the desperate effort to find a formula that would win back the readers, and with them their loyalty, successive editors tried everything, including "sophisticated muckraking" which brought it only libel suits. More and more it was the struggle for power in the board room that came to determine the magazine's future, just as it had in the case of Crowell-Collier. Editors were subordinated to that struggle, or became involved with it in a partisan way, and in such a climate it would have been impossible for any but the strongest editor to have established his supremacy and found a way out. A Lorimer might have been able to do it (one could not have imagined Lorimer doing anything else). As it was, the complicated battle reached its climax in April 1968, when Curtis came into the control of the Perfect Film and Chemical Corporation by virtue of a $5 million rescue loan, and Perfect's young president, Martin Ackerman, became president and chief executive of Curtis.

When that occurred, any student of modern communications could have predicted what would happen. It is axiomatic that editorial products coming under the control of large corporate enterprises cannot hope to succeed unless the executive officers of the parent company keep their hands off what is produced editorially. Their function, in these cases, is to provide capital, and wait a reasonable time for results. If none are forthcoming, they have a right to make a corporate decision that will end the life of the magazine or book-publishing house, or else put it into new hands. Anything else is almost always fatal. It was fatal at Crowell-Collier and it was fatal at Curtis. The enmeshing of editorial and business controls at a time of crisis proved to be the end of the *Post*—in an ugly atmosphere of mutual recrimination and litigation.

In August 1968, the *Journal* and *American Home* were sold to Edward R. Downe, Jr., a business entrepreneur anxious to get into magazine publishing. Curtis continued to publish *Holiday*, its luxurious and successful travel magazine; *Status,* its recently acquired snob-appeal periodical; and *Jack & Jill,* its long-successful children's magazine.

Oddly enough, a promotion ad running for a Curtis magazine in April 1969, when all the excitement was over and the damage done, underlined what it is that prevents disaster from overtaking magazines like the *Post*. The ad was for *Holiday,* and it was headed, "The S.O.B. at Holiday." The text, in part, read:

"There's an old saying in the publishing business that the biggest tyrants make the best editors.

"Henry Luce, Harold Ross, Bruce Gould, Ted Patrick—to name just a few—were all tough, uncompromising men who believed that democracy is great for America, but has no place in the editorial office of a magazine.

"Sharing this view is our own dictator in residence, Caskie Stinnett.

"Caskie has never been accused of killing anyone with kindness. And no one, to our knowledge, has ever suggested he enter the diplomatic service.

"He is a magazine editor, blunt, brusque, with strong opinions about his profession. He writes:

" '. . . We are firmly of the opinion that no great magazine will come from the deliberations of a conference. If it is to possess the invigorating qualities of honor and courage, a magazine must speak with a single voice and it must inevitably reflect the taste, the judgment, the boldness, and the scrupulousness of a single individual.' "

Even the grim picture of Stinnett running above the ad would scarcely convince his friends that he is an S.O.B., but the truth of the copy below it seems self-evident, and the many case histories in this volume provide ample documentation. It might be added that when the S.O.B. is in the board room and not at the editorial desk, and when he is in control of that desk, disaster is virtually inevitable.

Although the strong editor at the helm has always been the controlling factor in the life or death of a magazine, whether this will continue to be so is a question. In the first place, there is no longer a plentiful supply of strong editors. Only a few of the old breed remain, and team journalism is making steady progress.

In addition, the print media's share of advertising revenue has been declining steadily for ten years. Within a decade, television's share has risen from 13.1 to 16.9 percent, while magazines have dropped from 7.4 percent to 7.2 percent—not alarming in itself, until it is compared with television's substantial gain. In the same period, newspapers dropped from 31.1 percent to 28.4 percent, and radio remained the same after a brief dip.

The rise of the young to positions of power in our time is another important factor. Young media men, brought up on television, turn quite naturally to that medium, and young creative people in advertising find television a more exciting medium to work in than old-fashioned print.

Nevertheless, magazines continue to prosper in an overall sense, and, more important, they continue to improve. Further hope rises from such factors as the steady growth of education at higher levels, the continuing rise in income (even though it is sharply set off by inflation), the increase in leisure time, the growing cost of television advertising and the decrease in available time. Not everyone agrees that these are necessarily favorable factors. Some media men in advertising agencies believe that more leisure time and affluence will mean less reading, while others think the higher cost of television will result only in less money being spent on the print media.

In spite of all these imponderables, and the well-publicized failures, more magazines are begun every year, and begun successfully. Many of the new publishers are young men. Gilbert Kaplan, twenty-eight years old, started a magazine called *Institution Investor* in 1967, mailing it free to important businessmen. It is well established today. Nicholas Charney, of Del Mar, California, at twenty-seven is chairman of C/R/M, Inc., which began to publish, also in 1967, *Psychology Today,* a magazine designed for a small, college-educated audience, and already highly successful. It has a book division that Charney believes will surpass his magazine in profits, and a subscription list of customers who offer the basis for other ventures.

While these are further examples of the specialization that is becoming the dominant feature of magazine publishing today, they also exemplify the changing nature of the business. Neither of these young men regards himself as a magazine publisher. Kaplan's company was to be called Institutional Investor Systems, Inc., "a service company to the securities industry." Charney describes himself as in "the education and communications business."

New ideas, as always, continue to inspire potential publishers, and the best succeed. In 1967, while Kaplan and Charney were starting, another young Californian, Raymond F. Locke, was beginning *Mankind,* subtitled "The Magazine of Popular History," and published in Los Angeles. It started with a circulation of 175,000, of which only about 40,000 was subscription. By the end of 1968, it had 220,000 combined newsstand and subscription sales, and was still climbing. *Mankind,* exploring not only American but world history, intended to make history entertaining and readable—"to be read, not looked at," as the publisher put it. Its young staff has designed it both visually and in text to appeal especially to schools, where anything that would stimulate interest in history is certain to find a special welcome.

One of the most remarkable of the specialized magazines is *Atlas,* begun in 1960 by an idealistic lady publisher, Eleanor Worley, and edited for some time by Quincy Howe, the historian. Its intent was to survey and translate the world press for American audiences, and soon established itself as a unique service to writers, educators, and others as the only way to keep abreast of what was being published in foreign newspapers and magazines. *Atlas* covered not only politics and economics but the arts as well, including reviews and samplings of new books and critiques of new motion pictures.

Although it was a distinguished publication from the first, the magazine failed to achieve stability and had to be constantly subsidized until the late sixties, when its direction was taken over by an able and energetic young publisher, Malcolm Muir, Jr., who soon boosted it over the 100,000 mark. In 1968, Muir, acting as his own editor in chief, brought in as editor John Denson, a newspaper and magazine man whose notable talents, exercised on many of the leading publications in the country, had left their mark, particularly on *Newsweek,* the New York *Herald Tribune* and the Hearst papers in Los Angeles and New York. Denson did much to transform the magazine's format and further increase its circulation.

There is no doubt that magazines have improved in editorial content during the sixties, both in the writing and in the attempt to deal constructively and perceptively with the social issues that are the preoccupation of our time.

The best proof can be found in the pages of Gerald Walker's continuing annual anthology, *Best Magazine Articles.* Its table of contents for the 1968 issue (the stories were actually printed in 1967) displays not only a high level of writing but a broad spectrum of investigative reporting as well. Tom Buckley's *Esquire* profile of H. L. Hunt, the far-right Texas oilman; David Halberstam's "Return to Vietnam," from *Harper's*; Marshall Frady's examination of George Wallace in the *Atlantic* are examples.

One notices the inclusion, too, of articles from a new category of periodicals—the city magazines, bearing the names of their place of origin as title. Begun originally as puff sheets for chambers of commerce, there are now 67 or more of them, slick, well illustrated, extremely well written and edited, and no longer promoters of civic attractions. In fact, the city magazines these days dig into the social ills of their communities in a way that often puts local newspapers to shame. Some are more daring than regular consumer magazines. *Seattle,* for example, learning that the city was about to play somewhat unwilling host to a convention of homosexual organizations, decided that it could strike a blow for human tolerance and give its readers some unbiased information about homosexuality. The cover featured a picture of a young man sitting half-swung around in an executive chair, glancing quizzically at the camera. The title read, "This is ————[naming him]. He is a Seattle businessman. He is a homosexual." *Seattle* had found a man willing to sacrifice his anonymity for the cause, and the magazine had taken a step far bolder than most magazines would contemplate.

The city magazines may contain directories to local amusements and cultural events, which were chief among their original functions, but they are now competing with newspapers and radio and television stations in examining the social scene.

One of the most significant changes in magazines, as far as their awareness of contemporary life is concerned, is their changed attitude toward the black community. As Professor Theodore Peterson, the leading authority on twentieth-century magazines, has pointed out, only the journals of opinion and the crusading periodicals paid serious attention to black problems in the earlier years of the century, although *Esquire* carried the cartoon work of E. Simms Campbell, a Negro, in every issue since its founding. The rest of the magazines seemed to regard the black person as the stereotype personified by Amos 'n' Andy and Stepin Fetchit. In *Collier's* and the *Saturday Evening Post* during the thirties, the stories of Roark Bradford and Octavus Roy Cohen perpetuated the humorous, condescending view of the Negro as a shuffling, not very bright adjunct of the white community whose troubles were the materials of comedy, not tragedy.

Time was the first magazine to look at the black cause seriously, in the early 1950's, as Professor Peterson has observed, and it did so when it was neither fashionable nor of any particular interest to whites.

After the Supreme Court's integration decision of May 1954, magazines began to cover the black revolution in increasing depth, each one according to its own special audience. Thus *Business Week* examined the position of Negroes in the labor market, *Fortune* appealed to big business to help find a solution to ghetto problems, and the *New Leader* talked of the culture of poverty. *Look* was a leader among the mass-circulation magazines in exposing the plight of the black community to large numbers of readers.

In November 1967, *Newsweek* broke its tradition of news analysis to emerge into open advocacy when it produced a twenty-page section titled "What Must Be Done," and laid out a plan of action to meet the rising demands of the black community. The magazine's editor, Osborn Elliott, declared: "The reason for this marked change of approach is that the editors have come to believe that at this particular time, on this particular subject, they could not fulfill their journalistic responsibility as citizens by simply reporting what X thinks of Y, and why Z disagrees." *Newsweek* had, however, done a great deal of that kind of reporting, and done it well, in many cover stories.

The special section was well received, even by *Newsweek's* rival, *Time,* and as Professor Peterson notes, the National Advisory Commission on Civil Disorders cited it as a "brilliant exception" to the charge that the mass media had failed to present and analyze the basic causes of civil disorder. Polled by the *Magazine Industry Newsletter,* other editors and publishers applauded *Newsweek's* switch to advocacy, as long as it was clearly labeled. The *Newsletter* concluded in its survey story: "From another perspective, the current *Newsweek* highlights a new vigor in the mass magazines. They are becoming more exploratory, more dynamic, more concerned."

Other publishers followed *Newsweek's* lead. McGraw-Hill inserted a sixteen-page report on "Business and the Urban Crisis" in thirty-four of its trade, technical, and business publications in February 1968, urging business to take the lead, "now," in solving the ghetto problem, as *Fortune* had done, and outlining its own course of recommended action.

The black community has had its own magazines since 1837, as Professor Roland E. Wolseley, recently retired head of the Magazine Department at Syracuse University's School of Journalism, has pointed out in a valuable survey of black magazines (*Quill,* May 1969). In this summary, Professor Wolseley quotes Frank W. Miles, one of the few historians in this field, who cites the *Mirror of Liberty,* a quarterly begun in 1837 by David Ruggles, as the "first magazine to be both owned and edited by a Negro." Black historians do not credit an earlier publication, *The National Reformer,* as the first because it was owned by the white American Moral Reform Society. Other historians accept *The African Methodist Episcopal Church Magazine,* established in 1842, as the first, with *The Colored American,* begun in Boston in 1900, as the first general publication.

Aside from a few specialized periodicals, Negro magazines did not succeed from 1900 until 1942, when John H. Johnston, a black insurance salesman in Chicago, whose idea was to adapt successful formulas in white magazines to a black audience, started *Negro Digest* with $500 obtained from mortgaging his mother's furniture. He followed it three years later with *Ebony*, a picture-text magazine modeled after *Life*, which now has a circulation of 1,200,000; and in 1950 with *Tan*, a women's magazine based on confession-magazine formulas. *Jet*, the most recent Johnson entry, began in 1951 as a tabloid weekly newsmagazine, with its own energetic features. All these magazines do well except for *Negro Digest*, which suspended for a time in 1951, and is still a money-loser although it is militant in the black cause where the other Johnson publications are not. Two other ventures by the Chicago entrepreneur have failed: *Hue*, once described as the poor man's *Playboy*; and *Ebony International*, intended for the English-reading African market but defeated by African politics.

Another Negro magazine group are the four periodicals owned by the Good Publishing Co., of Fort Worth, whose publisher, George Levitan, is white. These include the monthly *Sepia*, a not very dangerous rival of *Ebony*; and three other monthlies, *Jive*, *Hep*, and *Bronze Thrills*, which combine sensational confession pieces with serious articles about Negro life.

Largest of all black publications is *Tuesday*, whose 2,000,000 circulation is derived from its use as a supplement to white newspapers that circulate in black districts.

Like the white periodical press, the black magazines are doing best these days with specialization. Among the new magazines designed to reach specific portions of the black market are *Negro Heritage, Black Theatre, Urban West,* and *Soul Illustrated*. These supplement the black business press, which is also growing, and the black scholarly quarterlies, the best known of which are the *Journal of Negro History, Journal of Negro Education, Phylon,* and *Freedomways*. Recently there has also sprouted a black equivalent of the white underground press—tabloid newspaper-magazines published spasmodically and, like their white counterparts, largely propaganda organs.

As Professor Wolseley notes, while it is hard to determine the number of black periodicals (because it is difficult to separate the magazines from the newspapers), there are probably about sixty of them.

The specialized publications have relatively small circulations, but the general magazines show substantial figures, and two of them are over a million.

In other areas of social concern, magazines have continued to take firm stands and to do outstanding reporting. *Commentary,* for example, printed Michael Harrington's "Our Fifty Million Poor" in July 1959, and touched off the war against poverty. In a few years, the subject had been treated in nearly every national magazine. The war in Vietnam, and the opposition to it, has been covered by the magazines from a variety of viewpoints. *Newsweek's* coverage of the conflict itself was particularly outstanding, measured best perhaps by the expulsion of its bureau chief in Saigon by the South Vietnamese government. In the public debate over the war, *Harper's* and *The Atlantic* were particularly eloquent voices, each devoting most of an issue to long articles about public reaction. *The Atlantic's* contribution was a book-length piece of reportage by Dan Wakefield, who toured the United States and Canada to find out how people felt about the war. *Harper's* carried Norman Mailer's equally lengthy report, which became a literary event, describing the peace march on Washington and the Pentagon.

Robert Stein, one of the best contemporary editors, formerly editor of *Redbook* and now with *McCall's,* has described the changed magazine world:

"It used to be that we could cover almost any subject in a popular magazine by assigning a very good writer to go to a number of obvious sources, get the necessary facts and figures and dramatize them with a few anecdotes or individual experiences, then put it all together in a neat, well-rounded way. The result would be that the reader would be superficially informed, would quite possibly be entertained, but would be left with very little of real value to him.

"Now, on some of the most serious subjects, we find that we are investing as much as two years of time; that we're using not only writers, but (often) teams of researchers to help them. In some cases we're working with research organizations to do basic research which goes far beyond reporting, simply to find out what the reality of the situation is before we can figure out what we're going to say about it, how we're going to treat it in a magazine. This is a growing trend because readers can discern the difference between an exploitation of their interest on the part of the magazine and the magazine's desire to serve their interests by clarifying confusion about issues that are important to them.

"When I first started writing magazine articles on almost any subject of direct concern to the reader, I finished with ten rules on how to handle the subject. Well, the ten-easy-rules days are over, because any issue that can be treated with ten easy rules isn't worth considering in the first place."

While some editors are not as convinced as Stein about the efficacy of research as compared with on-the-spot reporting by really talented writers, there is no question that many magazines are taking more time to do in-depth reporting about the social scene. But the ten-easy-rules days have not disappeared, by any means. There is still much that is trivial in magazines, and even some that is completely venal. Far too many stories, especially in the mass magazines, contain a proportion of 90 percent speculation and 10 percent fact, because magazines are still salesmen of ideas, and ideas can easily be presented as fact when they are largely fantasy.

In the area of sex, the periodicals have been casting off the blinders worn since they began, but in the process have not particularly distinguished themselves. They have reflected the new, permissive society to some extent, mostly in the greater use of nude pictures and some freedom with obscenity in the more intellectual magazines. As Enid Haupt, the editor of *Seventeen,* has remarked, "What was whispered about a decade back is now feature material." Her magazine, she recalls, was running in July 1957 a story called "Sex and Your Emotions," which dealt with the proper age to kiss a boy and the difference between necking and petting. Ten years later, in a discussion of teen-agers and sex, it was running the results of a national survey purporting to show that 15.4 of all girl teen-agers had had sexual intercourse.

But the magazines, in general, are not as permissive as some parts of society have become. They still, for the most part, reflect the middle-class values of the mass audience they reach, and in their way are just as unrealistic as *Playboy,* which deals with sex in terms of fantasy.

Playboy, in fact, has astutely broadened its scope well beyond its famed center-fold (which, as someone remarked, has given a whole generation of American boys the idea that girls come with staple holes in their midsections) to encompass a good many other aspects of society, while *Esquire,* which started out to be a sex magazine, has wound up being a periodical largely devoted to an examination of contemporary social problems.

The chief trouble with magazines in their discussion of sex is that they tend to perpetuate popular myths, and only give the appearance of discussing sexual matters seriously. This is particularly true of homosexuality, a subject treated by several of the large magazines. *Time's* essay on this subject, as one observer remarked, read as though it had been written by a parish priest. Others are simply not well informed. The fact, however, that magazines have had the courage to discuss the subject at all is encouraging.

At the other end of the scale, there is a substantial underground magazine press, most of it emanating from California and New York City, which is devoted to selling total freedom. Most of these publications have four-letter-word titles, and exist mostly by virtue of their classified advertising, which offers a wide sexual choice to its liberated readers. Most of them are also more or less allied with "the Movement," the social revolution of the New Left, which of course has its own magazine, *Ramparts,* the California radical publication, the chief muckraker of these times.

If one could summarize the major trends in magazine publishing in 1969, they might be set down as follows:

1. The trend to specialization, rising from the fact that in a country with more than 200 million people, already served by television, it is becoming increasingly difficut to edit a mass magazine. In 1968, of 48 new magazines in the general field and 46 in the business category, most were directed to specialized audiences.

2. The trend to regional and city editions, and the effort of large magazines to reach special segments of their audience.

3. The growth of controlled circulation methods, meaning that magazines are sent free to carefully selected audiences. For example, *Charlie,* a magazine for "coeds under twenty-five," was launched in

1968 to be mailed to lists of young customers in department stores who requested it—expected circulation, 150,000 to 200,000.

4. The exploitation of the youth market. There have been some spectacular successes in this field, and some equally spectacular failures. The most ambitious of the new ventures in 1968 was the Gulf Oil Company's *Wonderful World of Walt Disney,* a children's magazine to be distributed through service stations. A 25-cent quarterly, its first printing was 6 million copies.

5. The increasing number of magazines directed to young homemakers, the second largest market, after the young.

6. The increase in state and city magazines.

As the magazine industry itself puts it, "readers seek perspective in a changing world. They find it in magazines. Here, the ideas and products of American industry can enjoy their greatest moments of receptivity. Magazines are a point of view. A forum. A friend and counsellor. They offer an opportunity to examine in depth an infinite variety of subjects. Editor/reader rapport is strengthened by these inherent magazine values: Authority, with readers who believe and respect magazines; permanence, which allows unpressured time for consideration of ideas; and selectivity, that pinpoints the most valuable segments of the population for ideas and products."

On this foundation, the future of magazines rests.

Suggested Reading List

BAINBRIDGE, JOHN. *Little Wonder: Or, The Reader's Digest and How It Grew*. New York: Reynal and Hitchcock, 1946.

DREWRY, JOHN E. *Some Magazines and Magazine Makers*. Boston: The Stratford Company, 1924.

ELSON, ROBERT T. *Time, Inc. The Intimate History of a Publishing Enterprise, 1923–1941*. New York: Atheneum Publishers, 1968.

FORSYTH, DAVID P. *The Business Press in America, 1750–1865*. Philadelphia: Chilton Books, 1964.

HERSEY, HAROLD BRAINERD. *Pulpwood Editor: The Fabulous World of the Thriller Magazines Revealed by a Veteran Editor and Publisher*. New York: Frederick A. Stokes Company, 1937.

HOFFMAN, FREDERICK J., CHARLES ALLEN, and CAROLYN F. ULRICH. *The Little Magazine, a History and a Bibliography*. Princeton, N.J.: Princeton University Press, 1946.

LYON, PETER. *Success Story. The Life and Times of S. S. McClure*. New York: Charles Scribner's Sons, 1963.

MOTT, FRANK LUTHER. *A History of American Magazines,* Vol. I, 1741–1850, New York: D. Appleton and Co., 1930; Vol. II, 1850–1865, Cambridge, Mass.: Harvard University Press, 1938; Vol. III, 1865–1885, Cambridge, Mass.: Harvard University Press, 1938; Vol. IV, 1885–1905, Cambridge, Mass.: Harvard University Press, 1957; Vol. V, 1905–   (a collection of notes and essays published posthumously). Harvard: Belknap Press, 1968.

NOEL, MARY. *Villains Galore: The Heyday of the Popular Story Weekly*. New York: The Macmillan Company, 1954.

PETERSON, THEODORE. *Magazines in the Twentieth Century*. Urbana: University of Illinois Press, 1956; revised edition, New York: The Macmillan Company, 1968.

REYNOLDS, QUENTIN. *The Fiction Factory: The Story of Street and Smith*. New York: Random House, 1955.

RICHARDSON, LYON N. *A History of Early American Magazines, 1741–1789*. New York: Thomas Nelson and Sons, 1931.

SMITH, PAUL C. *Personal File*. New York: Appleton-Century, 1964.

STERN, MADELEINE B. *Imprints on History: Book Publishers and American Frontiers*. Bloomington, Ind.: Indiana University Press, 1956.

TASSIN, ALGERNON. *The Magazine in America*. New York: Dodd, Mead and Company, 1916.

TEBBEL, JOHN. *George Horace Lorimer and the Saturday Evening Post*. New York: Doubleday and Company, 1948.

VAN EVERY, EDWARD. *Sins of New York, as "Exposed" by the Police Gazette*. New York: Frederick A. Stokes Company, 1930.

WALKER, GERALD (ed.) *Best Magazine Articles* (a continuing anthology, published annually). New York: Crown Publishers, Inc.

WOLSELEY, ROLAND E. *The Magazine World: An Introduction to Magazine Journalism*. New York: Prentice-Hall, 1951.

———. *Understanding Magazines*. Ames, Iowa: Iowa State University Press, 1965.

WOOD, JAMES PLAYSTED. *Magazines in the United States*. New York: Ronald Press, 1956 (2nd edition).

———. *Of Lasting Interest: The Story of the Reader's Digest*. New York: Doubleday and Company, 1958.

WOODWARD, HELEN. *The Lady Persuaders*. New York: Ivan Obolensky, Inc., 1960.

Index